*Triumphs and Tragedies of Ninth Delhi*

# *Triumphs and Tragedies of Ninth Delhi*

JAGMOHAN

**ALLIED PUBLISHERS PRIVATE LIMITED**
NEW DELHI MUMBAI KOLKATA CHENNAI NAGPUR PUNE
AHMEDABAD BANGALORE HYDERABAD LUCKNOW

**ALLIED PUBLISHERS PRIVATE LIMITED**

1/13-14 Asaf Ali Road, **New Delhi**–110002
Ph.: 011-23239001 • E-mail: delhi.books@alliedpublishers.com

Khasra No. 168, Plot No. 12-A, opp. Wisdom Academy School, Kamta,
Surendra Nagar, **Lucknow**–227105
Ph.: 09335202549 • E-mail: lko.books@alliedpublishers.com

17 Chittaranjan Avenue, **Kolkata**–700072
Ph.: 033-22129618 • E-mail: cal.books@alliedpublishers.com

15 J.N. Heredia Marg, Ballard Estate, **Mumbai**–400001
Ph.: 022-42126969 • E-mail: mumbai.books@alliedpublishers.com

60 Shiv Sunder Apartments (Ground Floor), Central Bazar Road,
Bajaj Nagar, **Nagpur**–440010
Ph.: 0712-2234210 • E-mail: ngp.books@alliedpublishers.com

F-1 Sun House (First Floor), C.G. Road, Navrangpura,
Ellisbridge P.O., **Ahmedabad**–380006
Ph.: 079-26465916 • E-mail: ahmbd.books@alliedpublishers.com

751 Anna Salai, **Chennai**–600002
Ph.: 044-28523938 • E-mail: chennai.books@alliedpublishers.com

5th Main Road, Gandhinagar, **Bangalore**–560009
Ph.: 080-22262081 • E-mail: bngl.books@alliedpublishers.com

3-2-844/6 & 7 Kachiguda Station Road, **Hyderabad**–500027
Ph.: 040-24619079 • E-mail: hyd.books@alliedpublishers.com

**Website:** www.alliedpublishers.com

First Edition 2015



**ISBN 978-81-8424-981-1**

Published by Sunil Sachdev and printed by Ravi Sachdev at Allied Publishers Private Limited, Printing Division, A-104 Mayapuri Phase II, New Delhi - 110064

*To*

Radhicka, Sonali, Devika, Amayaah and Srijan
Five Budding Aspirants
Who, I hope,
Would find a more positive work-environment
To Realise Fully
Their Creative and Constructive potential,
In Service of the city, state and civilization

As in the case of his earlier publications, such as eleven editions of My Frozen Turbulence in Kashmir and its Hindi and regional languages translations, the author has donated the entire royalty of this book to a Charitable Trust set up in memory of his parents. The Trust, namely, **Amir Chand Dropti Devi Memorial Charitable Trust**, provides financial assistance to the poor and needy, especially the young students preparing for the competitive examinations.

## ACKNOWLEDGEMENTS

Sincere thanks are due to the India International Centre, particularly to Dr. S. Majumdar, Chief Librarian, and his highly helpful and humble staff—Ms Shafali Bhatt, Sarvshri Rajeev Mishra, Surinder Singh, Ms Hemlata, Ms Kanchan Nagpal, Ms Nupur Sharma, Sarvshri Rakesh Chand, Sunil Sharma, Jagdish Prasad Dabral and Amit Kumar. The facilities provided have been excellent. Special thanks are also due to former IIC Librarian Ms Sushma Zutshi and Dr. H.K. Kaul and Ms Sangeeta, Director and Network Manager, DELNET respectively.

I owe a deep debt to my family members—my wife, Uma, my daughter Deepika, my son Manmohan, my son-in-law Rajiv Kapoor and my daughter-in-law Nutan Manmohan. But for their reverential and encouraging attitude, I would not have found a congenial environment at home for undertaking an onerous task of writing a book in difficult times, covering a wide range of complex issues.

An outstanding and conscientious colleague of long-standing, Chaudhry Ranbir Singh, unfortunately passed away recently. His superb knowledge of land records and other matters, was indeed, without a parallel. The pages of the book would always remind us of his invaluable contribution.

Special thanks are also due to R.K. Bhandari, Pashim Tewari and R.K. Safaya who, despite their own preoccupation, spared time to attend to my queries at a short notice.

JAGMOHAN

## Publishers Note About the Author's Publications

Jagmohan's Publications are distinguished by three special features: first, by his objectivity based on documented and other irrefutable evidence; secondly, by his intellectual prowess, supplemented by intense ground-level experience; and thirdly, by his insightful understanding of the undercurrents of historical forces that largely shape the events occurring on the surface.

The following extracts from the Reviews that appeared soon after the publication of the First Edition of his book, *My Frozen Turbulence in Kashmir*, in 1991, bear ample testimony to the extraordinary combination of the aforesaid features in Jagmohan's writings.

> "... it is a brilliant work, written with verve which derives its power from [the author's] addiction to truth...."
>
> — **Dr. Mulk Raj Anand** in *Business & Political Observer*

> "It is a great book indeed and it tells me much more about Kashmir than I ever learnt from any other place."
>
> — **Michael Foot** (*British M.P. in a letter to Dr. Mulk Raj Anand*)

> "Frozen Turbulence is an evocative expression; the book chills the readers as it takes him through the heavy past, the dismal present and the bleak future. It is a work of monumental proportion and of great archival and historical importance.... Jagmohan has a mass of background information and documentary evidence to support his thesis...."
>
> — **V.N. Narayanan**, Editor-in-Chief, *The Tribune*

> ".... the one man who saved the Valley for the country last year, Jagmohan..... His book is one of the most important to have been published in India...."
>
> — **Arun Shourie** in *Economic Times*

"As a history of both modern and ancient Kashmir, his account is invaluable. In many respects this is the first detailed honest and forthright narration of the series of lapses and blunders which have led to the present situation.... The disclosures about corruption at the highest levels of the State administration and the vivid accounts of the politics of systematic deception leave one breathless."

— **K.R. Sunder Rajan** in *The Pioneer*

"One has only to read Jagmohan's awesomely documented book to realize the truth.... He has minced no words about the indifference and incompetence and worse of Indian political leaders of all hues.... The situation in 'Azad' Kashmir is no different...... There is no Jagmohan there to tell the truth......"

— **Bhabani Sen Gupta** in *The Hindustan Times*

"In any other country, the publication of a book along the lines of Mr. Jagmohan's recent offering would have triggered off a fierce controversy and political furor......"

— **Swapan Dasgupta** in *The Times of India*

The book has seen eleven updated Editions (upto 2014). It has been hailed as a definitive work. It has also been translated in Hindi, Urdu, Marathi, Malayalam, Telgu, Kannada, Gujarati, Punjabi and Assamese.

Similar has been the response to the author's other publications. With regards to his book, *Soul and Structure of Governance in India*, Professor B. Bhattacharya, in *Management and Change*, has commented: "Jagmohan's book forced me to go back to Plato's Republic, a classic...." And *The Business Standard* has observed: "Jagmohan's magnum opus is a work of immense research and scholarship."

About Jagmohan's total commitment to clean and nobility-oriented service as Union Minister, the views of eminent public figures, including senior Member of Parliament, belonging to non-ruling parties, quoted in the text at pages 95-97 and pages 149-150, speak for themselves. What is specially pertinent is

Fali S. Nariman's observation: "Whom can honest citizen turn to? The sad answer is that city's power-that-be care more for their wallets than they care for Delhi. That is why the citizens of this Capital owe Mr. Jagmohan a measure of gratitude. He is the only man who has had the guts to launch this long-overdue drive. And only he has the stubborness to see it through". In a similar appreciative tenor India Today's TODAY, the Capital Afternoon Newspaper, of April 29, 2003, chose Jagmohan as citizen No. 1, with the citation: "He takes on foes, he knows no friends. For him nothing or nobody is above Delhi, its beauty, its heritage, its historical places and public spaces. He's Citizen One".

# PREFACE

*History is us – and there is no alternative but to shoulder the burden of what we so passionately desire and bear it out of the depths.*

— A Solzhenitsyn[1]

It is the deeper layers of the Indian Reality that I have endeavoured to explore, analyse and comment upon in the books that I have so far published: *Rebuilding Shahjahanabad: The Walled City of Delhi; Island of Truth; The Challenge of our Cities; My Frozen Turbulence in Kashmir; Soul and Structure of Governance in India; Shaping India's New Destiny; Crisis of Environment and Climate Change; and Reforming Vaishno Devi and a Case for Reformed Reawakened and Enlightened Hinduism.*

In these eight publications, while the outward forms have been extensively sketched, greater significance has been accorded to the undercurrents that determine the course, colour and content of the events that occur on the surface. For example, *My Frozen Turbulence in Kashmir,* which has seen eleven updated editions, underscores the point that what has been happening on the ground is really an outcome of the forces that lie embedded in the soft and permissive nature of the Indian State, and in the general disposition of the nation to remain oblivious of even burning realities, such as terrorism and subversion, till they knock at its door. Likewise, *Soul and Structure of Governance in India* shows how in the absence of a healthy civilizational base and inspired ideology of work, the entire organizational framework created by the Constitution has been rendered frigid and fragile.

In this ninth book, which I have titled, *Triumphs and Tragedies of*

[1]Russian Nobel Laureate Aleksandr Solzhenitsyn's classic works like The Gulag Archipelago and Cancer Ward have profoundly influenced the contemporary world.

*Ninth Delhi*[2], I would take the readers with me on my long journey to both the outer and inner reality that pervades the Capital of the Republic. I would show to them quite a few scintillating products of a new urge to make Delhi an inspiring symbol of a new civilization, a civilization that synthesizes the regenerated purity of the 'long suppressed soul of India' and the ever increasing scientific, technological and organizational power of the modern times. I would also point out to them the dangers of being sucked into the 'death-traps' which are being simultaneously dug out by the regressive forces. At the end of the journey, beginning from Jawaharlal Nehru's time till date, most readers, I am sure, would be impelled to ask themselves a number of crucial questions about the fate and future of Delhi, such as those that follow.

- Why did Jawaharlal Nehru, despite his elevating and enlightened vision of the orderly and balanced growth of Delhi, extend only a weak implementational hand when it came to actualize that vision on the ground? As an eminent statesman, at the helm of affairs, should he have not fully realized that the constructive work by him and his followers was needed to inject new meaning into the veins of history and civilization of Delhi?
- Why was no leaf taken from Sardar Patel book of dealing with Ahmedabad's civic affairs, which showed that what mattered most, in the municipal arena, was the inner impulse to develop a street level touch with the reality, do selfless service to the needy and keep the greedy and indisciplined elements at bay?
- How was it that, while most of her senior party leaders of Delhi lambasted me and my colleagues for launching a drive to implement some of the clearance-redevelopment projects, Ms. Indira Gandhi experienced a sense of 'thrill and pride', when the results of that drive surfaced on the ground and enhanced the image of the Republic and its Capital, especially in early 1980s, the years of hosting ASIAD, NAM, CHOGAM?

[2]As indicated in the Introductory Chapter, I have named Delhi that has been built after mid-1950 as the Ninth Delhi. (For detailed particular, pages 5& 6 and footnote 7 on page 6 may be seen)

- Was there not a preponderous of evidence to show that whenever any firm and sustained action was taken to translate the accepted national/civic policies and programmes on the ground, the chronic infections in the diseased spots of Indian democracy flared up, rendering an already weak system still more weak and ineffective?
- Why were the few remnants of the Gandhian Truth that could be seen in Prime Minister Morarji Desai's stand, with regard to the Delhi's clearance works, butchered by his Home Ministry bureaucratic caucus and the Shah Commission who went to an unimaginable extent to suppress the contemporaneous records which showed that, in so far as the clearance-cum-resettlement cum redevelopment schemes were concerned, nothing was done in terms of procedure and provisions, during the emergency, what had not been done in the pre-emergency period?
- How did Turkman Gate Slum Clearance Scheme, sanctioned decades earlier by the Delhi Improvement Trust and Delhi Municipal Corporation, suddenly become communal and linked to the concocted lines such as: We would not allow second Pakistan? Is it not that, exasperated by the gross mismanagement of its funds, the Central Government, in February 1974, transferred the entire slum clearance scheme from the Delhi Municipal Corporation to the DDA for effective implementation; that is, about 16 months before the emergency?
- What led Prime Minister A.B. Vajpayee, a noble statesman, with an attachment to the principle of *rajdharma,* to act against his own beliefs and change my portfolio of Urban Development when, by all objective accounts and comments, Delhi was witnessing an unprecedented pace of clean, orderly, environment-friendly and culturally-uplifting development?
- And why did Mrs. Sonia Gandhi-Shiela Dikshit regime think that its principal plank for winning Delhi State Assembly Elections (December 2013) and Lok Sabha Elections (May 2014) should be a handsome reward to those who had ravaged, with impunity, the landscape of Delhi in form of thousands of unauthorized

colonies and illegal constructions? And why could not rival political parties think of any plan other than competitive negativity and announcing a still larger packet of rewards to the offenders?

- Was it not clearly a practice of bribing the voters of unauthorized colonies in kind and that, too, on massive scale? Did it not tilt the electoral contest in favour of the candidate who was out to undermine not only the rule of law but also the future of the city? Why would the Election Commission not move the government to amend the election law to empower the Commission to deregister political parties which declared, through their manifestoes or otherwise, that the violation of statutory provisions of central, state or local laws would be condoned, if such a condonation gave pecuniary advantage, in cash or kind, to a group or category of violators? Was inaction on the part of the Election Commission to check the existence of an unhealthy clientistic relationship between the land-grabber/illegal builder/voters and those seeking their votes justifiable? Was not the paradox apparent: if there was an individual act of illegality or corrupt practice, the Election Commission would take action; but it would look the other way if there were mass violations and mass corrupt practices?

The above are some of the posers that I have delineated in the various chapters of the book. The historical backdrop and civilizational legacy has been expounded in the introduction. The reader would find all this, in its full context, in the pages that follow. The curative action, based upon personal experience, has also been elaborated.

Unfortunately, the city, of late, has seen a massive onslaught of rapacious and ruthless elements. No principle, no norms, no value, no past solemn declaration, and no court-verdict or its repeated denunciation have mattered. All that is sought is power—power not for doing long term good to the city or the state but for attaining short-term personal and political gains, forgetting all the time that ignoble and unjust means could give birth only to a deformed and disoriented city and disoriented civilization.

Before I end this preface, I may underline: One of the basic lessons that history provides to its earnest students is that civilizations begin to debilitate, and eventually destroy themselves, when the wielders of political and bureaucratic power of the state and makers of public opinion in the society fail to turn their eyes on a seemingly insignificant speck of poison on the nation's plate.

**Jagmohan**

# CONTENTS

# INTRODUCTION

*The cities are destined to become the most significant phenomenon on the planet.*

—John Reader

*The farther backward you can look, the farther forward you can see.*

—Winston Churchill

The city is among the most imposing creations of man. It is the cradle of civilization. It has many facets. As an economic entity, it is a seat of business and industry; as a social organization, it is a creator of community and collective action; as a political unit, it is a centre of power and government; and as a cultural force, it is a repository of old traditions, a fountain-head of new ideas, an instrument of intellectual advancement, and a moulder of attitudes and thoughts. Its all-pervasive character was aptly brought out by Spengler when he observed in *The Decline of the West*: "World history is the history of the civic man. Peoples, states, politics, all arts and all sciences rest upon one prime phenomenon of human being, the town."

The face of a city is really the face of a civilization in which it exists. Delhi has often appeared to me less as a developing and disciplined metropolis than as a civic entity which manifests all major facets of the present-day Indian civilization – a confusing mix of contradictory values and a queer combination of antiquity and modernity, oscillating between the two worlds, "one dead and the other powerless to be born."

Viewing, on a larger canvas, the history of prominent civilizations, it would be noticed that each one of them is marked by a special attribute. The special attribute of German civilization is its organization, of the US its enterprise, of Japan its adaptability and of Great Britain its balance. The hallmark of Indian civilization, in its heyday, was the power and profundity of its mind. It was this power which led the celebrated Indologist, Max Mueller, to observe: "If I were asked under what sky the human mind has most fully developed the choicest gifts, has most deeply pondered on the greatest problems of life, I should point to India." It was this power that produced one of the earliest city-based civilization of the world. In archaeological parlance, it is known as Harappan civilization.

Excavations done since the early twenties of the last century have shown that as early as 3000 BC, a number of cities existed along the banks of rivers or vast water-bodies, such as Mohenjodaro on the river Indus, Harappa on the river Ravi, Dholavira and Lothal on river Saraswati.[1] About 1500 cities have so far been identified from Adi-Badri in Haryana to Dholavira in Gujarat.

Apart from the individual houses built with burnt-up bricks, the larger cities,[2] such as Mohenjodaro and Dhola-vira, had quite a few community facilities. The Great Public Bath of Mohenjodaro is an outstanding example of these facilities. The worth of having an organized civic life was well-appreciated. The lay-outs took care not only of the street-patterns but also of public amenities. An ingenious system of underground drainage had been evolved and the human and other wastes were disposed of in a planned way, taking care of health and hygiene of the people. In contrast to the position prevailing in corresponding arenas of social and political life in Mesopotamian and Egyptian pre-historic cities, there was no palace, no tomb, no temple, no organized army, no weaponry, no powerful monarch and no despotic rule in the area covered by the Harappan civilization. Obviously, the people inhabitating the Harappan cities were peaceful and disciplined. Noting the features of public facilities and public

---

[1] Some scholars dispute the existence of now submerged Saraswati, ignoring solid literary, archaeological, geological and hydrological evidence. But the issue is not being discussed here, as it would be outside the scope of this book.

[2] Notwithstanding the commonality of the basic features, the Harappan cities show substantial variation, both in sizes and functions. While the large cities encompass as much as 200 hectares, the smaller cities could be as small as one hectare. Out of about 1500 Harappan sites so far identified, only about 100 have been excavated.

architecture of a large Harappan city, the famous French historian and indologist, Amaury de Reincourt, has observed: "The colossal size of the capital cities reminds one of the Imperial Rome. The sheer size of the Citadel, the impressive Great Bath, the Collegiate building, the Pillared Hall, all these great monuments indicate that Mohenjodaro was a centre of religious and administrative life on a grand scale".

The estimates of the total area covered by the Harappan civilization range from 6,80,000 to 80,000 sq. km., and it existed for about 1000 years. Clearly, those who had produced and managed as advanced an urban civilization as the Harappan for about 1000 years were no ordinary people. They must have been endowed with a powerful mind and creative spirit. Was it not the same powerful mind and creative spirit that, over the years, produced the profound thoughts of Vedas and Upanishads in the Indraprastha – Kurukshetra – Hastinapur region and the area around?

While such questions of archaeology and pre-historic literature cannot be answered with absolute certainty, it could be stated with a fair degree of accuracy that the Harappan civilization was an outcome of the creative and constructive urges of indigenous people. This civilization started withering away when the rivers-system underwent a fundamental change, consequent to sedimentation and neo-tectonic movements.[3]

After about a thousand year of disappearance of the Harappan cities, the Ganga Valley saw the growth of a sizeable number of another category of pre-historic cities, such as Kashi/Varanasi/Banaras, Vaishali, Ayodhya, Rajagriha. Most of them were capitals of small kingdoms and republics which had come up in the region, except during the period of the Mauryan Empire (321 BC to 185 BC), when it was held by a single strong ruler. Apparently, over the

[3] The signatures of the sedimentation and tectonic movement are widespread in the geological formations of the sub-Himalayan and Shiwalik regions of Himachal Pradesh, Uttar Pradesh, Uttaranchal and Haryana. The waters of Sutlej shifted to the Indus system and Yamuna changed its course to north-east. While Saraswati practically dried up, Indus basin got additional water and saw frequent floods.

years, the small settlements[4] grew in size, attaining prominence in many spheres of economic, social and cultural activities. Some of them emerged as great centres for learning and intellectual discourse and gave birth to the three of the greatest thought-processes of the world; namely, the religions and philosophies of Hinduism, Buddhism and Jainism. These religions and philosophies are followed, even at present, by more than half the number of the human race, and bear testimony to the unique power and profundity of the Indian mind.

Varanasi is the strongest and most pervasive manifestation of the above phenomenon. This is what M.A. Sherring, famous Indologist and Protestant missionary, who stayed in Varanasi in mid-nineteenth century, observed about the antiquity of the city and its contribution to the vitality of the Indian civilization:

> Twenty-five centuries ago, at the least, Benaras/Varanasi was famous. When Babylon was struggling with Nineveh for supremacy, when Tyre was planting her colonies, when Athens was growing in strength, before Rome had become known, or Greece had contended with Persia, or Cyrus had added lustre to the Persian monarchy, or Nebuchadnezzar had captured Jerusalem, and the inhabitants of Judaea had been carried into captivity, she had already risen to greatness, if not to glory... Not only is Benaras/Varanasi remarkable for her venerable age, but also for the vitality and vigour which she has constantly exhibited. While many cities and nations have fallen into decay and perished, her sun has never gone down: on the contrary, for long ages past it has shone with almost meridian splendour. Her illustrious name has descended from generation to generation, and has ever been a household word, venerated and loved by the vast Hindu family... As a queen, she has ever

[4] How the principles of town planning and architecture engaged the attention of Indian intellectuals and thinkers of ancient times would be clear from the works of Manasara, Kautilya and Treatises of Vastu Shastra. The description of Ayodhya, Indraprastha, Pataliputra show that quite a few towns attained prominence. Havell has rightly observed: "The most advanced science of Europe has not yet improved upon the principles of town planning of garden cities of India based upon the Indian village plan as a unit."

> received the willing homage of her subjects, scattered over all India; as a lover, she has secured their affection and regard.[5]

Not only Varanasi but many other non-Harappan pre-historic cities served as important pilgrim centres and played a highly significant role in bringing about cultural unity of India. It has been rightly noted: "The Pilgrim's India reaches back many hundreds of years and brings to us an astonishing picture of land linked not by the power of the king and governments but by the footstep of the pilgrims".[6]

During the Turko-Afghan rule and the period of the Mughul Empire, premier cities were generally established as extensions of the rulers' dwellings and reflected their imperial will and sense of grandeur. Akbar's Fatehpur Sikri, described by Gascoigne as "the world's most perfectly preserved ghost town", is a telling example of this category. Such cities may be the monuments of the past despotism, but their cultural and architectural heritage has innate attraction of their own.

Delhi is also one of the oldest cities of India, though it does not fall in the category of Harappan cities or the pre-historic cities of the Ganga Valley. The Pandavas, the heroes of the Mahabharata, are believed to have founded a city by the name of Indraprastha or Indrapat at the site which is now covered by Purana Quila and Humayun's tomb. Recent archaeological excavation in the Purana Quila and the discovery, in 1966, of an inscription of Asoka (273-236 B.C.), engraved on a rugged rock, near Srinivaspuri, west of Kalkaji temple, leave little doubt about Delhi's antiquity. Its present name is, however, associated with Raja Dillu of the Mauryan dynasty who built a city in the first century B.C. near the present settlement of Mehrauli. Years later, "Dillu" came to be spoken as Dilli or Delhi.

Over a period of time, the Tomar Rajputs had extended their hegemony north-westward and established their regional headquarters at Suraj Kund. Their Chief, Anang Pal, built a citadel,

---

[5]M.A. Sherring: *Benaras, Past and Present*. p.7-8, L.P. Publication.

[6]Diana L. Elk: *A Sacred Geography*.

named Lal Kot, about ten kilometres west of Suraj Kund. In the early twelfth century, Vigrarhar Chauhan defeated the Tomar King and brought his territory, including Lal Kot, under Chauhan's control. When Prithvi Raj Chauhan, also known as Rai Pathora, became the King, he built a massive fort as an extension of Lal Kot. In the strict sense, it is the Lal Kot-Quila Rai Pathora, and not Lal Kot as a separate entity, which is the first Delhi.

Leaving aside the ancient pre-historic urban settlements, Delhi had six distinct cities: Lalkot-Quila Rai Pathora; Siri; Tughlakabad; Jahan Panah; Ferozabad; and Purana Quila. Lord Curzon described these cities as 'dreary and desolate tombs'. Shahjahanabad, the city founded by Mughul Emperor Shahjahan in 1638 on the bank of the Yamuna, near the old ruins of Ferozabad, is the seventh city. It is against this background that some historians speak of seven cities[7] of Delhi. The above six cities are now extinct. Only their ruins remain as mute testimony to their past. But Shahjahanabad, the seventh city, is still a living city, accommodating about half a million people in a limited walled area, nesting frozen memories of its past triumphs and tragedies, in a few hidden corners of its over-crowded lanes, bye-lanes and bazaars and occasionally speaking to us through the silent voices of its history.[8]

Shahjahanabad, though cast in a classical mould of a fortified city, acquired a distinct character of its own under the strong impact of

---

[7] Some scholars take the number of medieval Delhi cities as more than seven. In any case, before New Delhi was built, Shahjahanabad, the seventh city, was the only living city. All other cities, including pre-historic city of Inderprastha, were extinct. In some of my earlier books and newspaper articles, I have called Edwin Lutyen's New Delhi as the eighth Delhi, and Delhi that has been built after mid-1950, particularly after coming into force of the Delhi Development Act, as the Ninth Delhi. The size of the Ninth Delhi, in terms of population and urbanized area is now about ten times bigger than all the previous eight historic cities of Delhi built by the medieval or modern regimes. This would provide to the reader a broad idea about the tremendous expansion that Delhi has seen, after the DDA was set up.

[8] Kucha Ghasi Ram reminds us of the famous astrologer, Ghasi Ram, upon whose predictions the emperor always relied; Begum-ka-Bagh of the recreational facilities of the time and the manner in which the ladies of the *Herm* enjoyed themselves; and Ballimaran

its founder's power and personality who is remembered as a great builder of monumental buildings, such as Lal Qila and Jama Masjid. The main artery was Chandni Chowk through which passed a canal, lined with trees. A boulevard extended from the main gate of the Red Fort to the Fatehpuri Mosque. On both sides of this boulevard were the shops of merchants and their living places. Bernier, the famous French traveller, has described the scene as under:

> In the spaces between are open shops where, during the day, artisans work, bankers sit for the dispatch of their business, and merchants exhibit their wares. Within the arch is a small door, opening into a warehouse, in which these wares are deposited for the night. The houses of the merchants are built over these warehouses, at the back of the arcades: they look handsome enough from the street, and appear tolerably commodious within: they are airy, at a distance from the dust, and communicate with the terrace-roofs over the shops, on which the inhabitants sleep at night.[9]

The rich merchants and generals lived along the river and their large "villas" were near the Red Fort.[10] The comparatively under-privileged were pushed towards the fringe of the town. All the

---

of the *Ballimars*, i.e. those who used to row boats in the Yamuna. Ghalib's simple house in the Ballimaran locality still exists and reminds us of the finest, humanistic poetry ever written. Digamber Jain Temple and the Bird Hospital attached to it, which treats the sick and wounded birds and sets them free after cure, are expressions of Shahjahanabad conscience, its love and compassion. Katra Neel, Chawri Bazar, Bazar Sita Ram, all have their associations and traditions. And what expressive and colourful names are these: Gali Paranthe Wali, a street where *paranthas* of special type are cooked; Gali Mandir Wali, a lane with temples: Kucha Chakiwalan, a street of the flour-grinders; and Kucha Dhobian, a street of the washermen.

[9] Bernier, *Travel in the Mughul Empire*, 1656-1668, S. Chand & Co. p.245.

[10] In Chapter III, titled: *Ninth Delhi Greens and their Philosophic Pedestal,* I have brought out features of my Special Initiative Programme for setting up of Great Green National Cultural Hubs. Under this initiative, elements of history, heritage, environment and clean civic life were synthesized to create lasting assets in the form of natural and cultural wealth. Since the items pertaining to legacy of Turko-Afghan period and the period of the Mughal regime have been dealt with, as components of the Hubs, in the aforesaid Chapter, I am making here only a very brief mention of main events and trends of the said periods. This approach, I trust, would avoid repetition, while maintaining the continuity of historical backdrop.

buildings were not pucca. Even in Chandni Chowk, a number of buildings were of clay and straw. Suburbs of the poor, near the wall or even outside, were not very different from the 'jhuggi-clusters' of today.

The city reached its zenith during the early period of Aurangzeb's rule, when its population grew to about two lakhs. It was at that time that the wall around the city was completed and Shahjahanabad acquired its present shape and form. In the later period, however, the city began to show strains of Aurangzeb's puritanical personality; its life-nurturing functions weakened and art and architecture suffered.

With the death of Aurangzeb in 1707, the twilight of the Mughul empire began. The weakness of the empire, coupled with the wealth, beauty, and fame of Shahjahanabad, was a standing temptation to the adventurers, invaders, and other political forces that were emerging in and around India at that time. The city was brutally ravished and denuded of its charm and exuberance. It is sad to note that the city did not display the will to fight, the will to save its honour. Its citizens allowed themselves to be slaughtered like lambs. Their poetry, their art and culture, their skill as artisans, and their knowledge of science and medicine could not save them.

By the beginning of the nineteenth century, Shahjahanabad had acquired a new master – intelligent, subtle and calculating. Lord Lake, after defeating the Marhattas in 1803, established British control over Shahjahanabad. The Mughul empire lost everything except its sonorous title and ceremonial privileges. About Shah Alam's power and position, there was a popular distich of the time:

*Badshah Shah Alam*
*Az Delhi ta Palam.*
(King Shah Alam
From Delhi to Palam.)

The British control brought peace and moderate prosperity to Shahjahanabad. Though the life for the poor was hard, the middle and upper classes had comfortable time. The culture of the city was not very different from the Nawabi Lucknow culture so appropriately described by Mirza Mohammad Rusva in his novel *Umrao Jaan Ada.*[11] In the words of Percieval Spear, Delhi at that time was a German Weimar, with Ghalib for its Goethe. It was during this period that Ghalib, Zauq, and Zafar wrote their unforgettable poetry – full of romance, tragedy, humanism, and breadth of life.

Shahjahanabad was a charming place and the mood of the time was expressed by Zauq when he wrote: "*Kahan Jain Zauk Dilli Ki Gallian Chhor Kar*" (where should we go after leaving the streets of Delhi; they are so charming). Poetry, music, and sports dominated the life of the people. Favourite sports of the aristocracy were cock-fighting, kite-flying, and quail fighting. These sports evoked as much interest as do the cricket and football of our time. The common citizen enjoyed the spectacle.

While the Imperial Court was the centre of cultural activities, the Hindus dominated the local trade and commerce and the British controlled the administration. There was much give and take in daily life. This is what Percieval Spear has to say in this regard:

> Official garden parties at Metcalfe House were attended by Mughul princes and Hindu bankers equally with British officials and their wives. The Court celebrated the Hindu festivals of Diwali and Holi as well as the Muslim Id; the Hindus regarded the Mohurram ceremonies and procession as almost as much their own as the Muslims. Bahadur Shah followed his father in the semi-Hindu custom of making murids or disciples, who regarded him as a spiritual preceptor in virtue of his kingly office and the festival of Punkha, held at Mehrauli in the rains, was attended by Hindus and Muslims, who went in procession in turn to the Hindu temple of Jogmayaji and the tomb of the Muslim saint Qutab-ud-din. Communal life was tranquil but

[11]The novel narrates the life of a courtesan and portrays Lucknow's culture during the time of Wajid Ali Khan. Considered as a classic of Urdu story writing, it has been translated, under the auspices of UNESCO.

> not quite idyllic. There were no records of riots during the period, but there was always an undertone of tension.[12]

The upheaval of the year 1857 was a turning point not only in the political history of Shahjahanabad but also in its social and cultural life. The British officers instinctively turned away from it. After a short stay in Kashmere Gate area, inside the Walled City, they moved away to the locality of Civil Lines, leaving the vast space of Qudsia and Nicholson Gardens between the old and the new settlements.

Uptil 1890, the relationship between the Hindus and Muslims was marked by mutual trust and tolerance. In fact, in the early stages of freedom movement, particularly in 1918-19, the city saw scenes of reverential friendship between the two communities. It may seem unbelievable that, in the wake of protest meetings and demonstrations following the arrival of British Constitution Mission, Swami Shraddhanand, who later died at the hands of a Muslim assassin, was invited to address a prayer meeting from the platform of Jama Masjid. Of the happenings of 4 April 1918, the Swami had recorded:

> I was busy writing, when by 1.00 p.m., about 50 Musalman gentlemen hounded my humble lodging and lovingly forced me down. A tonga was waiting. In the way, they requisitioned several conveyances, one faster than the other, till an empty motor car was found. I was then hurried on, and reached the southern step of Jama Masjid. Maulvi Abdul Mujib was addressing the audience. He stopped, waiting for me to go up. I hesitated. A hundred voices urged me to go up. After ascending two steps, I again hesitated. The huge audience was up on its legs and with one voice asked me to go up. When I reaches the pulpit, they sat down....... It was an inspiring spectacle.[13]

Beneath the surface, however, the under-current of communal suspicion and strife continued to flow. The British rulers, were quick

---

[12]Percival Spear: *The Twilight of the Mughuls*.

[13]Swami Shraddanand, *Inside Congress*, Phoenix.

to boost this undercurrent and make it a key component of their policy of 'divide and rule'. As the freedom struggle gained momentum, the net of the 'divide and rule' policy was spread over a larger area.

On December 23, 1912, a bomb was thrown at Lord Hardinge's procession, when it was passing through Chandni Chowk, near Katra Dhulia. The attack had been planned and executed by a small group of 'revolutionaries' whose hardcore was arrested and put to trial. Three of them – Master Amir Chand, Avadh Bihari Bose, and Bal Mukand – were sentenced to death and hanged on 8 May 1915 in the local district jail. Later on, under the aegis of Mahatma Gandhi, Delhi, by and large, played a non-violent and disciplined role in the freedom struggle. It became a focal point of the struggle in northern India. It also provided to the national movement leadership of such stalwarts as Hakim Ajmal Khan, Dr. M.A. Ansari, Asaf Ali, and Desh Bandhu Gupta.

On a separate plane, the British rulers, notwithstanding their alienation, after 1857, from the people of Delhi, could not but be dazzled by the imperial tradition of the city. This should be clear from their decisions to hold the three imperial *Darbars* in Delhi. When Queen Victoria assumed the title of Empress of India, under the Royal Title Act (1876), Lord Lytton decided to celebrate the occasion by holding a grand Darbar. The venue selected was not Calcutta but Delhi, "since no city in the British Empire was so fitted as Delhi for the assumption of sovereignty of India". Twenty-six years later, Lord Curzon organized the second Darbar. The third Darbar was held on 12 December 1911 in the presence of Emperor George V who, on that occasion, announced the transfer of the capital of India from Calcutta to Delhi. The confidential note, dated August 25, 1911 of the Governor-General-in-Council had given the following reasons for transfer:

> On geographical, historical and political grounds, the capital of the Indian Empire should be Delhi. The political advantage accruing from the transfer of the capital could not be overestimated. Delhi was still a name to be conjured with. It is

> intimately associated in the minds of the Hindus, with sacred legends which go back even beyond the dawn of history... To the Muhammadans, it would be a source of unbounded gratification to see the ancient capital of the Mughuls restored to its proud position as the seat of the Empire.

Concurring with above views, Lord Crewe, Secretary of State, had noted: "The site of the new capital is rich in meaning and significance. It will assist the efficiency of the government, remove widely felt grievances and satisfy the historic sense of millions".

The decision makers belonged to a generation of 'thinkers and doers' who "aspired to bind the past and present and confidently sought to dictate the future". This would be clear from the unambiguous declaration made by Sir George Birdwood: "It is not a cantonment that we have to lay out at Delhi but an Imperial City – the symbol of British Raj in India – and it must like Rome be built for eternity". Herbert Baker, the principal colleague of Edwin Lutyens, measured the imprints, not on the time-scale of a century or two, but in terms of millennia: "In 20,000 years, there must be an Imperial Lutyens tradition in Indian architecture".

At the highest level, the thinking was not very different, though it showed greater awareness of India's indigenous building skills. At the time of laying foundation stone of the new capital, Viceroy Lord Hardinge, in his introductory address, entertained a slightly broader span of history: "Many capitals have been inaugurated in the neighbourhood of Delhi, some of which are so ancient that their origin is lost in the mist of antiquity, but none has risen under happier auspices than those which attended the ceremony that your Imperial majesties are about to perform, and assuredly none ever held promise of greater permanence or of a more prosperous and glorious future." The king, in his reply, said: "It is my desire that the planning and designing of the public buildings to be erected will be considered with greatest deliberations and care, so that the new creation may be in every way worth of the ancient beautiful city". Earlier, King George had articulated his thinking through his Private Secretary

Lord Stamfordham: "The Indian was of critical mind, fully aware of what Hindu and Mughul builders had accomplished. We must now let him see for the first time, the power of Western science, art and civilization".

It is of pivotal importance to note that every decision the authorities took, every declaration they made, reflected the positivity, pride and general strength of the British civilization of the times and the high quality of leadership that this civilisation produced, practically in all walks of life – public administration, architecture, town planning, etc. Their first priority, undoubtedly, was to serve the imperial interest of Britain. But this did not prevent them to give expression to their inner impulse to create a mighty and magnificent imprint on the Indian soil of British values of order, discipline, scientific precision, respect for eclectic and enlightened planning and firm and efficient governance. Is all this not in sharp contrast to what, of late, has been happening in Delhi, where powerful elements in the leadership of almost all the political parties have been virtually competing with one another in developing a messy civilisational tradition by encouraging creation of un-authorised colonies in the capital and then regularizing them on the eve of the civic, state or Parliament elections, caring little for the all-round destructive potential of their legacy?

The original site chosen for the new city was on the north of northern ridge. But the Town Planning Commission, comprising G.S. Swinton, Edwin Lutyens and J.A. Brodie, considered the original site unsuitable. On its recommendation, location of the new capital was changed to the area around Raisina Hill. The foundation stone, laid so solemnly, was quietly picked up at midnight by a young Punjabi contractor, Shobha Singh, and taken on a bullock cart, wrapped in a gunny bag, to Raisina hill.

Planning and construction of the new capital, at the new site, was mainly in the hands of Edwin Lutyens, an ambitious architect, who in his childhood had dreamt of constructing monumental buildings. "As Faith Wills, Fate fulfills." This is what Lutyens in his youth had inscribed upon a casket presented to his would-be wife. In his case, fate could not have fulfilled better what his faith had willed. He got the rare opportunity of building a new city, an "Anglo-Indian Rome," which would reflect the might, glory and vastness of the British Empire upon which the sun never set.

The story of the construction of New Delhi is fascinating and educative, too. In this story come alive strong personalities of planners, builders and administrators. But the story cannot be told here. I would, however, refer briefly to two episodes which are both interesting and instructive.

Swinton, Lutyens, and Brodie often went on elephant to survey the site. Once, near the ridge, they entered into an argument about the cost of tunneling at a point where the ridge was low. So fierce became the argument that Brodie refused to share the same elephant. He "slid off the elephant, walked five miles home with temperature nearing 117 in the shade." Such was his emotional involvement in the project.

Lutyens was keen to build on a grand scale. The cost of his projects mounted. Lord Hardinge, Viceroy, started curtailing his proposals. Lutyens was upset. He ruefully remarked, "Viceroy thinks only of what the place would look like in three years' time: 300 years is what I think of." But Lutyens was not a man to give up easily. He cultivated Lady Hardinge and got his schemes sanctioned through her influence. Once, however, she, too, got annoyed with Lutyens for side-tracking her suggestion. He employed humour where other skills failed. In an assumed posture of penitence, he told Lady Hardinge: "I will wash your feet with my tears and dry them with my hair. It is true that I have very little hair, but you have very little feet." Lady Hardinge burst into laughter. Her annoyance vanished like thin air. Lutyens got his proposals through. His commitment to the monumentality of his projects was so deep that he employed every method to secure their acceptance.

At one stage, Lord Hardinge, Viceroy, was attracted by the proposition of H.V. Lanchester, a British architect who had experience of Indian conditions, having worked in Delhi, Jodhpur and Gwalior. In April 1912, Lancehster was appointed as Consultant Adviser to the government. He saw the need for integration of the old and the new, the Indian and the English. His suggestion included a programme of future alteration and expansion of Shahjahanabad. Hardinge declared that he wanted the two cities – old and new – to be one. He discussed this proposition with Lutyens who did not deny its validity. Yet, in practice, neither Lutyens nor Hardinge did anything to integrate the two cities into one. Physically, socially and culturally, Shahjahanabad remained isolated and the wall remained the wall. It is, therefore, no surprise that the British art and architecture had practically no effect on Shahjahanabad. Begum Samru's Palace, now known as Bhagirath Palace, Skinner's Church, Kashmere Gate, and a few other isolated buildings of minor importance are the only structures which reflect the influence of British architecture on Shahjahanabad.

For dealing with the civic issues, the Delhi Municipal Commission, which later came to be known as Delhi Municipal Committee, was established in 1862. Writing in 1901, H.C. Fanshawe observed: "The Municipal Committee has always been distinguished for its enlightenment, and has spent twelve lakhs of rupees on its water works, and is about to spend as much on a complete system of city drainage. It consists of seven Hindus, ten Muhammadans, and seven European members, five of the last being district officials. Twelve of the members are elected and twelve nominated; the number of registered electors is 10,000."[14]

The Municipal Committee may have been enlightened but it did not have finance to deal effectively with the many civic problems of the city. Nor did it receive special assistance from the government. The average annual municipal income from 1896 to 1901 was only Rs.435,000.

Nevertheless, the government showed occasional concern over the congestion in the city. As far back as 1905, Major Parson, Deputy

---

[14]H.C. Fanshawe : *Delhi Past and Present*; John Murray, London 1902.

Commissioner, had referred to the congestion in Shahjahanabad and advocated that the city must have "room or burst." It was obvious, he said, that the city must expand in the western direction by breaking the wall and filling the ditch. For about 25 years, however, hardly anything was done in this regard, and Shahjahanabad continued to suffer from congestion. In fact, the decision to build Imperial Capital at Delhi aggravated the conditions. A.P. Hume, who was appointed as Officer on Special Duty by the Government of India to prepare a comprehensive report on the Relief of Congestion in Delhi, had said:

> The location of the Imperial Capital at Delhi introduced a new factor governing growth, the result of which has become very apparent in the last decade, and the future effects of which it is still difficult to gauge. If we take the average rate of increase of population for all enumerations since 1868 at 12.45 per cent, it is reasonable to suppose that 28 per cent of the increase in the last decade is due directly to the building of New Delhi.[15]

In 1937, the Delhi Improvement Trust was set up, and formulation and execution of Town Improvement and Town Expansion schemes were entrusted to it. But the resources of the Trust were limited. It had also no overall comprehension of the needs and no long-range programme to meet them. In the opinion of the Delhi Improvement Trust Enquiry Committee (1951), which was set up by the Government of India to assess the work of the Delhi Improvement Trust, the achievements of the Trust were not significant. The Committee observed:

> The achievements of the Trust during the thirteen years of its existence are not at all impressive. Two essential pre-requisite of the proper planning of a town are: (i) a civic survey, and (ii) a Master Plan. The Trust has been able to produce neither, with the result that the growth of Delhi has been proceeding in a

---

[15] A.P. Hume, *Report on the Relief of Congestion in Delhi,* Vol. I. Government of India Press, 1936. p.14.

haphazard way, with little foresight and imagination and without any coordination.[16]

Earlier, in pursuance of its long-term imperial interests and as a part of its plan to deepen 'the divide and rule' policy, the British rulers introduced the principle of communal representation in the public services and in legislature.

From 1922, the practice of nominating Indians from minority communities, who were unsuccessful at the examinations, was adopted. This development had the effect not only of undermining the purity and fairness of the selection process but also introduced a new loyalty – loyalty to one's own community – in the machinery of governance. It was on account of this factor that by the mid-thirties and early forties, the ICS and other services had virtually got divided into two broad camps – sympathisers of the Congress and the sympathizers of the Muslim League. "By the autumn of 1946, all Indians in Central Government were either Congress, more or less, or League, more or less".

It was mainly because of the deep fissures in the civil services that the last two years of the British rule in India turned out to be tragically inglorious. These were the years in which the steel frame degenerated into a moth-eaten bamboo structure. These were also the years which showed how inherently weak India's social structure was, how neighbours fell upon neighbours with the ferocity of mad dogs, how the public services themselves added to the fury and fire and how the governance machinery often acted as an instrument of disorder rather than of order and made the miserable even more miserable.

While Gandhiji and his band of dedicated colleagues had succeeded in strengthening the freedom struggle, and provided high moral and humanitarian values to it, they could not evolve an effective strategy either to counter the two-nation theory or to meet

---

[16]Report of the Delhi Improvement Trust Enquiry Committee, 1951 (Vol. II). Government of India Press, 1951. This Committee was set up by the Government of India in April 1950, under the Chairmanship of G.D. Birla. Its other Members were Dr. Bakshi Tek Chand, M.P., Desh Bandhu Gupta, B. Shiva Rao, M.P., Dr. Yudhvir Singh, and A.N. Nanda.

the challenge of violence embedded in 'direct action'. Consequently, when freedom came, it was embittered with partition. The tryst with 'destiny' was accompanied by a tryst with blood and bones. It led to one of the biggest migrations known to history.

With the influx, in 1947-48, of about half million displaced persons from Pakistan to Delhi, and development, on emergency basis, of 36 rehabilitation colonies, providing 69,000 residential units, ranging in size from 60 to 80 sq. yd, during the period, 1948 to 1953, the pressure on the two main civic bodies, Delhi Municipal Committee and Delhi Improvement Trust, mounted to a breaking point. In a short span of time, Delhi's population had increased from 7 lakh to 17 lakh. The G.D. Birla Committee, mentioned above, had earlier recommended setting up a single Planning and Controlling Authority for the Urban areas of Delhi. After considering these recommendations and realizing the urgent need for checking haphazard growth, the Government of India promulgated the Delhi (Control of Building Operation) Ordinance 1955 to constitute the Delhi Development (Provisional) Authority. It was followed by regular Act of 1957. The Delhi Improvement Trust stood abolished.

The Delhi Development Authority (DDA) was set up under the provisions of the Delhi Development Act, 1957. With the help of the Town Planning Organisation of Ministry of Health and Ford Foundation Team attached to it, the DDA finalised a Master Plan for Delhi (1962-1982) and notified it under the statutory provisions of the Delhi Development Act on 1 September 1962.

In the sphere of town planning in India, the Delhi Master Plan must be reckoned as a pioneering work. For the first time, a long-range urban plan was prepared after making detailed and scientific studies. The Plan assessed the existing deficiencies in various directions and estimated the requirements of the future. The back-logs and future needs were put together so as to provide a framework of development in an integrated and co-ordinated manner, keeping in view the existing resources as well as those that could be created. It also laid down the planning laws and regulations for the entire Union Territory of Delhi.

Ninth Delhi, the nomenclature and contextual parameters of which have been indicated by me earlier, had to reckon with the structural legacies of seventh and eighth cities. It had to face the problems of sprawling rehabilitation colonies which were hastily planned and developed in the wake of influx of displaced persons from Pakistan. Added to this were the problems emanating from the flood of migrants. Over-politicization of local institutions, emergence of new class of exploiters, with no regard either for the healthy heritage of the past or future of the city, created numerous other difficulties. Against these negative forces were the positive factors which manifested themselves in the inspired vision of a few individual leaders and civil servants who had both the courage and keenness to move to cleaner and nobler horizons.

Ninth Delhi has its planning foundations in the first Master Plan (1962-1981). But planning in itself would have hardly yielded any results. A creative approach, which could meet the challenge of physical, financial and institutional constraints, was called for. Accordingly, simultaneous to the enforcement of the Master Plan, a scheme of acquisition, development, and disposal of land, with a revolving capital of Rs.5 crores, was formulated and executed. The programme of acquisition, development and disposal of land was so deftly arranged that the revolving fund got replenished in time to keep the cycle of acquisition going. The key component of the strategy was to ensure that non-availability of finances with the government did not stand in the way, and additional resources were created from within the city by reaping advantage of the rising value of the urbaniseable land consequent to the investment made by public authorities in the urban infrastructure.

The strategy had many other salutary features. It facilitated distribution in accordance with the needs of different sections of the community. It equalized the impact of planning on the erstwhile landowners as everyone got compensation on the same principles, irrespective of the use prescribed under the Master Plan. It checked hoarding and speculation in land. It safeguarded the future and secured long-term planning objectives. It also helped the public authorities to ensure that issues pertaining to environment and ecology were taken care of at the time of allotment of land, allowing at the same time the private sector to do most of the construction.

It is on account of the above unique and courageous move on the 'land acquisition, development and disposal front' that the Delhi Development Authority/Government, starting with a small revolving fund, was able to build a solid and welfare-oriented land bank of about 72,000 acres. Thousands of crores were generated and lakhs of poor, low income and middle income persons provided with plots and houses and thousands of acres created not only as 'community greens' but also as protective shield to several hundred monuments.

Some of the biggest residential colonies of the world like Naraina, Mayapuri, Janakpuri, Vikaspuri, Ashok Vihar, Shalimar Bagh, Pitampura, Yamuna Vihar, Vivek Vihar, Rohini, Saket and Pushp Vihar and Dwarka have come into being. About 14 lakh dwelling units, largely of Janta, Low Income and Middle Income categories have been made available either by way of direct construction or through cooperative societies. This is in addition to 41 resettlement colonies for squatters and slum dwellers. Commercial Centres, such as Nehru Place, Rajendra Place, Bhikaiji Cama Place, Netaji Place, have also been built besides many educational, cultural and other institutions. The great city forests now serve as the healthy lungs for the metropolis. Ten regional parks, 104 district parks, 190 neighbourhood parks and 38 sports centres make their own contribution in preserving its environment and ecology. No private acquirer and developer of land would have entertained such a comprehensive vision or taken care of housing for the poor or green areas for the community. It is out of acquired pool of land that about 2,000 hectares was allotted virtually free to poor migrants under the special squatters' resettlement project of 1976.

Land, especially the urbanisable one, under the first Master Plan (1962-1981) and its two successor Master Plans of 2001 and 2021, was only one of the critical challenges which Ninth Delhi and its leadership in the political, bureaucratic, social and cultural arenas had to tackle. There were many other equally, if not more, critical problems embedded in the old and worn out structure of civic institutions. Then, there was a fundamental challenge, a mother of all challenges, of rekindling the power of the Indian mind, of recapturing the healthy strands of India's culture and of evolving a civilisational pattern, which is able to maintain dynamic equilibrium between the material and spiritual needs of the people.

How these challenges were faced or ignored, how new opportunities were seized or missed, and how some of the visionary approaches were accompanied by myopic ones, constitute the story of Ninth Delhi – its saga of triumph and tragedy, of fulfilment and disappointment. The seven chapters that follow would also unfold different layers of the current Indian reality, including the inner ones, and leave it to the readers to ponder over the fate and future of the capital city and the civilisational ripples that it is engendering and transmitting all over urban India.

CHAPTER I

# CITY AND ITS LEADERSHIP AND CIVILISATIONAL CONTOURS

***From Nehru to Indira Gandhi to Morarji Desai to Vajpayee to Sonia Gandhi-Manmohan Singh – Moments of Triumphs and Tragedies of Ninth Delhi.***

*Great cities are built by great leaders with a great vision which is illuminated by a civilisational surge and not by the birds of passage who could flutter for a while in uncertain winds and then arrowed down.*

— Author

As one who was concerned with the formulation and implementation of Delhi Master Plan, I had the good fortune to come in contact with Jawaharlal Nehru's thought on cities in general and Delhi in particular. In the middle of 1963, he very graciously visited my modest office in Vikas Bhavan, the first pre-fabricated structure put up in Delhi. This he did at the request of Bhagwan Sahay, Chief Commissioner, whom he held in high esteem. Bhagwan Sahay was keen to show to Nehru how office and field work, connected with the implementation of the Master Plan, were being organised on scientific lines, how new principles and practices were being evolved for securing integrated and sustainable urban development, and how financial self-sufficiency was being achieved by acquiring lands, with a small 'revolving fund', and leasing them out, on a rational and equitable basis, for residential, industrial, commercial and institutional purposes.

Despite his poor health, Nehru stayed in my office for about ten minutes, looked at various maps and charts, and asked me and Bhagwan Sahay a couple of questions, particularly about the opposition of strong vested interests to the acquisition of all urbanisable lands. His visit, though brief, animated our sense of mission and prompted us to go ahead with our projects with greater courage and convictions.

As a matter of general interest and also as a part of my duty, I have studied a number of books, reports, plans and projects about Delhi. But nowhere have I found a description of this city as captivating and insightful as the one penned by Nehru in these words:

> Here we stand in Delhi city, symbol of old India and the new. It is not the narrow lanes and houses of old Delhi or the wide spaces and rather pretentious buildings of New Delhi that count, but the spirit of this ancient city. For Delhi has been an epitome of India's history with its succession of glory and disaster, and with its great capacity to absorb many cultures and yet remain itself. It is a gem with many facets, some bright and some darkened by age, presenting the course of India's life and thought during the ages. Even the stones here whisper to our ears of the ages of long ago and the air we breathe is full of the dust and fragrance of the past as also of the fresh and piercing winds of the present. We face the good and bad of India in Delhi city which has been the grave of many empires and the nursery of a republic. What a tremendous story is here; the tradition of millennia of our history surrounds us at every step, and the procession of innumerable generations passes by before our eyes....

It is easy to see how these few lines capture not only the soul of a great city and great civilisation but also the soul of a powerful mind which was imbued with a poetic passion and a profound sense of history. They have moved me as nothing else has done during my long date with Delhi. Thereafter, I have always looked at this rapidly expanding metropolis as a spiritual workshop of the nation, a cultural crucible for fashioning out new ideas and ideals which would harmonise its past, present, and future into a dynamic web.

But it had also struck me that Jawaharlal Nehru had not spelt out how the 'good' of Delhi could be preserved; how its 'bad' could be incised; and how the fresh and piercing winds of the future could be prevented from getting polluted by the stinking garbage accumulated over the years in the vast and varied courtyards of its society. I had often wondered why the problems of implementation had not engaged Jawaharlal Nehru's attention with as much depth as he had shown in spinning out his ideals and propositions. Months earlier, I had read his foreword to a booklet of the Bharat Sewak Samaj, titled: *Slums of Old Delhi*, which contained the Socio-Economic Survey[1] of early 1950s *katras and bastis*. In it, he recorded:

> For the past several years I have been deeply interested in the slums of Delhi. Every time I have visited them I return with a certain feeling of numbness and an urgent desire to have something done to remove these slums. Action is initiated but progress is slow because of innumerable difficulties. Vested interests are always hard to dislodge and the law generally appears to favour them.

Clearly, Nehru was aware of the 'innumerable difficulties' and also of the long arms of the 'vested interests'. Was he, as a towering leader of a nascent Republic, aspiring to be 'mighty in thought, mighty in deed, mighty in culture and mighty in service to humanity', not expected to create a reform oriented society and state, and show to the nation an effective way of removing the difficulties and defeating the vested interests? Should he have not realised, in the background of his study of history, that the crucial issue that he faced was not what he knew and wished but what he did with what he knew and wished?

The questions of this nature and many other issues connected with the attitude and outlook of post-1947 leadership continued to trouble, and sometimes torment, me during my long dates, under different regimes, and in different positions and circumstances, with

[1]The Socio-Economic survey was conducted by a committee consisting of Shri Brij Krishan Chandiwala, as Chairman, and Shri N.K. Pant, Shri P.B. Desai of Delhi School of Economics, Shri M.S.Gore (of Delhi School of Social Work), Shri V.A. Phillipos of Town Planning Organisation and Smt. Aruna Asaf Ali as members. However, the main responsibility of the survey was shouldered by Shri Pant and Shri Desai.

the affairs of Ninth Delhi, especially those relating to slums, squatters and planned and disciplined urbanisation.

My first memorable date with Delhi, at the ground level, occurred, when I came here as a young refugee boy from West Pakistan. I used to go to Kudesia Garden[2], especially on Sundays and holidays, to study. There was acute congestion in the small government house where I and other members of the family had taken shelter, along with other displaced persons. On a very hot day in June, being tired and in weak health, I made a pillow of a small wooden plank, on which I used to fix papers for facility of writing notes, and adjusted it against the side arm of the bench, kept under a cluster of shady trees, and went to sleep. Suddenly, I was woken up by an intense rustle of the leaves underneath the bench. I found a huge snake lurking around. I virtually lost my breath. Luckily, the wooden plank, the make-shift pillow, slipped and fell on the ground. The noise disturbed the snake. It moved away. But I could not alight from the bench, so fear frozen was I. I shouted for help. An old gardener, who had seen the frightening spectacle from some distance, walked to me calmly and told me not to worry: "This aged and majestic King of the Cobras is an angel, who does not bite, but blesses. For you, it could be a good omen". But, then, he added: "Never, again, make the mistake of sitting in summer underneath this extraordinary dense and cool canopy of shady trees. It is a favourite spot of small and spiteful scorpions and poisonous snakes that abound in the crumbling monuments in the vicinity. No one cares. No one bothers. The garden is in disarray. A good part of it has already been encroached upon by the vendors of the Yamuna Bazaar. The number of morning and evening walkers has sharply dwindled".

---

[2]Kudesia Garden, near Kashmere Gate, was built on the western side of river Yamuna as a mini palace cum fort with a large pleasure-garden at the initiative and under the supervision of Begum Kudesia, Queen Mother and her son, Ahmed Shah. The buildings were extensively damaged during the attack of British Forces on Kashmere Gate in 1857, and these are in ruins now. But a sizeable part of the spacious garden with all its beautiful trees remained.

At the moment, the gardener's words had hardly any meaning for me. They just sailed across my mind. I hurriedly collected my two books and note-sheets, tucked them into my little bag, thanked the gardener and departed from the scene. I never went back to Kudesia Garden till, over two decades later, my job as Commissioner, Delhi Development Authority, brought me again near the same spot for organising a massive project of clearance of slums and squatters that had come to occupy the vast 'Master-Plan Green' area between Kudesia Garden and the bank of river Yamuna, including the Nigambodh Cremation Ghat. At that time Mrs. Indira Gandhi was the Prime Minister and Dr. A.N. Jha, the Lieutenant-Governor.

In the unauthorised occupation of above public lands were involved not only the multiple problems of woeful insanitation, savage environment and inhuman habitats of the poor but also those caused by powerful vested interests in politics, business and local administration. But no one paid any attention to it, though a clear policy decision[3], taken at the highest executive level, with the concurrence of major political parties, to free all public lands from squatters by providing alternative sites only to 'eligible occupants', had been in existence since 1960.

Earlier, the Lieutenant-Governor A.N. Jha and I had seen in the file a letter written by President Dr. Rajendra Prasad to the then Chief Commissioner A.D. Pandit, expressing his agony over the deplorable conditions, prevailing in the Nigambodh Ghat, where he had gone in connection with the cremation of his elder sister who passed away while staying with him at Rashtrapati Bhawan. The 'national shame' which the President felt could well be imagined, when he noticed that a number of friends and well-wishers, including Ambassadors and High Commissioners who came to attend the cremation-ceremony at the Ghat had to wade through garbage, mud and even human excreta and cattle waste.

[3]The background, the particulars of the policy-decision and the experimental stage through which the decision-making process had passed, have been given in chapter IV, *Slums: Physical and Mental.*

It was in this backdrop that Dr. A.N. Jha and I undertook a project which could legitimately be described as a pioneering venture to create a number of signposts of triumphs for the Ninth Delhi. Being a Sanskrit scholar, with his roots firmly planted in the family tradition of championing the values of ancient Indian philosophy, Dr. A. N. Jha was acutely conscious of the need to accord priority to the proposal of redeveloping Nigambodh Ghat. One day, after visiting the site with me, he asked: "Can we clear this?" "Yes, certainly," I replied, "provided political element can be taken care of." Dr. Jha took little time to decide. He said: "We must go ahead. Be careful. In the process, we may lose our jobs, even our heads."

I drew up a plan of action, within the broad framework of the above mentioned 1960's policy-decision of the Government of India. The plan took an integrated view of all related problems and provided for their simultaneous tackling through a well-coordinated project of clearance cum resettlement cum redevelopment. The detail of the plan and projects, the manner in which they were conceived, the precision and speed with which they were executed, the determined face of the implementational set-up that was shown to all kinds of vested interests, have been discussed in chapter IV titled *Slums: Physical and Mental.*

All that I may indicate here is that the comprehensive initiative and committed action resulted in the clearance of a huge slum; development of a neat Nigambodh Ghat, with solemn and soul lifting environment around; emergence of resettlement colonies of Seelampur, Seemapuri and Nand Nagari, with regular layouts and civic facilities, for providing permanent accommodation to erstwhile squatters and slum-dwellers; completion of the ring road; regeneration of the Kudesia Garden; and, in due course, construction of the state of art Inter-State Bus Terminus and bridge over river Yamuna. It was an unprecedented endeavour which was brought to a successful conclusion in a short time. But what did Dr. A.N. Jha and I get in return? Largely, brickbats and a barrage of fiery and false accusations, designed to denigrate and demoralise us.

Strolling at the eastern side of the Kudesia Garden on the last day of the clearance cum resettlement operation, my thoughts went back to the complaint of the old gardener: "Here, no one cares, no one bothers". This, I believed, was so, because those who attempted 'to care or bother' soon found themselves in a sea of trouble and needed extraordinary skill, stamina and steadfastness to swim out of it.

Over a period of time, Prime Minister Indira Gandhi came to the site to lay the foundation stone of the Master Plan bridge over river Yamuna. Looking from her high platform at the sprawling green complex, which had undergone full development by that time, including the Nigambodh Ghat-part of the river front, with beautiful trees and shrubs swinging nearby, she wondered whether she was in the same area where once a huge and horrible slum existed. A few years earlier, she had visited, with me and Lieutenant-Governor A.N. Jha, vast area around Hauz Khas monument which had seen even a more striking transformation, from a disease-ridden and muddy slum of cattle, inhuman habitation and polluting workshops, to an elegant cluster of parks, gardens and long shrubby walk-ways. She was so pleased with the innovative development that she light-heartedly suggested that she would wish to leave her 'hand-mark' in the complex. A seedling of Alistonia, her favourite tree, was immediately arranged, and she happily planted it. The graceful tree, now fully grown, with its commemorative plaque underneath, adds to the attraction of the visitors and provides an additional talking point to the regular morning walkers.

Indira Gandhi was eloquent in her praise of our work with regard to the Nigambodh-Kudesia Garden area and the Hauz Khas Green complex. I was puzzled by the tragic irony, implicit in the contradictions between her attitude and the stand taken by her partymen at the ground level. But I did not have the courage to tell her that when the hard crust of the seemingly intractable problem of slum and squatters' clearance and their resettlement was being tackled, at the two above sites, it was the senior leaders of her party, who had caused maximum obstruction and denounced us with such vehemence in public and Parliament that we nearly lost our jobs as well as personal esteem in the common man's eye. Nevertheless, her praise, though expressed at a much later stage, was a great morale booster, springing as it was from her own beliefs and inclinations.

As in the case of Nehru, whose concern for slum clearance and orderly development of the Capital of the Republic was not matched by the reform oriented push to upgrade the milieu of the society, that alone could have met his concern, Mrs. Indira Gandhi did little to ensure that her party-men shared her views about the growth of simple but clean and graceful settlement for the poor and helped, at least not obstruct, those who were endeavouring to give concrete shape to them.

Mrs Indira Gandhi had, in fact, started nursing a feeling of national pride in our path-breaking work, when it received warm appreciation of a number of eminent leaders and experts from abroad, who visited the newly developed areas in mid-1970s, either on their own or at the suggestion of the Prime Minister herself. This would be clear from the few cases cited below.

In September 1976, Mrs. Margaret Thatcher, who at that time was the leader of the Conservative Party in Great Britain, and leader of the opposition in the House of Commons, visited India. During her visit, she called on Prime Minister Indira Gandhi. In the course of their talk, they are believed to have discussed the rapid transformation that the Capital was undergoing. Mrs. Thatcher expressed her wish to see some of the newly developed housing colonies for the low and middle income groups and also the green areas in the vicinity. Mrs Indira Gandhi readily agreed, and asked me to accompany Mrs. Thatcher. After the visit, she noted in the visitors' book: "A lot was being done in the field of housing and development in Delhi which was not known to us. It is evident from the excellent work shown to me by Delhi Development Authority which was very much different from what I saw during my last visit. I wish I had more time to see the transformed city. Houses constructed by Delhi Development Authority are simply marvellous. I did not realise you are doing so well here, and so much."

In those days, whenever any foreign dignitary, VVIP or reputed intellectual met Mrs. Gandhi and spoke about the changing face of Delhi, she invariably suggested a visit to the sites. Those who agreed, and had time, went to see the areas and localities of their interest. In practically all such cases, Mrs. Indira Gandhi deputed me to go with the visitors. She, I believe, chose me because she thought that I could clearly explain the rationale of what was being done and also discuss with the visitors, at the academic and ideological level, the current theories of city-planning that were especially relevant to the problems of the developing countries.

The impressions recorded by the visitors, in almost all the cases, were remarkably warm and encouraging. This is what the President of the London Royal Town Planning Institute, who came to Delhi in February, 1976, said: "It is wonderful to see that the Delhi Development Authority has so much vision and its officers have so much enthusiasm". The views expressed by Mrs. Jill Foot, wife of top Labour Party leader, Britain, were no less laudable: "How encouraging to discover modern town planning and housing projects. Others have much to learn from Delhi planning. The public housing programme of Delhi Development Authority is the best seen so far in any country". In her comments, Mrs Gabrielle Kibble, daughter of the Governor General of Australia, herself an architect and environmentalist, observed: "We have a great deal to learn from you about how to preserve areas around historic buildings for the whole community to enjoy". In February 1975, Prince Charles and Lord Mountbatten visited Delhi. The latter, standing on the eastern side of the ramparts of Red Fort, pointed to me the green development in front and remarked: "Unless I had seen this – the area that was once a stinking slum – I would never have believed the transformation that has been brought about."

All this, though dazzling on the face of it, was no more than a side issue. The central issue of civilisational reconstruction of India and strengthening of positive forces in the society remained untouched; rather, the hostility of the negative forces increased. In fact, from the very inception of my implementation drive, I had realised that whenever any earnest attempt was made to translate declared principles and policies on the ground, the chronic infections in the diseased spots of Indian democracy flared up, rendering an already

Prime Minister Indira Gandhi, looking from the platform/dais at the vast cleared-area, near the Nigambodh Ghat of the Yamuna River Front when, years after the clearance, which was then vehemently opposed by her party's senior Delhi leaders, she came to the site to lay the foundation stone of major Master Plan Projects of Bridge, Roads and Green Areas. In the above photograph, the author (Delhi's Lieutenant Governor at that time) is answering Mrs. Indira Gandhi's query and elaborating the benefits of holistic approach.

(Reference: Section pages 28-29).

*Hauz Khas City-forest:* When Prime Minister Indira Gandhi asked, impromptu, for a seedling of Alistonia for plantation in the upcoming Hauz Khas City-forest, on September 10, 1970, it left Dr. A.N. Jha and I in no doubt that she was instinctively disposed towards implementation of the Green Projects of the Master Plan. This was in contrast to the attitude of her senior local party-men who even opposed clearance of disease-ridden muddy slum of cattle, shacks etc. in the area. Photo above provides a view of the fully grown city-forest with Alistonia tree in its amidst.

(Reference: Chapter 1, pages 28-29).

Prime Minister, Indira Gandi, presenting the all-India Essay Competition award, on October 22, 1971, to the author, (Vice-Chairman, Delhi Development Authority at that time), at the Indian Institute of Public Administration.

(Report-Photo: The Indian Express of October 23, 1971).

With Padma Award (January 26, 1971) being pinned by President V.V. Giri at Rashtrapati Bhavan on October 7, 1971.

*Indira Gandhi Indoor Sports Stadium:* This stadium, with linked infrastructure of modern roads, fly-overs and surrounding greens, all developed/built in a record time, for hosting the IX Asian Games (1982) at Delhi, became a symbol of effectiveness of governance machinery in early 1980s, and enhanced the prestige of the Indian Republic in the international arena.

*Boosting Sports at National level:* The Indoor Stadium also served as a befitting venue for holding public functions to popularize sports. The above photo shows a massive public reception held at this stadium to honour the victorious world cup cricket team 1983.

(Seen at the dais (left to right) are Kapil Dev, Balram Jakhar, Lata Mangeshkar, Rajiv Gandhi, the author (at that time Lt. Governor), Mahender Amarnath, Gavaskar)

When new grounds were being broken at a fast pace, with regard to the planned development of Delhi, a number of foreign dignitaries and experts from abroad, either on their own initiative or at the suggestion of Prime Minister Gandhi, visited newly developed colonies. The above photographs shows Mrs. Jill Foot wife of Miachel Foot on a visit to a low cost housing estate. The other V.V.I.P. who made similar visits, at different dates, to different colonies/estates, included Mrs. Margaret Thatcher and President of the London Royal Town Planning Institute.

(Reference: pages 29-30).

Purana Quila, after having been relieved of years of encroachments in the form of camps, timber stores and coal depots, became a shining example of restoration and clean environment

(Reference: Chapter IV, titled; Slums – Physical and Mental (pages 171- 176)

*Queen Elizabeth at the Red Fort:* Queen Elizabeth visited the Red Fort in November 1983. The author (Lt. Governor at that time) received and escorted her around. In the above photograph, she is seen at the rampart, having a panoramic view of Shahjahanabad: The Walled City of Delhi, and inquiring from the author about the Chandani Chowk through which a canal once passed.

Apprising Queen Elizabeth of some momentous events associated with history of Diwan-i-Khas and Diwan-i-Aam at the Red Fort.
(Reference: Three major events, including CHOGAM (1982-83); Page 36)

With President K.R. Narayanan, Vice-President Krishan Kant and Prime-Minister A.B. Vajpayee, after the author and Jaswant Singh and Pramod Mahajan were inducted in the Union Cabinet, in December 1998.

*With the two Presidents – R. Venkataraman and K.R. Narayanan.* The former was supportive of the care taken by us to protect and pin up signposts of regional cultures in Delhi such as Malai-Mandir Complex. The latter shared my disappointment over the change of my portfolio, first of the Tele-communication and then of Urban Development.

weak system still more weak to sustain action. It was this infection that was at the root of all the serious maladies that visited the Indian state and society in the three fateful periods of 1970s – the period shortly before, during and shortly after the Emergency.

The manner in which most components of the power-structure conducted themselves during these periods showed how fragile, at its roots, was this structure, how badly shredded was the moral fibre of the leadership at various levels of governance and how poor was the clay which the people, by and large, were made of. Was it Mrs Indira Gandhi or her son or a few advisors around them who were responsible for the imposition of Emergency and what happened during it? What about the Supreme Court Judges who, despite their high status, not only held that the declaration of Emergency was valid but also refused to safeguard even elementary liberties the denial of which would reduce the individual citizen to a 'state of utter rightlessness'? What about the pressmen who quickly changed sides and became 'the singers of the ode'? What about both the Houses of Parliament which endorsed the Emergency by an overwhelming majority – 336 to 39 in Lok Sabha and 136 to 33 in Rajya Sabha? What about those who adopted an excessively agitational approach to attain Jayaprakash Narayan's nobly conceived ideal of 'total revolution' but started wrecking, as Chaudhry Charan Singh did, the new government from inside to realize personal ambitions? And what about the people themselves, who just 'melted away' as soon as the Emergency was declared?

The crisis of character, of conscience and of value-system was too wide-spread to remain confined to the period of Emergency. What else could explain the continuance of the maladies in the post-Emergency period. In sheer arbitrariness, the Shah Commission out-performed the medieval Court of Star Chamber[4]. It selected and slanted pieces of 'evidence' that suited its bias and suppressed what did not.

---

[4] The Court of Star Chamber of sixteenth and seventeenth century has earned notoriety in English Law as a symbol of misuse of power for political purpose.

In so far as the city's clearance cum redevelopment works were concerned, I could assert from personal experience that nothing was done during the Emergency what was not done in the pre-emergency period. But the Shah Commission and its agencies were determined to turn a blind eye to everything that did not fit into its pre-drawn conclusions. An intimidating atmosphere, reminiscent of the days of McCarthyism[5], was whipped up. In the examination of witnesses, a pre-designed pattern was followed. Those who said anything to denigrate the Emergency-administration were encouraged, humoured, and even applauded. These obliging witnesses were not stopped by the Commission even when their statements clearly contradicted the written records. On the other hand, those who tried to defend their actions were jeered, taunted, insulted, and even asked to shut up. A deeply corroded iron in the soul of the Shah Commission was clearly visible.

It was because of steep and all round decline in value that, when, in accordance with the pre-Emergency orders of the Central Government and unanimous resolution of the Delhi Municipal Corporation, I cleared the Turkman Gate slums whose blighted misery had evoked Nehru's poetic frenzy, 22 years earlier, to such an extent as to call for their immediate burning, and accommodated even the illegal occupants in the newly built flats in Ranjeet Nagar-Patel Nagar areas and made allotments of about 600 residential and 200 shop plots to other rank encroachers in resettlement colonies, I was subjected to the most diabolical campaign of calumny known in contemporary Indian history. It was labelled as 'Emergency excess' and given a communal tinge, ignoring all written documents and contemporaneous record.

[5] The term McCarthyism has come to be commonly used for making reckless and prejudicial accusations. It is associated with Republican Senator Joseph McCarthy who, in 1950's, led an aggressive campaign against liberals in politics, bureaucracy and universities on mere suspicions of being sympathizers of communism and indulging in what he called Un-American activities. Many innocent persons lost their jobs or otherwise suffered prolonged harassment.

Ironically, most of the negative and nihilistic forces, notorious for exploiting religion from the opposite ends of the political spectrum, found themselves on the same side to butcher the truth and denounce me merely because I refused to unfairly blame Mrs. Indira Gandhi and Sanjay Gandhi for what I had done according to my own convictions.

When I was being besieged by utter-falsehood from all sides and no one was prepared to even look into the recorded decisions of the Union Government and Parliament, I thought of meeting Prime Minister Morarji Desai. He was the Finance Minister at the time the Union Cabinet approved the Master Plan and its accompanying Scheme of Large-Scale Acquisition, Development and Disposal of Lands in Delhi. This Plan/Scheme required a financial outlay of Rs.732 crore at 1962 price-level. The Finance Minister was on the point of rejecting it on the ground that not even a fraction of the money needed was available. At that stage, myself and Bhagwan Sahay met him and put up an alternative proposal for sanctioning a Revolving Fund of Rs.5 crore by way of which chunks of land could be acquired, developed and disposed of. The receipts would facilitate acquisition of more such chunks for development and disposal.

What it involved was the issuance of preliminary notification, under Section 4 of the Land Acquisition Act, covering all urbanisable lands envisaged in the Master Plan and acquiring them piecemeal, at an accelerated pace, as the Revolving Fund gathered momentum. Its ingenuity lay in creating resources from within the city by ensuring that the financial benefits of the investments, made by the public authorities in providing economic and municipal infrastructure and in developing new colonies, were reaped by them to augment the Fund. The proposal had other planning and environmental advantages. It could ensure effective enforcement of the land-uses prescribed in the Master Plan and also facilitate distribution of the acquired lands, at fixed rate, to meet the shelter needs of the deprived and the disprivileged. The rich speculators could be kept at bay.

Apparently impressed by the proposition that we had put forward, Morarji Desai gladly sanctioned Revolving Fund of Rs.5 crore. He also added a few words of appreciation; light-heartedly, he remarked to Bhagwan Sahay: "You have good advocate on your side. I hope you would use the Fund diligently and in the manner you have presented".

When I requested Prime Minister Morarji Desai to grant me an audience, my intention was to remind him of what he had said at the time of agreeing to our proposal of Revolving Fund, and also to underline that the Plan and accompanying schemes that I had implemented were nothing but what he had himself approved as Finance Minister. I had also expressed the hope that, being a votary of truth, he would appreciate how well-grounded were my assertions. However, soon after making the request, I felt a bit diffident. How could a Prime Minister be expected to recollect a comparatively insignificant item that was discussed years ago? Would he not be prejudiced by the bitterly hostile atmosphere and frown upon me for daring to pick holes in the version given to the public by his government? Fortunately, I had not to undergo the state of uncertainty for long. After three days, I was given time to meet the Prime Minister at his residence on coming Sunday at 12 noon.

At the time of the meeting, what happened was beyond my wildest imagination. With a saintly glow on his face, he talked with unmatched composure and expressed sympathy with my plight. While turning the pages of my book, *Island of Truth*[6], which had come out a week earlier and which I had presented to him at the very start of the meeting, his eyes fell on the chapter, titled: *The Disease That Afflicts Us All,* he asked me what did I mean by it. I replied that I was referring to the crisis of values, character and commitment and the overall spiritual and inspirational vacuum which prevailed around us.

This seemed to have touched a sensitive chord within his inner self. He reflected, for a while on what, in essence, was an echo of Gandhi's dictum: "Politics bereft of principles are like death traps; they kill the soul of the nation." Time conscious, he looked at his

---

[6] Island of Truth (1978): Vikas Publishing House, New Delhi.

watch and abruptly posed a question to me: "Why are you supporting these two....[7]? I learn, you are doing so".

"Sir", I replied, "I am not supporting any one. I am adhering to the truth and merely asserting that, in so far as Delhi's clearance cum resettlement cum redevelopment works during the Emergency were concerned, nothing wrong was done. Similar projects, following similar procedures, were carried out in the pre-Emergency days also. All the policies and procedures had been approved by the Union Government and Union Parliament about a decade before the declaration of Emergency. I have cited all the relevant documents and contemporaneous records in the book[8] in your hand. Neither Indira Gandhi nor Sanjay Gandhi had ever asked me to do anything that had no precedent". The only difference was increase in the speed of execution, because both Mrs Gandhi and her son had strictly instructed the local party leaders to cooperate fully with clearance and resettlement work. Earlier, every little politician, every little vested interest, could cause obstruction on every little excuse or plea.

Prime Minister nodded which indicated his appreciation. What seemed to have especially weighed with him was absence of hesitancy on my part to publish my contentions forthwith in *Island of Truth*, with all the supporting documents and precedents. His sympathy was obvious. But he did not say anything beyond assuring that he would ask his Secretary to take up personally my matter with the Home Ministry. Ultimately, nothing concrete resulted from the meeting. Nevertheless, Morarji Desai's dispassionate attitude provided new clutches to my dwindling faith in the morality and maturity of the Indian democracy. It made me feel that there were still some leaders around, who had preserved the 'distilled nobility' of the ancient Indian culture, and who could be relied upon to provide light and warmth to those who were struggling to inject the

---

[7] I do not wish to reproduce the expression which Morarji Desai used involuntarily. It was so uncharacteristic of him to invoke any pejorative term for senior politicians. All that I may share with the reader is that by the expression "these two", he meant Mrs. Indira Gandhi and Sanjay Gandhi.

[8] *Island of Truth;* 1978: Vikas Publishing House, New Delhi.

values of truth and justice in the political and administrative ethos of the country. I should not, I thought, give myself to despair and continue to strive, by way of writings and practical work, for strengthening what remained of the healthy forces in the Indian society and state.

Soon, however, circumstances took another fateful turn. The Morarji Desai government, and Charan Singh government that followed it for about six months, fell. Under the new government of Indira Gandhi, I took charge as Lieutenant-Governor in February 1980 and saw the Ninth Delhi through a triumphant march of development which ensured successful organization of the Asian Games at short notice. The deep wounds, which the city had suffered at the hands of disruptive forces under the previous regime, were promptly disinfected, bandaged and healed. Never before had Delhi looked so elegant and efficacious than it did in 1982-83 when it hosted three major international events, namely, Asian Games, Commonwealth Heads of Government Meeting and Non-Aligned Movement Conference. The execution of key components of the Master Plan, in a coordinated and cohesive manner, was in top gear when in April 1984, destiny beckoned me to Kashmir, then to Parliament and NDA government as Union Minister of Communication. In June, 1999, my portfolio was changed to Urban Development, thereby bringing me face to face once again with my first love – Ninth Delhi. Unfortunately, during my absence from the scene, the predatory forces[9], let loose by the exploitative practices of our democracy, had once again established their sway on the city and enchained it from all sides.

As already underlined, I had developed an intense emotional bond with Delhi and nursed it virtually like my child. Its planned and balanced growth had a special corner in my heart. When I saw how wantonly this child had been battered and how savagely the norms of healthy and harmonious development had been butchered,

[9]The depth and dimensions of predatory forces, and the devious manner in which they operate their machinery of exploitation, have been particularised in a subsequent chapter.

I was bitterly disappointed. I wondered whether all the creative, constructive and hard work done, in the earlier phases, in evolving a grand vision for the capital city, and for actualising it on the ground, had been worthwhile.

Having suffered deep disappointment, though of a different kind, at the time of my exit from the Ministry of Telecommunications, and also at the time of my resignation as Governor of Jammu and Kashmir in the course of my second term, I thought of giving up my efforts to put across to the nation what I believed was the right model of governance. A pall of hopelessness seemed to be descending upon me. But the idea of abandoning my child was no less distressing. Moreover, by that time, fighting against heavy odds had become a second nature of mine. Soon I collected myself and decided to take up the formidable challenge of putting the derailed engine back on the track.

I undertook the challenge after explaining to Prime Minister Atal Behari Vajpayee how necessary and urgent it was to not only save the city from sinking deeper and deeper into the snake pit of civic lawlessness but also to make it a model of regenerative spirit of contemporary Indian civilisation, combining in itself the best of the East and the best of the West. Poetic, like Nehru, at the core of his personality, Vajpayee readily concurred with my line of thinking. His support facilitated the Cabinet's approval to all the measures that I had intended to enforce. But when the 'approved measures' were enforced on the ground, a fierce counter offensive was mounted by the vested interests and myopic elements within the ruling party. The familiar technique of slant and slander, of distortion and disinformation, of brow-beating and bullying was deployed on an extensive scale and the matter was agitated in both the Houses of Parliament through Call-attention notices.

The scale and intensity of the trumped up agitation; the way I encountered it in Parliament, press and other public fora; the manner in which the 'let down' came, and the reaction that this 'let down' encountered from the Supreme Court and enlightened section of the media, have been described, with all its social, moral and intellectual overtones in chapter II, titled: *Tragedy of a Self-Destructive Democracy: Phenomenon of Unauthorised Colonies and Constructions.*

All that I would share with my reader here is that the fear of Bharatiya Janata Party losing the coming election to the Municipal Corporation was successfully planted in the Prime Minister's mind. What used to sometimes happen during Indira Gandhi's Prime Ministership, when she, overcome by the apprehensions of losing elections, acted against her own instincts, happened again. Vajpayee, keeping aside his own better judgement, telephoned me on September 1, 2001 to ask me whether I would have any objection to moving to the Ministry of Tourism where, as he put it, a new initiative and dynamism was required. I understood. Noting, perhaps, my sense of being let down, he tried to humour me out of my dejection. I had, however, little doubt that it was only a decent way of consoling me. I knew the real cause. Contrary to what happened at the time of change of Telecom portfolio, I made no attempt to hide my bitterness. Time and again, I had earlier apprised him of the positive impact of my efforts to create a new civic culture, a new civic commitment, throughout the country, and he invariably expressed his warm appreciation of what was being done, particularly with regard to fresh and forward-looking thinking that was being disseminated through periodic conferences of city-Mayors and Ministers of Local Self Government and Urban Development of States and Union Territories. On September 3, I wrote to him a letter[10] the contents of which are reproduced below:

> Dear Prime Minister
>
> As I mentioned to you on the evening of September 1, 2001, I am deeply hurt over what has happened. The message given is that, in our set up, there is little place for efficient, effective and principled governance. Even otherwise, I would request you to consider whether petty considerations, propagated on false

[10] D.O. 377/RCJ/2001: September 3, 2001.

assumptions of winning elections or the larger issue of nation building, should prevail. I hope you would agree that at this critical moment in our history, nothing should be done to provide a stimulus to those forces which, on account of short-sightedness or nihilistic outlook, are out to take the nation in the wrong direction.

With respectful regards,<br>Yours sincerely,<br>Sd/<br>(Jagmohan)

The following day, I did not go to my office. Thinking that I was about to submit my formal resignation, Prime Minister sent his Principal Secretary, Brajesh Mishra and the Minister of State in his Secretariat, Vijay Goel, to my residence to persuade me not to think of leaving the Cabinet. They spoke of compulsions of politics, especially of local politics, and hinted that, later on, some other Ministry, possibly Culture, would be added to my charge.

At that time, in fact, I had not made up my mind, having been trapped in two different sets of emotions. Both Vajpayee and L.K. Advani had been very kind and always treated me with a great deal of respect. To discard their advice and undermine their position in public could be construed as an act of defiance. At the same time, I could not adjust myself to their short term thinking, especially when they and their party swore by Ram Rajya, that is, to the principle of fair and just governance by fair and just means. What, moreover, baffled me was their inability to understand my deep and passionate commitment to the idea of planned development of Delhi and of making our capital an inspiring symbol of a new civilisation, a civilisation that combined, in a unique way, the reawakened strength of the long suppressed soul of India and the ever-increasing technological and organisational might of the modern times.

If, I thought within myself, the new assignment provided me scope for creative, constructive and value-based work, and enabled me to propel the country, even in a very small way, towards a new civilisational path, I would continue; otherwise I could leave. As it usually happens in such cases, passage of time relieved me of pain and state of uncertainty which I had initially experienced. When, after a few days, the Ministry of Culture was added to my charge, I took the final decision to stay on and make another attempt to put my ideas into practice.

As coincidence would have it, prior to the change of my portfolio, a meeting of all the Chief Ministers of the States and Union Territories had been fixed for September 12, 2001. It was to be inaugurated by Prime Minister. In my address, which I had to deliver after a couple of days of the change in my assignment, I dwelt on the pivotal role of planned and organised cities in promoting tourism and in presenting a positive image of our way of life. The following excerpts from my address are pertinent and would elucidate my proposition:

> Tourism is an issue that is closely linked to the civilisational and cultural traits of the nation. Much depends upon how we behave; how well-ordered and disciplined we are as a society; how we preserve, protect and project our history, heritage and architectural and artistic legacy; and how honest, effective and service-oriented is our machinery of governance.
>
> If an intending tourist, sitting in United States, Germany, France or Japan, reads in the newspaper or hears on television that Delhi has become the fourth worst polluted city in the world, that its traffic is obstructed by unending encroachments on roads, that the approaches to its monuments are littered with slums and semi-slums and are surrounded by pestering beggars, and stray cattle roam around even important intersections, he would not be attracted by our brochures or publicity-material, howsoever glossy and well produced they may be. He would first think about his health, safety and security.
>
> But if, on the other hand, he learns that Delhi has 'Nine-Cities' rolled into one, each with a history and heritage of its own, each with scores of incomparable monuments, frozen in time and space, approachable through graceful boulevards and bye-lanes and studded with enchantingly laid down greens, then

he would be attracted to it as a metal to the magnet. He would return home with happy memories and transmit to his countrymen the saga of India's past, her present resurgence and exhilaration, her creative mingling of the old and the new and the great future that awaits her. He would be the best ambassador of India's Tourism Industry.

What Paris is today is largely due to what Baron Haussmann, encouraged by Louis-Napoléon, did to it, during his Prefecture from 1853 to 1870. By rebuilding Paris and making it a symbol of national pride and elegance, he gave a new life to the entire nation. Paris is France and France is Paris. It is the brightest jewel of her civilisation and culture. It brings millions of tourists to France from all over the globe and is the mainstay of her economy.

In sharp contrast, we have the case of Varanasi. It is the oldest living city of the world. Its antiquity has been eloquently described by the noted Indologist and Protestant missionary M.A. Sherring, in these words: 'When Babylon was struggling with Nineveh for supremacy, when Athens was growing in strength, before Rome had become known, or Greece had contended with Persia, Varanasi had already risen to greatness, if not to glory".

Varanasi is a store-house of cultural treasures – a city where the Great Trinity – the Ganges, Siva and Kashi – have ever been watchful; where 'eternal India' has always been present; and where mysteries of existence and the meaning of both life and death, of creation and destruction, have been explored with unmatched depth and subtlety. And what have we made of it? When Mark Twain visited it, he, in his inimitable style, observed: "Varanasi is older than history, older than tradition, older even than legend, and looks twice as old as all of them put together".

Even a day's walk around the main part of Varanasi would show how the city is on the verge of total civic collapse, how its skyline is lacerated by ugly hoardings and jumble of overhanging

> wires and how most of the 70 or so ghats along the five kilometre 'Ganga River Front' are in a state of total disarray.
>
> As Urban Development Minister, I had drawn up a rejuvenation plan for Varanasi, the central thrust of which was to ensure not only its civic reconstruction but also its emergence as a new hub of cultural tourism. I was confident that its fruition would have brought about a radical improvement in the image of the city and its economy.
>
> May I request this august Conference to reflect in depth whether a great potential for tourism development and economic prosperity is not being lost by our inability to stand up against the extremely selfish and short-sighted elements in our politics and administration.

Many in the audience and the media thought that this was my way of protesting to the Prime Minister about the change of my portfolio and gently reminding him that what I was doing to improve the landscape and mindscape of Delhi had a larger purpose and included a special service to the tourism industry. But any protest was far from my thinking. I was merely emphasising that dishevelled and disorganised cities had harmed India in every conceivable way, and would continue to do so in future if the current trends and attitudes persists.

My deep concern for the emergence of a clean, orderly, law-respecting, environment friendly and culturally awakened city, and its link with the growth of a healthy society and ethically strong state, was seldom seen in perspective. But it did not go unnoticed, either. On quite a few occasions, it was warmly supported by a knowledgeable and perceptive section of the public, especially the media. As an example, I reproduce below a few excerpts from the *Indian Express* Editor-in-Chief, Shekhar Gupta's article published in daily's issue of September 8, 200:

> They have got the head of Urban Affairs Minister Jagmohan who is widely acknowledged, even by Congressmen, as the one BJP minister who was making a difference. He was generating

> such a positive buzz with his clean-up of Delhi that even the Congress was beginning to see him as a threat. Unfortunately, so did his own partymen and got him in the jugular.
>
> The real story is not that the Delhi's BJP party leaders should hold the view that Jagmohan's kind of assault on the illegal builder mafia's unauthorised construction, polluting industries and encroachments was going to lose the BJP votes. The more alarming truth is that Vajpayee and his advisors bought that argument. If they still believe that our capital is a city run by the mafias, for the mafias and other special interest thugs who care a damn for the quality of the air we breathe, the congestion on our roads, power failures, water shortage, mess in the hospitals and so on, as long as property prices can boom, they live in very old times indeed.
>
> Then, they opposed the removal of polluting industries – what else could they do when it was well known that a large number of the polluters were also power-thiefs, financiers and friends of the politicians and patrons of the ruling party? Then they sat on dharnas against the demolition of encroachments.
>
> The wide-spread support to Jagmohan...When was the last time when you saw such dismay at the departure of a Cabinet Minister anywhere? The only reason this happened is that we Dilliwalas have now begun to appreciate quality-of-life issues better than we traditionally do elsewhere in India. Recent years have convinced us that even in a city as chaotic as ours, it is possible to clean the air, remove the squatters – the rich with the clout of connections and equally the poor with the power of votes.

The following Editorial comments, made in the *Statesman* of September 5, 2001, were more pertinent and extensive:

> That Jagmohan has been persuaded or pressured to overcome his resistance to accepting another portfolio in no way dilutes the negative side of the clear signal sent out by his removal from the Urban Affairs Ministry. Over the next few days the line likely to be put out is that the spirit behind entrusting

tourism to Jagmohan was to inject dynamism into a department that has floundered despite all the attractions of this land. It simply will not wash. Even those who do not accept Jagmohan as a genius in the management of urban affairs will concede that he has always displayed total commitment to his job – whether during his assignment with the Delhi Development Authority, as Lieutenant Governor, or finally as Cabinet Minister whose task centres around critical aspects of the Capital. Not for nothing did Indira Gandhi recall him to boost the flagging construction projects for 1982 Asian Games. Not for nothing did VP Singh dispatch him to Srinagar to fire the first shots against the gunmen who had come close to taking control of the Kashmir Valley.

It is true that almost all through his career he has run foul of politicians whose racketeering he disrupted, as well as that section of the bureaucracy that believes with a religious faith not unmixed with self-interest that it is duty-bound never to rock the boat. Yet when he did enter electoral politics he was a three-time winner from what is deemed the most intelligent electorate in the country – the New Delhi constituency.

The politicians' equivalent of thieves-honour is what has united them against Jagmohan for it was under their patronage that the master plan was rendered meaningless and encroachments flourished. And when the apex court found no local agency seriously following its instructions it was Jagmohan who filled the breach. There may be some truth in the charge that he was demolishing vote banks, in the process he was also cutting off the funding-line that runs between the various disreputable lobbies and their politician associates. The grapevine has it that adding to the tirade against him were a host of media persons who claim protracted occupation of government accommodation as a birthright.

All that added up to the kind of pressure that the Prime Minister chose not to resist – even at the cost of his promise of good governance losing all credibility. The talk of the town

> suggested that shifting Jagmohan was utterly questionable but perhaps a sound political decision. This newspaper refuses to accept that interpretation of "politically correct."

Harish Khare, Associate Editor of the *Hindu*, in his edit-page article of September 5, 2001, titled: *The Hindu Rate of Governance,* analysed my case in the larger context.

> The extent to which the BJP leadership has happily house-trained itself in the Hindu rate of governance can be judged from the ejection of Mr. Jagmohan from the Ministry of Urban Development. Here was one administrator who was willing to follow the classic textbook approach: spell out the larger vision of a city two or three decades down the line, conceptualise a plan of action in tune with that vision, prioritise the tasks in the plan of action, summon the supervisory energy, attend to the nuts and bolts of details, stay unwavering in achieving the task at hand, despite the opposition from the vested interests.
>
> There has been not a single rumour, leave alone an allegation, that in his drive to clean the capital out Mr. Jagmohan was susceptible to the familiar charm of the slumlords and the builders lobby. He obviously had the mandate of his Prime Minister and his Government. It was the backing of his Prime Minister that enabled Mr. Jagmohan to stand up to a whole array of opposition voices, from within and outside his own party. And just when he was on the verge of proving the point that it was possible for a good man, with the requisite dedication, integrity and competence, to move an agenda, he finds himself thrown out.
>
> The presumed political costs of Mr. Jagmohan's anti-encroachment drive have apparently been cited to the Prime Minister, and the local party bosses have been allowed to have their way. The half-hearted explanation that Mr. Jagmohan's successor in the Ministry of Urban Development would not tinker with his priorities does not wash. The Hindu rate of governance would not let a Jagmohan break out of the stranglehold. The Jagmohans of this world would always

displease some sections; after all the society is forever engaged in an intense struggle over collective resources. The idea of good governance is to ensure that the choices this struggle produces are in the larger interest (as collectively defined at any particular time) as well as are morally defensible.

Even more pertinent a question presents itself: can individual Ministers – however competent, however dedicated, and however sincere – break out of the Hindu rate of governance without the Prime Minister of the day providing a hands-on leadership. Even if they could create little islands of ministerial efficiency, they would hardly change the fundamentals without a new collective approach.

Without a Prime Ministerial commitment, courage and clarity about our national vision, about what is right for India in the long term, what are the costs and who would pay these costs and who need to defer gratifications, there would be no breaking out of the Hindu rate of governance.

While the appreciative comments of eminent journalists[11] and other knowledgeable and public spirited individuals and organisations[12] were reassuring* and engendered quite a few sparks of animation and brought in fresh confidence, the overall inconvenient reality encountered at the operational level thickened

---

[11]The full texts of Editor-in-chief of Indian Express, Shekhar Gupta's article of September 8, 2001; of the Statesman's editorial comments of September 5, 2001, captioned: Junking Jagmohan: Politically Correct Gets New Meaning; and of Harish Khare's edit page article of September 5, 2001,with the heading, The Hindu Rate of Governance, have been given in Appendices CI-(i), CI-(ii) and CI-(iii) respectively.

[12]A few typical comments and views of this genre have been reproduced in Appendix C-IV. These comments confirm my belief that a sizeable number of concerned citizens and their associations are longing for a clean, principled and effective governance of the city.

* I hesitated a great deal before reproducing extracts from the comments of the eminent journalists and other public spirited individuals and organisations because they could give an impression that I was indulging in self-praise. But, on final count, I decided to do so because truth had been butchered by the vested interests through a highly tendentious publicity campaign which sought to portray my fight for cleanliness in public life and orderliness in our cities as a mere demolition drive.

the haze of cynicism around me. What particularly disturbed me was the rising trend amongst talented and well-meaning leadership to live with the diseased limbs of Indian democracy, instead of running the risk of losing office by being righteous which would make them truly victorious in the service of the State.'

In the circumstances in which the change in my portfolio occurred, the idea of resignation from the Union Cabinet had been entertained by me. But it was soon given up. The reasons for the 'decision' and 'revision' have already been indicated briefly. A couple of friends thought that had I resigned, my point would have gone home to the public more forcefully. But my own beliefs, the respect which was generally accorded to me by the Prime Minister and Deputy Prime Minister, and the prevailing social and political ethos in the country made me to decide otherwise. Nor could resignation fit into the overall framework of my fundamental objective of presenting to the nation a model for the principled and planned development of our cities and make them nerve-centres for a healthy change in our civilisation.

Subsequent events proved how right I was. Had I resigned, I might have been talked about in the media and at chattering tables in the coffee houses for a few more days. But it would not have altered either the outlook of our political leaders or produced any concrete improvement at the ground level. I would have merely deprived myself of the opportunity to evolve a *New Initiative Programme* under which I was able to synthesise elements of history, heritage, environment and clean civic life and create *Great Green Hubs* for historical sites and monuments in culturally significant cities, spread all over the country[13], from Mahabalipuram in the South to Leh in the North, and from Ajanta-Ellora in the West to Bodh Gaya in the East. Delhi's historical sites and monuments, such as Red Fort and Quila Rai Pathora, were the biggest beneficiaries under the

[13] Those readers who are interested in acquainting themselves with the implementation of the New Initiative Programme at the all India level may go through chapter XIV of my book, titled: *Soul and Structure of Governance in India*, published by Allied Publishers, New Delhi, 2005.

*New Initiative Programme*. All this and connected matters have been dealt with in chapter III, titled: *Ninth Delhi's Greens and their Philosophic Pedestal*.

While some aspects of my clean up drive, launched as Urban Development Minister, continued to yield wholesome results, under the Tourism and Culture Ministry's *Special Initiative Programme*, as detailed in aforesaid chapter, titled: *Ninth Delhi's Greens and their Philosophic Pedestal*, a virtual epidemic of lawlessness descended upon the city with regard to the provisions of the Master Plan and Municipal bye-laws.

The city became sick, dangerously sick, both in body and soul. Not only it suffered periodic bouts of high fever, in the form of unauthorised colonies and constructions, but also its doctors became the purveyor of the infection, making the sickness still more pervasive. No action whatsoever was taken at the ground level even against the most serious violators of the Master Plan. Worse, an atmosphere conducive to their multiplications was created by the political masters of the State.

The Supreme Court was unhappy over the unsavoury turn of events. At the very first hearing of the matter, after my exit from the Ministry of Urban Development, the Court, while inquiring from the Additional Solicitor General, Harish Salve, as to what action had been taken by the local authorities on the directions of the government issued during my charge, observed, albeit orally, 'You have got rid of him; how would you get rid of us'. The Court ordered that the infringement of Master Plan and Municipal Bye-laws should be proceeded against, and it appointed its own monitoring committee to ensure compliance on the ground.

But the Supreme Court had clearly underestimated the long arms of the vested interests and the extent to which their political patrons in the power-structure could go to protect those interests. As would be seen from what I have narrated and analysed in chapter II, titled: *Tragedy of a Self-Destructive Democracy : Phenomenon of Unauthorised Colonies and Constructions*, the Manmohan Singh-Sonia Gandhi regime, which had come into being by that time, started the practice of amending, with retrospective effect, land-use regulations and bye-laws and also notifying new Master Plan (2001-2021) from the back date. The strategy was to confront the Supreme Court with the argument that the erstwhile infringements in the form of unauthorised colonies, constructions, etc. were no longer so as they now conformed to the provisions of new Master Plan (2001-2021)[14].

I do not think there is any other case in the town-planning history of the modern world where the mixed land use regulations of a lapsed Master Plan had been amended with retrospective effect, and where a new Master Plan had been formulated, primarily with the ulterior purpose of extending unmerited benefits to all those who, in pursuance of their personal and pecuniary interests, had recklessly violated the basic principles and provisions of the preceding Plan. The amended regulations and the new Master Plan (2001-2021), virtually declared, that 'illegal' would be legal, 'foul' would be fair, the established principles of town planning would be followed in breach and it would not be the ravishers of the city but their victims that would be penalised. If, for instance, a law-breaker had constructed five storeys where only two or three were permissible, it was stipulated in the new Plan that five storeys would be permissible. In other words, under the cover of the new Master Plan, the law had been tailored to fit into illegalities, no matter if in the process the very *raison d'être* of the Plan was destroyed and the ideals of justice and equality, inherent in our constitutionalism, were submerged in the hypocritical adherence to the words of the Constitution.

Further, to elicit sympathy in the name of the deprived, the cases of squatters/Jhuggi-Jhompris and street vendors were mentioned in the same breath as those of the land-racketeers and profiteers. Could a more deceptive device than this be thought of to deflect the beam of truth from the core and corruption ridden issue of unauthorised colonies and their political godfathers?

---

[14] This Master Plan was finalised/notified in 2007 but made applicable with effect from 2001.

As the Delhi Assembly Elections (December 2008) and Lok Sabha Elections (May 2009) neared, head of the ruling party at the Centre, Mrs Sonia Gandhi, was invited by the Delhi Chief Minister, Mrs Sheila Dikshit, belonging to the same party, to hand over, at a public function, provisional regularisation certificates to all '1639' unauthorised colonies. Obviously, they believed that by being first permissive in the creation of unauthorised colonies and then regularising them was a great achievement of their regime, something to be flaunted about to the people, the voters of Delhi.

I wish both these otherwise admirable and modernity-oriented leaders had paused for a moment to think whether they were not resorting to cynical expediency and betraying Nehru's vision of planned development of Delhi, whether they were not deceiving themselves by extending bounties, at the expense of honest tax-payers' money, not to the poor Jhuggi-Jhompri wala, but to the land-racketeers, speculators and profiteers; and whether, along with their friends and foes in the political leadership of the city, state and Centre, they would be presented before the bar of history as contributors to the tragedies of Ninth Delhi.

Similar disturbing reflections, as briefly indicated earlier in this chapter, had weighed upon my mind when a venerable leader of the stature of Prime Minister Atal Behari Vajpayee had agreed, under pressure, to ignore the larger issues of city-planning and value-based growth of Delhi to serve as a model for a clean and disciplined urbanisation in the country. At that time, as a Union Urban Development Minister in A.B. Vajpayee's Cabinet, I was merely following the norms of *Rajdharma*, that is, of principled adherence to my moral and legal obligations and discharging them earnestly through a coordinated and result-oriented mechanism of governance. I was assailed in Parliament by a number of Members, including those belonging to the ruling party. I was saddened by the motivated denunciation which showed little respect either to facts or to law. But I kept cool and confined my response to appealing to the Members of all hues and colours to address themselves the following question:

> In what type of Delhi do we want to live, and what type of legacy do we wish to bequeath to posterity and to our children and grand children? Do we want our city to become a junk-yard of unauthorized constructions, mirroring civic and moral chaos, or an orderly and disciplined capital of a Resurgent Republic, embodying values of justice and honesty on the basis of which we have often claimed a pre-eminent position for our culture and civilisation?

But these words and the documented facts that I cited and the arguments that I advanced in my speech[15] had no meaning for most of the Members of Parliament. All that they could unleash was a barrage of simulated anger, replete with vague generalities. The other Members kept a studied silence. I found myself on a choppy sea, plying a lonely furrow, with an uncertain future staring in my face.

The above narration and analysis of events, based upon personal experience, from Nehru's time till date, throw up a number of issues of fundamental significance. These issues have been compressed by me into *nine pivotal questions in para 3 of the Preface.* The reader may find it instructive to go through them once again and reflect on the dispositions of the post-1947 leaders, such as Jawaharlal Nehru, Sardar Patel, Ms Indira Gandhi, Morarji Desai, A.B. Vajpayee, Sonia Gandhi – Manmohan Singh, and also consider to what extent these leaders were affected by the cultural and civilisational arthritis of their times, and what approach, if any, they adopted to contain or cure this arthritis; or negatively, add to its gravity.

A dispassionate look at the above nine questions and their corollaries, I am sure, would cause immense worry to all the well-wishers of Ninth Delhi. This worry would also extend to the type of democracy that we are practicing, the quality of leadership that this democracy is producing, the manner in which "we – the people"

[15] The contents of the speech, which are revealing in more than one respect and which show, how fast is the Indian political soil turning into an intellectual, cultural and moral waste-land, have been given, with its detailed background, in chapter II, titled: *Tragedy of A Self-Destructive Democracy: Phenomenon of Unauthorised Colonies and Construction.*

are conducting ourselves, displaying either our greed or our indifference, and engendering a disoriented civilisation which in turn would add to the sickness and soul-lessness of the city, thereby setting in motion a vicious circle in which mutual infirmities of civilisation, city and its leadership get multiplied, leaving no room for reform and regeneration.

In the chapters that follow, I have discussed, in detail and in proper context, different aspects of Delhi's development and brought out the staggering dimensions of the problems that have to be faced with regard to each of these aspects. But one worrisome issue is common to all of them. The city is fast losing its sense of direction and acting like an entity with an impaired vision. Despite a powerful lantern in its hand, it cannot see beyond its own shadow.

What is still more ominous, the dark clouds on the horizon of urban India are getting thicker. By 2030, about 590 million people would be living in our cities. This would constitute 40 per cent of the total population at that time. In terms of number of people, it would mean a scale and speed of growth which has not been witnessed anywhere in the world except in China. There would be 68 metropolises with more than a million population, and Mumbai and Delhi would be amongst the five largest cities of the globe, encompassing about 3.3 crore and 2.59 crore people respectively. About 900 million square meters of additional residential and commercial space and about 2.5 billion square meters of new roads would have to be built.

If Delhi has to emerge as a great city and be worthy of inspiring to all other urban centres of the country, it must attend to its core maladies. Apart from intensive physical treatment, it must subject itself to a long spell of cultural and civilisational therapy at all levels with a moral compass in its hand. But does a precise prescription for such a treatment, such a therapy, exist? In my opinion, it does. And I have indicated items of the prescription, wherever relevant, while discussing key events and developments in the subsequent chapters.

The cure is not going to be easy. The chronic diseases have long and multiple roots. They have to be fought with patience, skill and, above all, with a new mind and motivation. The challenge is to move to a higher orbit and create an inextricably enmeshed web of thought and action, in which strands of regenerated civilisation and reawakened leadership reinforce each other to serve as a sanctuary for a clean and just city – clean not only in body but also in soul; and just not only to the present but also to the future.

## CHAPTER II

# TRAGEDY OF A SELF-DESTRUCTIVE DEMOCRACY: PHENOMENON OF UNAUTHORISED COLONIES AND CONSTRUCTIONS.

*Jagmohan is the Only Sane Voice, says Supreme Court*[1].

— Report of the Indian Express September, 14, 2000.

Delighted to read the Indian Express report with the above cited caption, my wife, Uma, thrust the newspaper in my hand and said, "Look what has appeared about you; unnecessarily you remain disturbed and dejected". For a moment, I was also overtaken by a surge of happiness within. Then, as if from nowhere, a waft of apprehensive thought crossed my mind. With amiable irony in my tone, I turned to Uma and commented: "This could spur forces inimical to my stand against unauthorised colonies and constructions in Delhi to exert greater pressure for my removal and I might suffer another change". And this is what exactly happened. I was soon out of the Ministry of Urban Development.

One of the most agonizing tragedies that has, of late, visited Ninth Delhi is the phenomenon of unauthorised colonies. In it are manifested the ugliest elements of Indian polity and administration. It shows of what insubstantial clay are a large number of our citizens,

[1]At that time, the Supreme Court was hearing a number of PIL cases pertaining to unauthorised colonies, constructions and conversions. The report of September 14, the full text of which has been given in Appendix-I was about one such case. The context and significance of the matter have been discussed in the subsequent portion of this chapter and need to be grasped fully by all those who want to vanquish the negative forces that have caused the tragedies of Ninth Delhi and to simultaneously provide stronger muscles to the positive elements that have brought about its triumphs.

a large number of our city-fathers, and a larger number of state and national leaders made of, how frequently are they betraying the constitution and laws of the young Republic and how lying to themselves, lying to the nation, lying to history, is fast becoming an integral part of their ethos and outlook. The phenomenon also demonstrates, in a classic way, that a society, like ours, which has a noble heritage embedded in its ancient bones but which has suffered devastating degeneration for centuries, cannot attain, in contemporary setting, a fair, firm and forward-looking system of governance if its modern Constitution and institutions established thereunder are not underpinned by a new awakening in the realm of culture and values.

To a common observer of the scene, all the illegalities and immoralities that I have recounted in this chapter, may appear to be temporary, though massive, aberrations which would find their balance in due course. But to me who has gone through the mill, with all its rattles around, these are nothing but warning shrieks of a coming storm which, if not encountered immediately with ameliorative measures, would cause a colossal damage to the civic and moral fabric of the entire community. The tragedies of Ninth Delhi would be deepened and its triumphs would run the risk of being uprooted. And it would be a mere matter of time, when the nastiness of the storm penetrates every nook and corner of the country.

In essence, the capital city is the spiritual workshop of the nation. The values that are moulded in this workshop soon become a model for other metropolises, towns and even rural habitats. It is, therefore, of utmost importance that the visible as well as the invisible contours of the phenomenon of unauthorised colonies in the Ninth Delhi are studied and understood in depth. To ignore or take this phenomenon lightly would be tantamount to a grim betrayal of the great destiny that we had sought for post-1947 India.

One of the basic lessons that history provides to its earnest students is that civilisations begin to debilitate, and eventually destroy themselves, when the wielders of political and bureaucratic power of the state and makers of public opinion in the society fail to turn their eyes on a seemingly insignificant speck of poison on the nation's plate.

How do unauthorised colonies constitute the speck of poison which I am bewailing over and which practically all shades of leadership in the country are refusing to see?

According to the Municipal laws, a coloniser who intends to develop land in his legal possession for setting up a new colony has first to prepare a layout plan. In this plan, he has to show, as per scales and standards prescribed under the bye-laws, the position of various plots, roads, open spaces, parks and other items of civic and social infrastructure, such as water and sewer lines and also, in case of sizeable colonies, sites for schools, health centres etc. After getting his lay-out plan approved from the municipal authorities, he has to submit and obtain approval of detailed services plans. It is only after developing the land and providing services on the ground, in accordance with the aforesaid approvals, that the coloniser could be permitted by the authorities concerned to offer plots for sale to the prospective buyers.

In the case of an unauthorised colony, none of the above legal requirements are complied with. What to speak of development of land or provision of services, the coloniser[2] does not even care to prepare any plan for submission to the sanctioning authority. He may not even have a valid title over the land; it may be public land or land under acquisition or land which has been obtained by violating the provisions of Delhi Land Reforms Act. He simply cuts the plots on a map, in a rough and ready manner, and sells them at rates which are comparatively lower than the rates prevalent in the nearby developed colonies.

Since the coloniser sets apart virtually no land for infrastructure and civic facilities and carries out no development on the ground, he secures huge financial gains. In the process, he also creates a group

---

[2]I am using the term, 'coloniser', on account of its common usage. The correct expression should be 'land racketeer'.

of buyers who, later on, pretend that they were not aware of the wrong-doings of the coloniser and had been cheated. Actually, they are accomplices who, in pursuance of their greedy ventures, do not hesitate to ravage the organised civic life. They buy plots at what may be termed as "stolen property rates". They do not ask the coloniser to show his title deed over the land or copies of the plans sanctioned by the municipal authorities. Nor do they demand regular sale deed in their favour. No complaint is ever lodged with the police against the coloniser for having trapped them. Their main aim is to obtain undue financial gains by circumventing laws and by posing as poor who are desperately in need of a shelter. They are confident that, politics of the country being what it is, the illegal colony of the coloniser and the illegal purchase of plots therein, would get regularised by way of a general political decision on the eve of elections to the Municipal Corporation, State Assembly or Parliament.

Since the unprincipled game of regularisation has been continuously played with impunity by the dominant sections of almost all political parties and since all the unscrupulous actors involved in it have been attaining their ends without any fear of law, the pace of growth of unauthorised colonies has, over the years, accelerated. On the eve of the last general elections (2009), the number of such colonies, after excluding those which had been earlier regularised, stood at 1639. In them are now involved thousands of vested interests who constitute a huge vote-bank. These interests are bound to have a negative impact in shaping the future contours of the power-structure at the municipal, state and central government level.

How has all this come about? In what way, has the tragedy of Ninth Delhi occurred and blighted both its landscape and mindscape? And who has failed its beautiful, balanced and buoyant vision, originally conceived as a Master Plan, in the wake of free India's tryst with destiny?

Before I deal with these crucial questions and provide a perspective to various unsavoury developments that have occurred in the connected spheres of public life, let me make it clear that the cases of squatters' settlements/Jhuggi-Jhompri[3] clusters are different from those of unauthorised colonies. While the former category of settlements/clusters generally emerge out of compulsions of poverty, the latter are a product of the propensity of persons, mostly belonging to lower middle class, to get rich quickly by not caring for the larger public good. They may be in need of a house or a plot, but they are not so resourceless as not to be able to pay either for the cost of development of land or for the provision of municipal services thereon. They are propelled more by greed than by need. Quite a few of them are unabashed land-racketeers who reap huge pecuniary benefits by cornering a large number of plots and then selling them at high prices by assuring regularisation in due course.

Reverting to the crucial issues and their perspective, I may indicate that the malady of unauthorised colonies sneaked into the civic set up, rather unobtrusively. In the late 1960, a heavy-weight political leader of the ruling party in the trans-Yamuna area was approached, through his local worker, by a group of persons to use his influence in persuading the officers concerned not to remove them from a piece of public land which had been in their occupation for a while and upon which they had put up a few makeshift structures for their residences and shops. The worker himself was in occupation of a large slice and was the biggest beneficiary. On behalf of the group, he advanced the plea, albeit falsely, that most members of the group had been uprooted on account of partition of the country, and their removal from the site would cause grave hardship. Eager to ingratiate his worker, the political leader obliged. He used his influence with the political and bureaucratic executives of the Municipal Corporation to ensure that the unauthorised occupation of the public land by the group continued.

---

[3]The problems pertaining to Delhi's Squatters' settlements/Jhuggi-Jhompris have been dealt with in chapter II. The nature of these problems and the issues connected with them are distinct. They are juxtaposed with those of unauthorised colonies by the sponsors of such colonies with the malafide intention of confusing the public and eliciting its sympathy on grounds of poverty and dire need. It is a different matter that the squatters/jhuggi-dwellers are also exploited politically to secure their votes en bloc. But this exploitation, as explained in the said chapter, is of another kind.

In the course of the next elections, which were held a few months later, the leader noticed two significant fall-outs of the help he had extended to the aforesaid group. First, the members of the group voted, en bloc, for his party; and secondly, they would continue to do so in the subsequent elections, if the promise of regularisation was held out and if local agencies were pressurised to provide, free of cost, a few municipal services, which would have the effect of increasing the price of occupied land. The political leader and his worker soon realised that they had, at their disposal, a large group of 'bonded voters' who would invariably support them. And, as a consequence, they added a larger dimension to their patronising attitude towards the process and pattern of carving out unauthorised colonies. A number of the political workers/leaders, including those of non-ruling parties, themselves started sponsoring such colonies, collecting huge unaccounted money in the process and providing further strength to their financial muscles. All this, coupled with frequent announcements about 'regularisation' by the political elements in authority, caused further spurt in the growth of unauthorised colonies and also made the speculative purchase and sale of individual plots therein far more profitable than hitherto. The unwholesome venture soon assumed the classic form of a case, where evil begets evil, grows exponentially, spreads its infection in other arenas of governance and becomes uncontrollable.

The first major decision[4] of the government of India to regularise the unauthorised colonies was notified on February 16, 1977. The cut-off date for regularisation was fixed as June 15, 1974. To assuage the hurt feelings of those like me, who were passionately involved in the process of planned development of Delhi and also of those who were aghast at the brazen disregard by the government of its own laws and norms of justice, it was simultaneously declared: Government will not countenance any activity or action on the part of any individual or body to put up fresh structure, whether in the existing

[4]There were quite a few other cases of regularisation of unauthorised colonies prior to February 16, 1977. But for the purpose of building up of the proposition that I have in view, the major decisions taken by the Government of India, beginning from February 16, 1977, would do.

unauthorised colonies or in any other area, within or outside the urbanisable limits of Delhi. Any attempt in this direction will be viewed seriously and defaulters will be dealt with severely.

The declaration of the government that it would not tolerate any unauthorised colony or illegal construction in future, as many suspected, turned out to be hollow and hypocritical. It was never enforced. By that time, expediency rather than moral compass, had become the guide for our political set-up. The elevating vision that the Indian Republic had entertained in the earlier phase of its life had been badly fogged by unprincipled and power-hungry leaders who, later on, appeared, in a large number, on the political stage of the country and dominated it. In line with the general downward trend, a substantial segment of bureaucracy, too, lost its appetite for clean and just governance. The political and administrative environment that ensued was contemporaneously captured by me in a newspaper article in these words:

> The racketeers and law-breakers prosper because of the subtle and crafty manner in which vested interests operate. The officers generally prefer to swim with the current. Even when the prescribed procedure is completed and action at the ground is about to commence, pressure groups come into play, crowds are gathered at site, the racketeers summon human considerations in their favour, and ultimately succeed in frustrating action. The city-scape is ruined. No one seems to bother. The ordinary law-abiding citizen remains a passive spectator. Even those who bewail all that is happening hardly take any concrete step to stop the menace. The city has, in fact, no lovers, no committed well-wishers, to protect it from its ravishers. Its lovers, if any, are cowards. All this shows a morally sick city, a city without a clean conscience or a clear commitment.

The moral sickness of the city was bound to worsen with the ever-increasing disposition of the government to virtually trade its laws for votes and not to stand by officers who were willing to fight the predatory elements and ensure a great future for Ninth Delhi.

While functioning as Vice-Chairman, Delhi Development Authority, I myself had an extremely bitter experience of being let down. My action against a group of powerful land racketeers, who were weaving a vast network of new unauthorised colonies in West Delhi, not even sparing acquired lands, was in pursuance of government policy and announcements made in Parliament. But no senior political leader in authority or in opposition was willing to say so in the public. The press reports, superficial or biased or sponsored as they were, converted a straight-forward issue into an item of public controversy. I was largely left to fend for myself. To deter me from persisting with my drive, civil and criminal cases[5] were foisted against me in courts. There was, in short, no end to personal harassment. Government of India knew the truth. And yet it kept mum. Fear of losing a few votes was sufficient to sacrifice all norms of just governance and healthy town-planning.

Even Prime Minister Indira Gandhi sometimes yielded to the vote-bank-oriented political pressures of her partymen, though her personal instincts leaned heavily towards the growth of well-designed cities. This became abundantly clear to me by the extraordinary interest she took in 1973 for setting up of a statute-based Urban

---

[5]One such case was Suit No.455/02, Raghubir Singh, Mohinder Singh and others (Plaintiff) versus Jagmohan (Defendant). Herein, attempt was made to fabricate evidence by showing an acquired land as an unacquired one. The local workers of the political parties did not hesitate to appear as false witness. Truth ultimately prevailed. But it took thirty five years. A brief extract from the final evidence submitted to the Court by me would provide a broad idea of the type of harassment faced: "The Plaintiffs (Colonisers) have not approached the Hon'ble Court with clean hands or clean conscience. They have no respect for the law of the land. On their own admission, they have put up illegal constructions without caring for the statutory requirements of getting the layout plan, the services plan and building plans sanctioned and also in total disregard of the provisions of the Master Plan. Raghubir Singh, PW-1 had admitted: 'The construction on these Khasras was raised unauthorisedly':. Clearly such persons' minds are tuned to illegalities and to secure their illegal ends, including illegal financial gains, they do not even hesitate to institute false cases, produce false evidence and browbeat and harass honest and well meaning elements in public services. For example, in this case, the evidence of PW-19, Vijay Kumar Sethi, is clearly false and documents referred to by him are fabricated. He says that he took 1974 CPWD Schedule of Rates while preparing the estimates, though the said Schedule of Rates had not even been published by that time".

Arts Commission[6], the main object of which was to ensure that an aesthetically pleasing and environmentally congenial metropolis was developed to serve as a worthy capital of the Indian Republic. When myself and late Patwant Singh[7] met her in this connection with the proposed commission, she reflected, for quite a while, on the care and commitment with which European cities were being planned and managed, and regretted that no such care and commitment for our cities was visible in India.

In July 1974, Prime Minister herself called a meeting of senior political leaders and civil servants to express her serious concern over the increasing encroachments and illegal constructions in Delhi. She instructed that firm action must be taken to ensure that the planned and orderly development of the Capital was not undermined in any way. But this concern and instructions remained only on paper. Whenever any officer took action on the ground, as I did in the 1974 case particularised above, he found himself isolated and in trouble. Mrs. Gandhi's party-men invariably flaunted electoral considerations before her to make her hesitant to pursue what she considered was good for the future of Delhi. Her true beliefs in the matter found clear expression when, in May, 1976, during the Emergency, she addressed the All India Congress Committee and spoke warmly about the clearance and redevelopment work that was being carried out in Delhi at that time. She candidly observed: "Earlier, there was no cooperation even from Congressmen for such works which were postponed on one plea or the other". She described this non-cooperation as anti-national[8].

---

[6]The principal statutory obligation that devolves on the Urban Arts Commission is to "advise the Central Government in the matter of preserving, developing and maintaining the aesthetic quality of urban and environmental design within Delhi, and to provide advice and guidance to any local body in respect of any project or building operations or engineering operations of any development proposal which affects or is likely to affect the sky-line or the aesthetic quality of surroundings or any public amenity provided therein".

[7]Patwant Singh, an eminent journalist and author, was at that time the Editor of the Magazine named Design.

[8]The Hindustan Times: Report appearing in its issue of May 31, 1976.

With the imposition of Emergency in the country on June 25, 1975, encroachments on public lands, illegal constructions and unauthorised colonies ceased in toto, only to return with a vengeance when it was lifted in March, 1977, conveying another kind of message about the incompatibility of our brand of democracy with honest and disciplined observance of its own laws.

Much before the imposition of Emergency, and as an adjunct of the First Master Plan for Delhi, which came into force with effect from Ist September, 1962, a scheme initially named as 'Jhuggi-Jhompri Removal Scheme'[9], was approved by the Union Government, Parliament and all statutory organisations concerned, such as Delhi Development Authority and Delhi Municipal Corporation. Later on, while working first as Commissioner, Implementation and then as Vice-Chairman, Delhi Development Authority, I liberalised the provisions of the Scheme with regard to resettlement of squatters, linked it with relevant development and redevelopment projects and rechristened it as 'Clearance cum Resettlement cum Redevelopment Scheme'. Under it, years before the declaration of Emergency, several land-mark projects, which produced spectacular results on the ground and were warmly applauded by the public in general, had been executed. These projects include slum-infested Nigambodh Ghat where now a well designed and well-equipped crematorium, studded by large green spaces, exists; Kela-Godam, where a vastly extended New Delhi Railway Station has been built; and Purana Quila Complex, where history and heritage have been made to breathe again, with refreshing parks and clean water-bodies around.

During the period of Emergency, particularly in the year 1976, the pace of work under the said scheme, attained tremendous speed and was carried out with efficiency and dynamism generally unknown to the Indian administration. It yielded remarkable results for the

[9]The background , context and full particulars of the scheme and connected projects have been given in chapter IV titled: Slums-Physical and Mental.

planned development of Ninth Delhi. But, after the termination of Emergency, the scheme was subjected to a vicious campaign of disinformation and distortion by the critics and denigrators of Mrs. Indira Gandhi and her son Sanjay Gandhi. It was included in the list of Emergency excesses and denounced as anti-poor.

Undoubtedly, Emergency, June 25, 1975 to March 21, 1977, was a tragic aberration, and excesses did occur in the form of misapplication of Maintenance of Internal Security Act, unwarranted Income Tax raids and intensified campaign for family planning. But with regard to the so called demolitions/bulldozing of Jhuggi-Jhompris and poor-man's structures, there was absolutely no excess. On the contrary, the squatters and slum-dwellers received a liberal treatment and got a hugely beneficial deal in shape of 41 resettlement projects. The resettlers gratefully acknowledged what was done for them. In the elections to the Delhi Metropolitan Council and Municipal Corporation, held soon after the General Elections of March 1977, these resettlers, as would be evident from election office documents, voted overwhelmingly for Indira Gandhi's party. Does it stand to reason that they would do so if they had been bulldozed as was made out? At that time, Indira Gandhi's party lost in almost all the constituencies except those that covered the resettlement colonies.

In fact, in so far as allegations of demolitions/bulldozing are concerned, the boot is entirely on the other foot. Knowingly and intentionally, crucial facts were suppressed, evidence concocted and wrong end of the stick picked up to paint development as demolition, dawn as doom and humanism as harassment. The post-Emergency establishments, particularly those under the Home Ministry and the Shah Commission, were so possessed of anger and bias against Mrs. Indira Gandhi and Sanjay Gandhi that they could not imagine that there could be an officer who performed his functions in a fair way, in accordance with the precedents of the pre-Emergency era, and was in the good books of Mrs. Gandhi because of the spectacular results he achieved in implementation of the Master Plan and that, too, with the meagre amount of Rs.5 crore. All this and the connected issues of negative and nihilistic politics of the country have been discussed in depth in chapter IV which deals with the special challenges that Ninth Delhi has been facing in the arena of slums and squatters' settlements. Here, only a limited reference is being made to the attitude of post-Emergency establishments which had provided a big fillip to the growth of unauthorised colonies and constructions during its regime.

The first year of the post-Emergency period saw the ugliest face of unhealthy politics, when the hapless city was ravaged by the worst form of urban anarchy. Reflecting upon the scenario, the reputed national daily, the Statesman of September 28, 1977, commented:

> Never before has "unauthorised construction", an euphemism for encroachment on public land, enjoyed such a boom as at present. Word has spread that the janta stealing the janta's land will be immune....

In similar tone and tenor, the Hindustan Times, in its issue of November 12, 1977, described the prevailing conditions as follows:

> The manner in which unauthorised shops have re-appeared in Tilak Nagar is totally shocking. Similarly, large-scale unauthorised encroachment on public land in the trans-Yamuna colonies during the past six months has gone unchecked. Hundreds and thousands of people have started building houses in different parts of the city without bothering to get the construction plans sanctioned from either the Corporation or the DDA. The stock reply from the police, the DMC or the DDA is 'We don't want to repeat Emergency excesses'.

One of the significant reasons for the speedy disintegration of the Janta government (April 1977-January, 1980) was its total disregard of the need for discipline, and its unabashed distortion of even the finest development cum improvement works carried out earlier in Delhi. In the name of democracy and freedom, it committed its own kind of excesses[10].

In January, 1980, after taking over as Lieutenant-Governor of Delhi, I undertook an extensive tour of the resettlement colonies. Everywhere I noticed that the resettlers had nothing but contempt for all those who had spoken utter lies about the Scheme under which their colonies were set up. Even today, few realise that the successful holding of Asian Games Delhi (1982), which enhanced the prestige of the country considerably, would not have been possible if massive clearance-cum-resettlement-cum-redevelopment projects[11] had not been earlier executed with unmatched speed and efficiency.

Mrs. Indira Gandhi was elated over the all round praise showered on her country's Capital. It was at that time that I perceived, far more clearly than hitherto, that Mrs. Indira Gandhi attitude towards Delhi's development was marked by a streak of Hamletian dilemma and self-contradictory impulses pushed her in different directions at different times. A good part of her mental make-up sought order, discipline, heritage preservation and healthy and elevating future. She was aghast at the recklessness with which the Janta government proceeded to damage the edifice of the Master Plan and allowed brutalisation of Delhi's landscape by virtually encouraging lawlessness in the municipal arena and giving birth to a climate of disdain for the civic officialdom. And yet, on other occasions, she could let her weakness for political power prevail over the provisions of planning laws. When the Delhi unit of her party suggested that regularisation of unauthorised colonies would bring a substantial chunk of voters to the party fold and help it to retain political power in the capital,

---

[10] For details, three sections with captions, 'Period Shortly Before Emergency', 'Period of Emergency' and 'Period Shortly After Emergency' of chapter VI titled: The Gods That Failed, of author's book, *Soul and Structure of Governance in India*, (Allied Publishers, New Delhi), may be seen.

[11] Chapter III, chapter IV and chapter V may be seen.

she agreed to play the negative card. In the name of pragmatism, a sizeable hole was caused in the physical and moral fabric of the civic set up. Nevertheless, she hardly left any one in doubt that her own instincts leaned heavily towards sophisticated planning and solid implementation.

My appointment as Lieutenant-Governor of Delhi in January 1980, after Janta's disastrous interlude, was a clear pointer in that direction. With my known commitment to the implementation of Master Plan and equally known aversion to illegal constructions and carving out of unauthorised colonies, the land racketeers beat a hasty retreat. The avalanche of illegalities and encroachments suddenly camc to a halt, leaving me to concentrate my energy and time to treat the numerous wounds which had been inflicted on the landscape of Delhi during the last three years and prepare the city and its agencies for meeting the formidable challenge of organising Asian Games Delhi (1982) at a short notice. How this challenge was met and what other development cum improvement works were done till my departure from Delhi to Jammu and Kashmir in April, 1984 have been dealt with elsewhere in the book. All that I may underscore here is that my administrative separation from Delhi for a few years did not diminish my concern for its fate or future; nor did it any way cool my poetic ardour for presenting the capital of the Republic as a sparkling sign-post for showing the right way for building a new India and a new civilisation.

In the intervening assignments, be it in Jammu and Kashmir or elsewhere, I attempted, with all earnestness at my command, to present a model of creative, constructive and just governance. But everywhere I was hit by the hidden claws of a self-centred, superficial and unprincipled political system, leaving me injured but at the same time more determined to fight back and inject at least a healing dose in the ethos of work and service environment of that system. In the 1990s, on account of an unexpected combination of circumstances, I found myself in Parliament, and joining, in 1998, the Union Cabinet led by Prime Minister A.B. Vajpayee.

When, in June 1999, as Union Minister, my portfolio was suddenly changed[12] from Telecommunication to Urban Development, I came face to face with the deeper layers of civic and moral chaos to which, over the last few years, a large part of Delhi had been pushed by a set of predatory forces, each working for its narrow and selfish ends. I had known from the press reports that, for quite some time, unfavourable winds had been blowing to sweep away whatever respect had been generated in the first half of the 1980s for the provisions of the Master Plan, and powerful vested interests in the creation of illegal colonies had once again acquired an upper hand. I had also known that, on the eve of 1996 General Elections, government had announced its intentions to regularise new unauthorised colonies that had been set up between the period, June 15, 1974 to March 31, 1993, and that this was bound to increase the tempo of land-racketeering and civic corruption. But what I found on the ground was much worse than what I could imagine.

To update my knowledge, I visited the sites extensively and held regular public hearings[13], at least twice a week. Cases after cases of gross violations of laws and injustices done to the honest section of citizenry unfolded before my eyes. To bring home, the preponderance of illegalities, the brazenness with which they were committed and

---

[12]It was amidst a fierce public controversy that this change in Portfolio occurred. At that time, a powerful group of Telecom Companies were pressurising the government to change the terms and conditions on the basis of which they had obtained licences. I saw no justification for the change; nor did I consider it right to deviate from the principle of granting licences without competitive bids or tenders. Those who, later on, did not adhere to this principle found themselves in trouble in what came to be known as 2G Scam.

[13]I set apart at least one day a week for meeting, between 2.30 p.m. to 6.30 p.m., without any prior appointment, members of the public who had any complaint or grievance with regard to matters with which my Ministry was concerned, directly or indirectly. The officers heading the departments or branches or field offices were present. The grievances were heard, the officer concerned had his or her say and the file pertaining to the case was called, if necessary. The matter was settled, one way or the other, at the time of public hearing itself. If the facts of the case so warranted, I personally visited the spot. This practice dramatically improved the work and conduct of the officers.

the consequent injustice and harm they caused to the honest and law-abiding citizens, I would give here two examples.

At one of my aforesaid public hearings, a representation was made to me by a group of persons, alleging that, in gross illegal use of green land in historic Kudesia Garden and in utter violation of all basic civic laws – master plan, zoning, parking and environmental regulations, municipal bye-laws etc. – a huge marriage-party *pandal* of practically permanent nature, fitted with a number of air-conditioners, kitchens, pantries, living quarters for staff, had been put up and allowed to exist for over five years, and all their complaints to various authorities had not produced any result. On examination of the records and photographs of the area, serious mal-practices were noticed. I personally visited the site and found that every word of what the representationists had told me was true. I recorded a note, the concluding portion of which, reproduced below, would show the extent of rot which had set in almost all the spheres of governance:

> Here is a case in which a huge structure has been constructed in defiance of all laws. This has been done in the heart of the civil lines, in the heart of Kudesia Garden and despite the bewailing of the respectable citizens in the neighbourhood and also despite the fact that the massive illegal complex falls on the road frequently taken by the top political and bureaucratic functionaries of the Delhi government for going to their offices. Why had all these functionaries allowed their conscience to sleep for so long and shown no moral or intellectual respect to their constitutional oath of office?

The second example pertains to a DDA flat. On May 19, 2000, a retired school teacher, an allottee of a group housing unit, accompanied by her near blind husband, represented to me that the allottee of an adjoining flat, an influential person in local politics, had constructed an additional floor on the scooter garages and an additional toilet in the common stair-cases, thereby blocking light, air and passage to her house. The builder was also illegally running a security-service from the same premises and his employees caused nuisance all around. The old couple bewailed that they had been crying hoarse for years to seek justice but no one listened. The issue in this case was not only of illegal construction which violated the basic norms of health and safety but also of ensuring that might was not allowed to prevail over right.

The other cases of blatant violations of law included running of illegal and polluting industries in residential premises and carving out of unauthorised colonies, even in the areas around protected monuments. Seeing all this from close quarters, caused a great deal of anguish to me. Had the holders of power in politics or bureaucracy any love for the city or inner commitment to justice, such violations would not have, in the first instance, come about. If they did, action would have followed in no time. It took me only two days to get the Kudesia Garden site cleared and also redress the grievance of the old teacher. The basic issue in city planning or nation-building is not merely of legal provisions but of commitment to enforce them with a clean conscience.

As more cases of blatant violations and grave injustices came to my notice, more visits to the sites I undertook. The reality on the ground was for more tragic than could be perceived during the public hearings or from perusal of the files. The faces of the victims, be they of poisonous fumes from the polluting industries or of extreme insanitation and fire-hazards caused by illegal eating houses in narrow lanes and on foot-paths, haunted me for days. Tension within me abated only after I had made up my mind to take the bull by the horns and launch an all-pronged drive not only against the self-centred and unsavoury elements in politics but also against civil servants who had acquired an expertise in the art of evading responsibility in the legal as well as administrative arena.

I drew up a comprehensive plan of action, giving priority to ending the menacing and mafia-ridden racket of unauthorised colonies. With regard to these colonies, I took the matter to the Cabinet and persuaded it not to extend the 'cut off' date for regularisation which had been last fixed as March 31, 1993. I was aware that some of my cabinet colleagues as well as other influential leaders whose politics over the years had got linked to 'competitive negativity' in the arena of regularisation were opposed to my line of thinking. But law, morality and past declarations, vowing strong action by government itself, were so clearly in favour of my stand that they had no option but to agree. Perhaps, they thought that there could be other ways of getting over my insistence and frustrating my plan of action on the ground. Apart from it, they had come to know that before bringing the case to the Cabinet, I had shown my site-inspection notes and accompanying photographs to Prime Minister Atal Behari Vajpayee and convinced him of the urgent need for approving my Plan of Action and following it up with Delhi government and local bodies.

I also secured the approval of the Cabinet for issuing instructions of Government of India to the Government of National Capital Territory of Delhi, Delhi Development Authority, Delhi Municipal Corporation and other authorities concerned to enforce strictly provisions of law and prosecute coloniser-racketeers with vigour and speed. I myself drafted the letter of instructions, taking care to make it so comprehensive that all aspects of illegalities were covered and no circumvention by the political and bureaucratic elements at both the central and state level was feasible. I had it issued, on August 28, 2000, in the form of an order of the government of India. It contained, inter alia, the following directions:

I. All illegal constructions should be demolished not cosmetically but in toto.

II. The cost of demolition should be recovered from the illegal builders within 15 days of demolition.

III. Prosecution should invariably be launched against the sponsors of unauthorised colonies under the Delhi Municipal Corporation Act, Delhi Development Authority Act, etc. and the cases followed vigorously with the police authorities/ courts.

IV. In cases, where after demolition, reconstruction is done, personal responsibility of the officer incharge should be fixed and departmental action taken against him.

V. In cases where illegal constructions have taken place on rural-agricultural lands, action under the provisions of the Delhi Land Reforms Act, 1954, should also be taken and such lands should be taken over as per provisions of the Delhi Land Reforms Act. Action in this respect should be taken as soon as the plots are cut by the colonisers and construction done in the shape of boundary walls, etc.

VI. All Senior Field Officers should be asked to carry out physical inspection of the area under their charge and the Supervising Officer should also make surprise checks to ensure that the subordinate staff takes immediate action to check/demolish unauthorised construction. Deterrent action should also be taken against the subordinate staff who do not take prompt action.

VII. Field officers should be asked to maintain field diaries and submit them to the Supervisory Officer regularly.

VIII. A monthly report should be sent to the Ministry of Urban Development by the 5th of each succeeding months.

IX. A Flying Squad has been constituted in the Ministry and if, as a result of findings of this Squad, it is found that subordinate staff has not done its duty or not carried out the aforesaid instructions, strict action against the Subordinate/Supervisory staff would be taken by the Government.

The pivotal importance of the above letter and the comprehensive and specific directions it contained was approvingly noted by the Supreme Court[14] in the course of its proceedings pertaining to various writ-petitions which were entertained by it as off-shoots of the Yamuna Mailey writ petition (725/1994). The letter showed how effective action could be taken under the existing laws but was not taken on account of unprincipled politics, poor commitment of senior civil servants and deep penetration of corrupt practices in a sizeable segment of public life. By referring to it, the Supreme Court,

[14]The Supreme Court referred to the letter of August 28, 2000 in its orders of May 9, 2001, then of 31st July, 2001.

later on, pin-pointed the responsibility of the individual officers and organisation.

Separately, since 1996, the Supreme Court had been issuing directions to the government of National Territory of Delhi and its local agencies to close down polluting industries operating in the residential areas or to shift them to special areas earmarked for them in the National Capital Region. These directions were given while hearing a Public Writ Petition which was also connected with the above mentioned Yamuna Mailey Case. The Supreme Court was exasperated to find that, despite solemn assurances, held out to the Court for over four years, none of its directives had been implemented. In its orders of August 30, 2000, the Court lamented:

> The continued infraction of the law appears to be encouraged and this has given rise to vested interests who appear to be so powerful as to see that even the orders of this Court are not implemented. The state of lawlessness continues with impunity with complete disregard to the interest of overwhelming majority of residents who have to tolerate such illegal industries in their midst.

Again, in its order of September 12, 2000, the court underlined:

> One thing is quite clear that there is a systematic effort which has been made in seeing that this Court's orders are not implemented or complied with and somehow there is in situ regularisation of the polluting industries. In other words, the wrong doer should not be punished, but they should be helped to retain the advantage of their wrongful acts. There is obviously no will or effort either on the part of the National Capital Territory or of the Municipal Corporation of Delhi in implementing and maintaining the rule of law.

During the proceedings of this case in the months of August and September, the general drive launched by me against the unauthorised colonies and other infringements of the Master Plan, came to the notice of the Supreme Court. It warmly applauded this drive, and also appreciated the strict and all-pronged instructions contained in my Ministry's letter of August 28, 2000. In this connection, I can do no better than reproduce below the relevent excerpts from the Indian Express report[15] about the Court's proceedings of September 13, 2000 which appeared in its issue of September 14 under the caption: Jagmohan's is Only Sane Voice, says Supreme Court:

> The Supreme Court has lauded the stand taken by the Union Urban Development Minister Jagmohan on the shifting of non-conforming industries out of Delhi, saying he seems to be "echoing our words" and was the "only sane voice" in the usual humdrum.
>
> In contrast, the three-judge bench headed by Justice B.N. Kirpal observed yesterday that the government of National Capital Territory of Delhi, the MCD and the DDA seem to be adopting a stand which would make the apex court totally helpless as various orders passed by it had gone totally unimplemented....The Court also directed that a nodal cell, headed by Jagmohan, should be set up and have members selected by him.....The nodal cell would have all the powers to close the illegal units.
>
> In response to the Delhi government's proposal to regularise these industries by carrying out changes in the Master Plan, the Urban Development Ministry had, in its affidavit to the court, said: "No amendment in the Master Plan of Delhi may be done to cover inaction or failure on the part of local government or local agency to enforce their by-laws."
>
> Any changes in the Master Plan or its norms to accommodate illegal activities, the Ministry said, would not only put premium on lawless activity but would also cause injustice to the law abiding citizens. The court agreed with the Ministry's viewpoint and strongly pulled up the Delhi government, saying it wanted

[15]The full text of the Indian Express report of the Supreme Court's proceedings of September 13, 2000, which appeared in its issue of September 14 under the caption: Jagmohan is only Sane Voice, says Supreme Court, is given in Appendix C-II-(i).

> to "encourage legalisation of illegal activities which resulted in the prevailing 'jungle raj' in the Capital as far as violation of law was concerned".

Reports on similar lines appeared in other national dailies also. The Times of India especially underscored the Supreme Court's warm approval of my assertion that no amendment in the Master Plan should be brought about merely to accommodate illegal activities, as it would mean putting premium on lawlessness and result in injustice and inconvenience to law-abiding citizens for a long time to come.

When the Supreme Court praised me as 'the only sane voice in Delhi', I was elated. I took it as a moral victory for values of scientific city-planning and for principles of fair and firm governance. At the same time, however, I feared that this could provoke my opponents and other vested interests who had become habitual violators of civic laws and to whom false assurances to the Court and false declarations in the public had brought rich dividends in the past in the shape of electoral and other gains.

It did not take long for my worst fears to come true. As soon as my drive against unauthorised colonies gained momentum and my work as Supreme Court's Nodal Agency resulted in the closure of quite a few illegal and polluting industries, the manipulative skills of the land racketeers and their 'political godfathers' were put in top gear. An extensive campaign of disinformation and distortion was launched, public agitations were engineered and an overall atmosphere hostile to my functioning was created. The local leaders of practically every hue and colour sided with the agitation. Legal merit of the issue or interest of the silent majority had little place in their consideration. The political posturing of the time was accurately reflected in a contemporaneous press report[16] which appeared under the caption: When Jagmohan Follows Rules, Colleagues Sulk. A few excerpts from it, which speak for themselves, were as follows:

---

[16]Pioneer : September 22, 2000.

There is significant heartburn in the city Bharatiya Janata Party (BJP) brass on the stand taken by Union Urban Development Minister Jagmohan on a number of issues, including relocation of polluting industries and the hefty penalty announced for regularisation of unauthorised colonies. Interestingly, the Congress too is criticising the Minister on the same issue.

The reasons which the leaders give out for heartburn are incidentally Mr. Jagmohan's biggest assets. He has the distinction of playing by the rules, not being swayed by populist demands and schemes and being a no-nonsense Minister. The perfect chemistry to achieve whatever he sets out to do is a good enough reason for his party colleagues to squirm and be upset with his style of functioning.

Mr. Jagmohan's reluctance to give in to the demands of the city government and Delhi units of the BJP and the Congress on the issue of relocation of polluting industries, has seen the other BJP MPs from the city fidgeting in discomfiture. Though the BJP and the Congress have joined on the issue to demand that the Master Plan be amended, the Union Urban Development Minister will have none of it.

Though the murmurs of discontent against his 'adamant attitude' were muffled for quite some time even his party colleagues could bear it no more and have now come out in the open with their demand for amendment to the Master Plan due to expire in 2001. The most prominent among these leaders are Delhi Sadar MP Madan Lal Khurana, leader of the Opposition in Delhi Assembly, Prof. Jagdish Mukhi and former Industry Minister Harsharan Singh Balli.

Add to this list of 'detractors within' all the leaders of city Congress and the members of the Delhi Vidhan Sabha.

Underneath this façade of attempting to retain the trade-city character of Delhi, however, there are the faces of only those people who either own huge chunks of land or have stakes in a number of industries running in the city or those whose family members, relatives, friends or financiers are likely to be

> severely affected by Mr. Jagmohan's decision. Since the Union Minister has no personal interest in the matter, he is rooting hard to pull out all the eyesores in the city.
>
> Paradoxically, his 'sincerity' and 'good work' are being applauded by lakhs of citizens, citing whose 'cause' the city's politicians have been trying to derail Mr. Jagmohan's endeavour to beautify Delhi.

But the sponsors of illegal and polluting industries and their supporters in politics were adept in the art of slant and slander. Money and muscle power was deployed on a large scale to organise processions and disturb public order in one locality or the other. False data were coined. It was given out that lakhs of workers would be rendered jobless and half of Delhi would be ruined. The vital information that non-polluting and cottage industries were permissible in residential premises was suppressed. The Master Plan was ridiculed without specifying any provision or procedure which was considered faulty. The issue was raised in both the Houses of Parliament through Call-Attention Notices, first in the Lok Sabha on November 24, 2000 and then in the Rajya Sabha on November 27, 2000.

The members of the ruling National Democratic Alliance and those of the opposition vied with one another in assailing my stand, without mentioning even once why the Supreme Court had found it necessary to appreciate my lonely furrow against the flood of illegalities and why it had passed several orders for closure of industries which were not only polluting but also had been unauthorisedly set up in residential premises. I was determined not to be brow-beaten either by intentional distortion or by criticism based upon ignorance or superficial knowledge. Nor was I tempted to win applause from any one at the cost of planned development and future of the metropolis. Politely but firmly, I responded to my critics as follows[17]:

[17]This is not an exact, but an edited and amplified, version of what I said in the Lok Sabha on November 24, 2000 in response to the Call-Attention Notice. It is, in fact, a resume of what I said and was recorded; plus what I said but what was not properly heard or recorded due to repeated interruptions; plus what I wanted to say but did not

The basic issue around which my drive revolves is: In what type of Delhi do we want to live, and what type of legacy do we wish to bequeath to posterity and to our children and grand children? Do we want our city to become a junkyard of unauthorised constructions, mirroring civic and moral chaos, or an orderly and disciplined capital of a Resurgent Republic, embodying values of justice, truth and rectitude on the basis of which we have often claimed a pre-eminent position for our culture and civilisation?

You have described the Master Plan as bureaucratic, sticking to a rigid time span of 20 years, caring little for practical and human considerations. Nothing could be further from the truth. It is you who have approved it in both the Houses of Parliament, after the Union Cabinet had found it in order and after the Screening Board of the Delhi Development Authority, with sizeable representation of prominent non-officials, had heard and disposed of hundreds of public objections against the draft-provisions. Nor is it inflexible. Apart from five-yearly periodic review, it can be amended any time by following the simple procedure prescribed under the statute provided it is in public interest to do so.

But here the real issues are: Should the Master Plan be amended to the extent of destroying its basic aims and objects, its soul, its raison de'etre ; and that, too, for pandering to the selfish interests of those who have no respect for any law, be it of town-planning or of municipal organisation or revenue

---

say, having been exasperated by the obstructive attitude of those who inwardly knew that truth was not on their side; and plus what I said in the newspapers in my interviews and write-ups especially the two write-ups which I penned for the Hindustan Times and were published under the title: Why I am Doing what I am Doing.

I have done so to avoid repetition and facilitate easy comprehension of all the material facts that I placed and all the arguments that I advanced in Parliament, Press and other public fora, in justification of my drive.

To maintain the continuity of thought as expressed in my response, I am retaining the first para of my resume, though I have quoted it in chapter I, titled: *City and its Leadership and its Civilisation Contours.* I hope, the reader would bear with the slight repetition.

department? Should the paramount considerations of public health, public safety and overall environment of the community be sacrificed at the altar of short-term political expediency? And should we not take into account that at present about 40,000 premature death, 17 million respiratory hospital admissions and 1.2 billion restricted activity days occur every year in our cities due to degraded living? These are the real issues, and not the inflexibility of the Master Plan or non-consideration of new requirements that are bonafide and in public interest. We must not allow our judgement to be clouded by the dust and din raised by the 'godfathers' of unauthorised colonies and polluting and illegal industries and other invalid constructions.

Some of you say that the population of Delhi has increased beyond the Master Plan projections. This is, undoubtedly, true. But you must ask yourself: why is a good portion of the ongoing migration to Delhi not getting deflected to the National Capital Region? Does it not stand to reason that no one would think of this Region, when all kinds of impermissible activities are being regularised here and even rewarded? By not taking any action against the land racketeers, not only a substantial part of Delhi is being made unhealthy and ugly but also a fatal blow is being dealt with on the very concept of National Capital Region. To facilitate speedy development of the area of the neighbouring States of Rajasthan, Uttar Pradesh and Haryana, falling within this Region, is our national commitment. Are we not betraying that national commitment?

I am not sure whether you are conscious of the contradictions in the arguments you give in support of different categories of violators of Master Plan and municipal laws. Whenever unauthorised colonies are to be regularised, you say that there is an acute shortage of houses. If it be so, then why are thousands of houses being allowed to be converted into commercial units and why should scores of hectares of commercial land, such as in Rohini and Dwarka city centres, lie unconstructed and unused? Did any illegal builder of commercial space ever represent to the authorities that in the proper commercial areas more land should be added as extensions, or did he even submit a building plan before resorting to construction or conversion? Why at the time of every regularisation of unauthorised colonies, has it been declared: "In future, illegal activities would not be tolerated and the offender would be dealt with severely"? What were the top executive and legislative agencies doing when their own declarations were being ignored with impunity and the capital of the Republic was being robbed of its social, cultural and environmental assets?

No Member countered, in specific terms, any of the facts or arguments put forward by me. As it usually happens in the course of such discussions, a lot of simulated anger was displayed and crude generalities were resorted to. Interruptions were galore. The attempt was to dissipate the truth and augment the vote-bank even if it be at the cost of all norms of organised civic life, all values of our Constitution and all the little residues of ancient nobilities that still form a part of our social and cultural spectrum. I was saddened not as much by criticism of my drive and unabashed distortions as by the increasing narrowness of the Indian political vision and increasing disregard of probity in public life.

On December 19, 2000, another attack was mounted on my stand in the weekly morning meeting of the Parliamentary Group of the BJP. A non-Delhi MP, who had apparently been prompted by the powerful lobby of vested interests, fulminated against what he called my ambition to go down in history of Delhi as a 'Europeanised Shah Jahan'. Besides being banal and boisterous, he was totally off the mark. He did not touch any issue relevant to my drive. Instead, he resorted to untenable generalities, and even went to the extent of saying that I should shed my bureaucratic baggage of rigidity and non-cooperation. Obviously, those who had egged him on from behind the screen had failed to equip him with any valid argument. Perhaps, the strategy was to bully me and run down my campaign before the senior leaders of the party.

I was taken aback by the suddenness of the fulmination and intemperate language used. Never before had I been criticised at the meeting of the Parliamentary Group of the B.J.P. Whenever any item pertaining to my Ministry came up for consideration, my work was eulogised, and if any suggestion was put forward, it was done with a positive frame of mind. What disappointed me most was the silence of A.B. Vajpayee and L.K. Advani.

I did not respond. Apart from the inadequacy of the time[18], no relevant or concrete fact had been mentioned that needed to be rebutted. My reply to general denunciation, I also thought, would have injected more tension in the atmosphere and resulted in mere hot exchange of words.

Sad and sullen, I sat in the Lok Sabha in the forenoon, reflecting upon the sordid game which the vested interests play by exploiting the infirmities of our democratic set-up. It seemed to me that the 'sense of reverence' which Herbert Baker[19] wanted to impart to the institution of democracy, through his grand creation of Parliament House, could not go beyond the 'circular grandeur' of its structure. The mind and soul for this reverence had to be discovered by the Indians themselves. And it was here that the post-1947 generations had failed their country. I could not concentrate. I went to my office in Nirman Bhawan and dictated a brief letter to the Prime Minister. The contents of this letter were:

> With regard to what was said this morning at the BJP Parliamentary Group meeting, I have only one simple request to make. If any one has any grievance against my decisions, he may communicate the same to me in writing. This would give me an opportunity to reply to specific points. Oral statements, I find, leave a lot of scope for ambiguities, factual inaccuracies and tangential observations.

My drive, briefly indicated earlier in this chapter, was not merely confined to illegal and polluting industries and unauthorised

---

[18]The Parliamentary Group meeting had to end a few minutes before 11.00 A.M to enable Members to reach the Parliament House in time.

[19]Herbert Baker was the famous architect who designed the monumental building of Parliament House and gave it a circular form. At that time, it was named the Council House.

colonies, it extended to huge clusters of encroachments on public lands, especially on the embankments of river Yamuna[20] and around historical monuments. All this was bound to subject my campaign to fiercer resistance. Apart from the opposition of the influential political leaders, the land-mafia moved heaven and earth to paint a false picture and whip up demonstrations here and there. But neither the mafia groups nor the political elements could cut much ice with the enlightened sections of the public, as the Supreme Court's pronouncements, made around that time, in quite a few cases, connected with the Yamuna Mailey Civil Writ Petition, showed to them what the truth really was. The only way to succeed, the vested interests seemed to have calculated, was to get me out of the Cabinet. They worked on the mind of Prime Minister Atal Behari Vajpayee who had earlier agreed with my views and without whose support I could not have secured the approval of the Cabinet to do what I was doing.

Unfortunately, as given in detail in the chapter I in the section dealing with the period of Prime Minister A.B. Vajpayee, he, against his own better judgement, changed my portfolio from Urban Development to Tourism. I was deeply disappointed. So was a large segment of citizenry. It gave rise to an intense public controversy the context and circumstance of which have already been discussed in the aforesaid section of chapter I.

Amidst the dust and din of this controversy, Prime Minister, at a press conference called in another connection, was asked by Shekhar Gupta, Editor-in-Chief, Indian Express: "Why did you change Jagmohan from Urban Development when by all accounts he was

---

[20]The existence of the biggest cluster on the embankment of river Yamuna presented the biggest paradox in the arena of planning and environment. On the one hand, the government was spending thousands of crores of public funds on cleaning of river Yamuna, on the other, its local leaders were keeping lakhs of squatters on embankments, who were daily polluting the river in the form of open defecation and industrial effluents. When I pointed out this paradox and drew up a plan for clearance cum development of river front, in accordance with the provisions of the Master Plan, I was badly pilloried by vested interests who seized this opportunity to spread more disinformation about my drive.

doing so very well in that area?" A.B. Vajpayee replied impromptu: "The compulsions of coming elections in Delhi". On learning this, a feeling of 'gloomy pride' silently seeped into my thoughts, assuring that in Vajpayee's reply there was an implicit recognition of the correctness of my stand against the unhealthy practice, adopted by political parties, of trading municipal and planning laws for votes.

My departure from the Urban Development Ministry and the signal it sent to the well-meaning section of bureaucracy at the local level could not but result in reversion to the old method of taking action only on paper and doing nothing on the ground that would bring it in clash with their political masters. The Supreme Court was unhappy and minced no words about it. At its hearing on February 20, 2002 the Bench, headed by Chief Justice B.N. Kirpal, was so exasperated that it described Delhi as 'the worst example of lawlessness in the world' and asked the government council to name 'any civic or planning law' that was being observed in letter and spirit[21].

Despite the Supreme Court's repeated denunciation of scant respect shown to the provisions of the Master Plan and Municipal and other laws by the Central, State and Local governments, violations were not only not checked but also an atmosphere conducive to their multiplication was created. As the Delhi State Assembly Elections (2004) neared, practically all the political parties competed with one another in declaring, as they had done previously at the time of every local, state or central election, that they would regularise unauthorised colonies and extend the cut-off date. In due course, they would include this declaration in their election manifestoes.

It was clearly a case of bribing the voters of unauthorised colonies in kind and that, too, on massive scale. It tilted the electoral contest in favour of the candidate who was out to undermine not only the rule of law but also the future of the city. But the Election Commission would not take any notice. Nor would it move the

---

[21]Times of India February 21, 2002.

government to amend the election law to empower the Commission to deregister political parties which declared through their manifestoes or otherwise, that the violation of statutory provisions of central, state or local laws would be condoned if such a condonation gave pecuniary advantage, in cash or kind, to a group or category of violators.

The inaction on the part of Election Commission to check the existence of an unhealthy clientistic relationship between the land-grabber/illegal builder/voters and those seeking their votes, was not understandable, when it had, of late, been showing a marked disposition to amend rule after rule to ensure purity and fairness of the means employed by the candidates and the political parties sponsoring them. The paradox was apparent : if there was an individual act of illegality or corrupt practice, the Election Commission would take action; but it would look the other way if there were mass violations and mass corrupt practices .

The contradictions which the Commission's attitude was throwing up was specifically brought to the notice of the Chief Election Commissioner and two other Members by way of note which I sent to each one of them, with photographs which supported my arguments. It was followed by my personal meeting with the full Commission. The main point placed by me before the Commission was that squatting on public land and carving out of unauthorised colonies had virtually become a part of election exercise in Delhi. It had led to the growth of the evil phenomenon of 'induced squatting'. Apart from the unfairness which it had injected in the electoral contest, it had destroyed many salutary provisions of the Master Plan and foreclosed even options for improvement in future. My concluding poser was: How was it that the Commission which frowned-rightly so-even upon minor infringement of law or norms on the part of a candidate or a political party, did not deem it necessary to take notice of the heavily polluted river of corruption and malpractices that flowed underneath the surface and poisoned the very roots of the system? Could a healthy harvest grow out of such poisonous roots, particularly when the polluted river went on accumulating more and more muck with every election to the Municipal Corporation, State Assembly and Union Parliament?

Nothing came out of my efforts. Neither was any reply sent to my note nor the validity of my facts and arguments contested by any of the three Election Commissioners during my meetings with them. The reason for all this was not because the Election Commission was not aware that the squatting or carving out of unauthorised colonies was a legal offence, civil as well as criminal; not because it did not understand that large scale corruption and malpractices were involved in the case; not because it did know that there was no difference between inducing the voter by cash and inducing him in kind; but because, like other key decision makers, it had no inner urge to look into the troublesome reality and take hard decisions to exterminate electoral evils from their roots. The Commission's outlook was determined not by its constitutional position but by the general national ethos of contenting itself by dealing with softer crusts of the problem, and leaving the hard crusts unattended.

In the elections years–2003 State Assembly and 2004 Lok Sabha Elections–due to assurances given, in an cavalier fashion, by the political leaders for regularisation of all kinds of infringements of civic laws and Master Plan land-uses etc., there was a virtual gold rush for land-grabbing and carving out of unauthorised colonies and also for construction of additional storeys and spaces in the existing buildings. When on February 16, 2006, one of the off-shoot cases, arising out of the pending writ-petition, M.C. Mehta Vs Union of India and Others, came up for hearing before the Supreme Court, the three judges Bench, presided over by Chief Justice Y.K. Sabharwal, severely criticised, as the earlier Bench, headed by Chief Justice B.N. Kirpal, had done, the authorities of the municipal, state and central governments which had assumed power after the aforesaid elections, for virtually conniving with the violators. The Bench raised a crucial question: "What happens when the violators and/or abettors of violations are those who have been entrusted by law to prevent them?" And, then, it proceeded to provide the answer: "The Court has a constitutional duty to intervene and ensure that the law-abiding citizens do not lose faith in the rule of law and to discharge this duty it could set-up its own monitoring mechanism". The Court, however, noted that, since violations had been committed, and connived at, on a vast and varied scale, action at the ground level could be taken only in phases. It directed that, in the first phase, big commercial establishments[22] on the main road should be sealed on the basis of the findings given by the monitoring committee appointed by the Court. On similar lines, the Delhi High Court, appointed its own monitoring committees in different zones to ensure compliance of its orders by the authorities concerned.

With the Supreme Court and the Delhi High Court getting their orders enforced on the ground and with the network of illegalities and corruption getting exposed, the beneficiaries–the racketeers in land and building and their collaborators in bureaucracy and politics – became jittery. Using their money and muscle power, they organised aggressive agitations in public, practically on the same line as they had adopted against my drive, particularised in chapter I and earlier part of this chapter. They knew how easily even the top leadership of national parties succumbed to the temptations of securing short-term electoral gains. They persisted with their pressure tactics and soon succeeded. And the national leadership once again demonstrated how quick it was in abandoning its national obligation to look at the larger picture.

A special Bill to legalise all 'unauthorised developments and constructions' was approved by the Union Cabinet. It was hurriedly passed, first by the Lok Sabha on May 12, 2006 and then by Rajya Sabha on May 15, 2006. On both the occasions, the passage was by way of a voice vote. It was unanimously supported by all the political parties. The President accorded assent to it on May 19, 2006. It was put on the Statute Book as the Delhi Laws (Special Provisions) Act, 2006.

The moral bankruptcy to which the highest executive and the highest legislative bodies of the land had been reduced to by our brand of democracy was self-evident. No one raised his or her little

---

[22]These establishments included even large show rooms, stores, galleries etc. of rich and powerful business houses of long standing and whose managers generally came from the class of educated elites.

finger against the inherent unfairness of the new law. No one drew attention to the solemn declarations, made by the central, state and local governments and the top leaders of political parties, at the time of earlier regularisations, that no infringement of civic or planning or environmental laws would be tolerated in future. No one took the trouble of referring to, or even refuting, any one of the several critical points raised in scores of articles written by me around that time for widely read national dailies in which I, inter alia, had brought out how treacherously Nehru's vision for the planned development of Delhi was being betrayed and buried under the dung heap of corruption ridden illegalities. There was no remorse, no prick of conscience, not even an expression of regret. The fatal weakness for power had clearly numbed all sense and sensibilities.

To provide a facade of justification to a wholly unwarranted act, pre-determined recommendations were procured from a convenient Committee of 'experts', with variable commitment. The Committee resorted to untenable generalities, ignored all relevant data, documents and declaration, blurred the true picture with regard to unauthorised colonies by linking it with issues of other categories of violations of the Master Plan. It did not care to explain how any change in law could help in retrieving a situation where no application for seeking permission or approval of any authority is ever made.

The pre-disposition of the committee predictably led to a number of serious factual errors and contradictions in their report. In a perceptive paper, circulated by Dr. Ashok Kumar, Professor in the Department of Physical Planning, School of Planning and Architecture, at a symposium, held to deliberate upon the Khanna Committee Report[23], it was pointed out that the said report was based on hearsay and the conduct of its two expert-members had

[23] The Committee was headed by Tajendar Khanna, former Lt. Governor of Delhi. Its other four members were S.S. Shafi, former Chief Town Planner, Town and Country Planning Organisation, E.N. Rebeiro, former Planning Commissioner of DDA, Dr. S.C. Vats, MLA (Congress) and Dr. Harsh Vardhan, MLA. Soon after the submission of the Committee's report, Tajendar Khanna was again appointed as Lt. Governor of Delhi.

been wholly unprofessional. He underscored: "Both the experts had headed the Town and Country Planning Organsiation, New Delhi, at different times. Both had also been general consultants for the formulation of Master Plan. This raises ethical questions regarding two diametrically different positions that these experts have taken: one position while making contributions to the draft of the Master Plan and the other as members on the Khanna Committee. Both views seem to be irreconcible." The other serious lapses of the Khanna Committee brought out by Dr. Ashok Kumar in the above mentioned 'discussion paper' are summarised in Appendix-CII-(ii).

The colourable exercise of power by both the executive and legislature was writ large on the face of the Delhi Laws (Special Provisions) Act, 2006. Its constitutional validity was soon challenged by the Delhi Pradesh Citizen Council and others in the Supreme Court on the ground that it had over-ruled and set aside the orders of the highest Court of the land and virtually permitted the instrumentalities of the state to disobey or disregard even its specific directions. Recognising the merit of petitioners' contentions, the Supreme Court granted partial stay and directed that implementation of the specific orders, earlier issued, should continue. The new statute was, however, not stayed in toto, though its 'unique' character was frowned upon, leaving its vires for in-depth examination at subsequent hearings.

With the grant of partial stay by the Supreme Court and its likely invalidation of the new statute, the Central Government and its local agencies, in line with their no-holds-barred approach, decided to amend the land-use regulations, prescribed under the Master Plan for the period 1982-2001 in September 2006, that is, five years after its time-frame had ended. Concomitantly, the preparation of the next Master Plan, that is, for the period 2001-2021, which had remained in limbo even after the expiry of the preceding Master Plan, was speeded up at an unprecedented pace with the intention of providing what was called relief to the poor violators, though most of them were plain racketeers and profiteers.

Several thousand objections received from the public against the aforesaid amendments of the land-use regulations and the provisions of the Master Plan for the period 2001-2021 were disposed of with unseemly haste, first by the Screening Board of the D.D.A. and then by the D.D.A. itself. The Central Government, too, put its stamp of approval in a couple of days and notified the new Master Plan (2001-2021) on 7-2-2007. Every item of the procedure prescribed under the statute was carried out with pre-conceived conclusions in mind. The intention was to merely observe the formalities and later on claim before the Court that the changes have been brought about within the frame-work of law and the regulations made thereunder.

The statement of objects and reasons, appended as preamble to the aforesaid Delhi Laws (Special Provisions) Act, 2006, was itself an exercise in tendentiousness. It was nothing short of an attempt to quote from the scriptures to build up a case for the devil's proposition. All the factors and forces set therein, such as migration and increase in population, were known and accounted for at the time of finalisation of the original Master Plan, 2001. If these factors and forces were the real cause, they would continue to exist in the days to come also; then how could it be declared that in future no unauthorised development or construction would be tolerated?

Aware of its constitutional infirmity, the Delhi Laws (Special Provisions) Act, 2006 was initially projected as a temporary legislative measure to provide interim relief to those who were adversely affected by the Supreme Court orders, and its time span was fixed as one year, from May 19, 2006 to May 19, 2007. It was stipulated that, notwithstanding 'any order or judgement of any court, status quo as on the Ist day of January 2006', would be maintained with regard to unauthorised development[24]. This status quo was extended[25] upto December 2014, by passing, on one plea or the other, similar Special

---

[24]As per definitions laid down in section 2 of the Special Provisions Act, the term 'unauthorised development covers a number of illegal activities. It means "use of land or use of building or construction of building carried out in contravention of the sanctioned plans or without obtaining the sanction of plans, or in contravention of the land use as permitted under the Master Plan or Zonal Plan or layout plan, as the case may be and includes encroachment".

[25]These Acts were: Delhi Laws (Special Provisions) Acts., 2006, 2007 , 2009 ,2011 and 2012.

Provisions Acts as and when the earlier Act lapsed. In other words, what was, in first instance, given out as temporary relief, has been virtually made permanent.

Clearly, the entire exercise was a legal fraud. The political master and their collaborators had, in fact, never intended to take any action as it would have put at risk their own Master Plan of retaining, and even augmenting, the huge balance of unauthorised developers and builders in their vote-banks. This was particularly so in the case of unauthorised colonies. These colonies contribute most to the vote-banks of the politicians and also enable the land-racketeers and their associates to make large amounts of easy money. That is why, while the main case pertaining to the constitutional validity of the Delhi Laws (Special Provisions) Act, 2006, is yet to be decided by the Supreme Court, the political elements in authority have been encouraging, albeit indirectly, growth of unautorised colonies, both in number and size. They have virtually ignored the stipulation of the aforesaid Act itself that its protection would not be available to unauthorised development and construction done on or after January 1, 2006.

These elements in political authority have also seen to it that the contents of the Master Plan, 2001-2021, in so far as they relate to the unauthorised colonies, allow them to continue playing their unprincipled game of fiddling with the norms of modern town planning, development and constructions. The Plan merely says: "In all unauthorised colonies whether on private or public land, regularisation should be done as per the government orders issued from time to time. It must be ensured that for improvement of physical and social infrastructure, the minimum necessary/feasible level of services and community facilities are provided".

What do the terms 'minimum necessary', 'feasible level' etc. mean? Have such imprecise terms any place in a planning document which aims at unfolding a scientific, sustainable and environmentally congenial pattern of development for about 20 years to come? The vague and incongruous expressions were used to avoid stipulating even reduced but distinct scale of planning and building bye-laws on the basis of which unauthorised colonies and building constructed therein could be regularised by the authorities concerned. The approach was to have unfettered discretion. It was only after the intervention of the[26] Supreme Court and the Delhi High Court that a set of guidelines was framed by the Central Government. But these guidelines, too, were subjected, under the pressure of vested interests, to quite a few revisions from time to time, especially when the elections to the Municipal Corporation (2002), State Assembly (2003) or Lok Sabha (2004) approached.

The guidelines, which would suffice for analysis here, are the ones that were notified by the Ministry of Urban Development on March 24, 2008. These guidelines, in main, lay down that the cut-off date for regularisation would be March 31, 2002; that the colonies, which have been set up on notified or reserved forest land, or which violate the provisions of Ancient Monuments and Archaeological Sites and Remains Act, 1958, or which pose hindrance to the development of infrastructure or fall in the right of way of Master Plan roads, trunk water-supply and sewerage lines, or where more than 50 per cent of the plots are unbuilt on the date of formal announcement of regularisation scheme would not be regularised. It was also prescribed that for every unauthorised colony, a registered Residents Society would be constituted, and that the said society would get the lay-out plan prepared from an Architect/Town Planner and submit the same to the local body concerned, with land ownership documents etc., for approval. An undertaking had also to be furnished that the land-costs and development charges, calculated on the basis of the criteria indicated in the notification, would be paid by the society.

In an atmosphere, which had been thickened over the years, by the dust and haze of unprincipled power-politics, where competitive negativity in bribing voters in kind, instead of cash, was not seen as an electoral offence by the constitutionally protected Election

[26]In this regard, the Supreme Court's orders of February 14, 2006 in writ petition No.725 of 1994, and the Delhi High Court's orders of February 27, 2001 in writ petition No.4771 of 1993 may be seen.

Commission and where practically every element of the civic and state machinery of governance was for itself and no one was for the city, no-guidelines, no declaration, no notification, even when issued on the directions of the High Court or the Supreme Court, was likely to get actualised on the ground. And this was what exactly happened.

In course of time, every material condition, set out in the 'guidelines', was whittled down or altered or not enforced. For example, the 'cut-off' date for regularisation was extended to March 2007 from March 2002. By sleight of hand, the DDA[27] was made to pass a resolution which, by implications, brought about the said extension. The resolution instructed the officers concerned that for determining the qualifying criterion for regularisation of unauthorised colonies, the aerial survey of 2007, instead of the earlier aerial survey of 2002, should be followed. Further, as briefly indicated in chapter I (section dealing with the regime of Dr. Manmohan Singh-Mrs. Sonia Gandhi-Sheila Dikshit), Chief Minister Sheila Dikshit organized a public function at which Congress President Sonia Gandhi distributed provisional regularisation certificates to all '1639' unauthorised colonies, though the case of a large number of them could not even be considered[28] on account of their location in the 'prohibited zones' of the reserved forests and protected monuments. The notification, stipulating the regulations and guidelines, was treated as no more than a scrap of paper.

All acts of the type, sampled above, had the effect of not only reducing to dust once again the solemnly declared 'final' policy but

[27]In respect of the items connected with unauthorised colonies, it is the non-official members of the DDA who aggressively assert themselves and get the resolution passed on political rather than planning considerations. The passive acquiescence of civil servants and professional town-planners and architects is generally available; if necessary, it is secured through brow-beating tactics.

[28]Later on, during the course of an inquiry, it was discovered that in a number of cases 'provisional regularisation' certificates were issued when there was no colony at the site. Clearly, when populism- oriented decisions, which are at variance with the regulations formally in force, are hastily announced, a lot of scope is provided to the corrupt elements in the society and administration to resort to mal-practices.

also of swelling the ranks of land speculators and illegal builders. More unauthorised colonies came up, either as extensions or as separate entities. The plots which were unbuilt at the time of 'final' declaration or notification of the guidelines were rapidly built over. Not even the area which could have been used for providing civic services and social infrastructure was spared. Besides rendering the overall problems all the more intractable, the issuance of provisional regularisation certificates and the special publicity given to Sonia Gandhi-Sheila Dikshit's function had the effect of enlarging the scope for the subordinate municipal and other field staff to manipulate records and resort to corrupt practices. Allegations and counter-allegations were galore. The political and administrative environment was further vitiated, causing execution of even worthwhile projects on the ground irritatingly slow and wasteful.

In the three-four-year period, following the elections of 2008/ 2009, there was much fretting and fuming, many more discussions and declarations, but no way could be found to satisfy a very large number of plot-holders in the 1639 unauthorised colonies. With the rising tempo of civic indiscipline in these colonies, and with the continued propensity of the political parties to agree even to most blatantly illegal and selfish demands, as long as they could corner group-votes, no decision could attain finality. When the time for 2013 State Assembly and 2014 Lok Sabha neared, the political authorities, both at the State and Central levels, who had often been making irresponsible and virtually unimplementable pronouncements in the public, could do nothing but move for more unwarranted concessions and rewards by sacrificing the larger public interest.

Pressures were put on the Archaeology and Forest Departments to amend their laws and regulations to ensure that unauthorised colonies set-up in the 'reserved forests' and 'protected areas' were also regularised. Definition of public/government land was changed to exclude Gaon Sabha land, land acquired for the planned development of Delhi but encroached or built upon by original owner/occupiers or even by rank outsiders, during the acquisition proceedings[29] and lands vesting in the Revenue Department under the Delhi Land Reforms Act.

Further, knowing full well that it would be extremely difficult, if not impossible, to recover development and other charges after the so called regularisation, the government of National Capital Territory of Delhi started spending huge amounts, from its general budgetary allocations, on constructing roads and laying down water, sewers and power-lines. It had also permitted 'sale' and 'purchase' of plots and houses even before the layouts and services plans were sanctioned by the 'competent authority' and precise particulars of the property were given in the municipal records.

The most pernicious consequence of these decisions was that the honest tax-payers' money, meant for financing welfare projects for the general public, were diverted to extend wholly unjustified concessions to lawless elements whose lands/houses saw sudden rise in prices and brought huge speculation gains to them. What could be worse than this? The state, instead of firmly checking illegalities, immoralities and resource-wastage, was actually promoting them, exploiting, in the process, the general culture of apathy and indifference prevailing in the society.

Before my drive, detailed particulars of which have already been given in the earlier portion of this chapter, was halted by changing my portfolio of Urban Development, I had made it amply clear to the public, the press, Parliament and Prime Minister that my fundamental objective was not merely confined to saving the vision of planned development of Delhi; it was also to present a model and to ignite fire of rectitude and commitment in the hearts and minds of the people and to remind them of an ancient saying: 'the only thing necessary for the triumph of evil is for good men to do nothing'; and thus awaken the well-meaning intellectuals and community leaders to their social and moral responsibilities.

---

[29]In most cases, land-acquisition proceedings are obstructed by the vested interests by raising one frivolous objection after another and by misusing the procedures laid down by law.

There are already some 'good men', though in microscopic minority, who are doing a lot to check the triumph of evil and encouraging those who are determined to move forward, the rising fury of the opposing storm notwithstanding. In this regard, I may give an example. Former Member of Rajya Sabha, Fali S. Nariman, who is a top jurist and thinker of the country, has been playing the role of 'good man' and warmly applauding the principle and firm stand of those who want to bring about clean governance in the country. Here it may not be out of place to reproduce what he has written in his latest publication, *The State of the Nation*[30]:

> We must also never forget to applaud public officials when they do the right thing.
>
> I offer an illustrative instance. In early 2000 there was a strong builders' lobby in Delhi - there still is! But at that time, there was an honest-to-God 'bulldozing' Union minister, Jagmohan, who stood firm against all the shenanigans of the builders. An editorial in the Hindustan Times (29 April 2000) set out why Delhi citizens owed a debt of gratitude to the minister:
>
> A Measure of Gratitude
>
> The Urban Development Minister has a reputation for being stubborn. When Mr Jagmohan was in charge of the Communication Ministry, many of his colleagues despaired of ever being able to persuade him to change his mind. Eventually they had to move Mr Jagmohan out before they could change the policy. Mr Jagmohan may or may not have been right in refusing to alter the telecom policy but few people will dispute that it is good to have an Urban Development Minister who is as stubborn as Mr Jagmohan. Ever since he announced a drive against unauthorised constructions, members of his own party have been using every trick in the book to get him to desist from following through with his crusade. A less stubborn man may have been amenable to some kind of compromise. But

[30]Fali S. Nariman's book, titled: The State of the Nation in the context of India's Constitution, page 327-330.

fortunately for the people of Delhi, Mr Jagmohan has lived up to his reputation for stubbornness.

Nobody who lives in Delhi can deny that a mafia of unscrupulous builders, corrupt municipal officials and venal politicians has conspired to destroy the character of this beautiful city. Some of the greatest architectural vandalism has occurred in south Delhi where quiet and pleasant colonies have been transformed by the illegal construction of ugly multistory apartments and hideously repulsive shopping centres. The law states that residential premises must not be used for commercial enterprises. Yet, in such previously charming localities as Defence Colony, this law has been flouted with cheerful impunity. Greedy house owners have pulled down their bungalows to construct ugly four-storey complexes, where room are let out to offices, slimming clinics, restaurants, computer institutes, so-called 'health clubs' and grocery stores. Those who run these establishments have paid off the municipal authorities so they do not even bother to be discreet. Large neon signs, banners and hoardings litter the frontage of these houses, breaking the law with an arrogant indifference to its provisions. It is clear, by now, that municipal officials are on the take. It is as clear that politicians also get their cut of the bribes. So, who can be honest citizen turn to? The sad answer is that city's power-that-be care more for their wallets than they care for Delhi. *That is why the citizens of the Capital owe Mr Jagmohan a measure of gratitude. He is the only man who has had the guts to launch this long-overdue drive. And only he has the stubborness to see it through* [emphasis added].

I wrote a letter congratulating the editor of HT. It was published on 4 May, 2000:

Doing The Right Thing

Sir,

I CONGRATULATE you on your leadig editorial in the Hindustan Times (29 April) as to why citizens of Delhi owe

Mr. Jagmohan a measure of gratitude. It needed to be said. Corruption must not only be fought by laws and through courts, but must be combated through the hearts of men and women.

Jean Monnet, father of the European Union, used to say there are two types of people in this world – those who want to be somebody and those who want to do something. Being somebody, the Urban Development Minister has also done great things - notably the drive against unauthorised constructions. Doing the right thing has a trickle-down effect.

Fali S. Nariman, Delhi.

There is an old school song made famous by Rudyard Kipling whose last stanza reads:

*Bless and praise we famous men*
*Men of little showing!*
*For their work continueth*
*And their work continueth*
*Broad and deep, continueth*
*Great beyond their knowing.*

When good people, people in positions of power, sometimes do the right thing, it does have a trickle-down effect for the common man, the proverbial man-in-the-street. For as the great book says:

'Whatsoever a great man doeth, that other men also do; the standard he setteth up, by that the people go.

The need of the hour is... And quite frankly they are in short supply.

*India Today's TODAY,* the Capital Afternoon Newspaper, of April 29, 2003, chose me as citizen No.I, with the following citation:

> He takes on foes, he knows no friends. For him nothing or nobody is above Delhi, its beauty, its heritage. Its historical places and public spaces. He's Citizen One.

This choice, too, was another indication that there were 'good men' who would not let earnest efforts of the motivated individuals to go unsung and thus spur them to continue with their mission no matter how overwhelming is the strength of the negative forces at present.

All said and done, the crisis of values remains, and remains in acute form. The symptoms of the irreversibility of the malady are, indeed, frightening. In any case, what could one think of future of a city, where the intellectual foundations of a new vision have been destroyed before they could develop firmness and strength, where mounting challenges posed by super-urbanization are sought to be tackled, not by relying on meticulous planning, not by respecting laws and constitution, not by engendering nobility of temper amongst the citizens, not by enforcing civic discipline and environmental sustainability, but by allowing an unprincipled and self-serving coalition of land grabbers and vote grabbers to swindle a large part of its resources and set most of its civic and planning institutions on an insane and self-destructive course?

CHAPTER III

# NINTH DELHI'S GREENS AND THEIR PHILOSOPHIC PEDESTAL

*What a perfect planner and architect the cosmic spirit is. Millions of items of life — of mountains, meadows and forests; of snows, streams and seas; of soil, space and air; of plants, animals and energy, etc.– have been spun into an astonishingly cohesive pattern which has poise, precision and dynamic equilibrium of its own. But we are violently disturbing this equilibrium.*

— Author[1]

*A nation reveals itself not only by the men it produces but also by the men it honours, the men it remembers.*

— John F. Kennedy[2]

I have never looked at the idea of urban greens from the restricted angle of honouring a town planning principle of keeping a certain percentage of land, in a colony or a zone, for development as parks, playgrounds, formal gardens, etc. To my way of thinking, the idea must be spread over a larger canvas and serve multiple objectives. It must promote citizens' health, preserve the city's historical memory, protect architectural legacy and help in rediscovering and absorbing the core message of the Upanishadic philosophy that our existence on this planet is an enmeshed part of the cosmic web in which every item of life and nature, animate or inanimate, is organically

[1] From the speech delivered by the author on February 21, 2000, on the occasion of distribution of Prime Minister's National Award for Excellence in Urban Planning and Development.

[2] John F. Kennedy: *In Praise of Robert Frost,* October 27, 1963.

integrated. "Whether we are rich or poor, black or white, young or old, humans or animals, fish or fowl, trees or rocks, everything is sustained by the same air, the same sunshine, the same water, the same soil."[3] There is, as the Upanishadic thought sums up, "One in All and All in One".

With this approach, the urban greens, created through city-forests, regional parks and vast gardens, do not remain merely as town-planning greens. They also become venues for receiving silent messages from the distant towers of what is most noble and profound in our ancient thought, and thus serve as an instrument for transfusing fresh and pure blood in the emaciated veins of the present social system and make it stronger and more balanced and benign.

The core issue is of 'root and branch' reforms and the need to recognize the pivotal importance of the base from which the attitudes, outlook and ethos of the citizens emerge. It must be kept in mind that:

*Culture springs from the roots*
*And seeping through to all the shoots*
*To leaf and flower and bud*
*From cell to cell, like green blood,*
*Is released by rain showers*
*As fragrance from the wet flowers*
*To fill the air.*[4]

The healthy roots and congenial environment are necessary for the development of the urban greens of the kind discussed in this chapter. But, once brought into being, they must make their own contributions in adding to the strength of the roots and improving the congeniality of the environment. The ultimate objective must be to disseminate cultural fragrance in the society, after filtering it through the lessons of history, and build a powerful urge to propel the Indian polity to a higher and healthier orbit of thought and action and for creating a new civilization which would synthesise

[3] S. Kumar: *Spiritual Imperative; Resurgence* – Issue of March/April 2005.
[4] Hassan Fathy, *Gourna: A Tale of Two Villages;* pg. 34.

the best in the Indian heritage and the best that is available to it from modern advances in science and technology.

Whenever a suitable opportunity came my way, I made my views on the subject known to the public in general and professionals in particular. For instance, in my inaugural address to the All India Conference of Horticulturists which, incidentally, was held by me at the Ministerial level, on June 29, 2000, after 45 years[5] of the first conference convened by Dr. C.D. Deshmukh, I spelt out the framework of my thought on greening of urban India, and underlined its philosophic pedestal:

> We must draw nature to our cities, develop a number of woodlands and parks, create 'rivers of green' by way of green belts, clean-up water-fronts and water-bodies and inject overall tranquility and elegance into the urban fabric. We must also consider how to upgrade the profession of horticulture and landscape architects and how new technologies should be introduced in this area, so as to enable the profession to play an effective role in evolving an elevating urban design....
>
> Above all, we must learn to go to the "basics of thing", respect the ancient traditions of balance and harmony and recreate a national mindscape which is in tune with our objectives and also conducive to their materialisation on the ground. I am aware that the approach that I am advocating would have little attraction for those who are bitten by the bug of present-day consumerism; or whose outlook is determined by the belief: 'The world is a machine, composed of inert bodies, moved by physical necessity, indifferent to the existence of thinking beings'. But we, on our part, must continue to prioritise measures which help in creating a healthy mind – a mind that is sensitive to finer aspects of life and leads to acceptance of higher value system.

[5] This fact was made known by the veteran horticulturist, Dr. G.S. Randhawa, who was one of the distinguished participants of the Conference, which I organised as Urban Development Minister, as well as the conference convened by Dr. C.D. Deshmukh in his capacity as President of All India Horticultural Association.

> The crucial challenge that we all face today is to create a sense of mission. And this sense of mission would not be forthcoming if the current ideological and inspirational vacuum persists. We must, therefore, not only absorb the basic tenets of Upanishadic philosophy as individual officers or functionaries but also educate the community about these tenets through the information cum interpretation cum conservation centres. Only then, a sense of dignified pride in our heritage would emerge....., and the current work-culture of casualness would get replaced by the culture of commitment.

As an executive head of the Delhi Development Authority, as a Lieutenant-Governor of Delhi, and, later on, as a Union Minister, I was associated with the development of a large number of Delhi's green spaces, be they in the form of city-forests, woodlands or regional parks. In all these cases, I had endeavoured to provide facilities to the citizens not only for oxygenating their lungs and strengthening their limbs but also for understanding and imbibing the core content of India's philosophic heritage; viz. the belief in the divinity of life, unity of existence and all life being interdependent. Let me elaborate.

A spark of divinity exists in every individual and in every element of nature. And if this inner spark is activated by the individual and if existence of such a spark in nature is also recognised, a deeper meaning of life would emerge. The common thread of divinity passing through all creatures, would become visible and the level of understanding between man and man, and between man and nature, would go up, paving the way for a harmonious and balanced pattern of life on earth.

In times immemorial, the Upanishadic sages moved to mountains, meadows and streams and experienced the elevation of mind that close contact and communion with nature produced. They felt the exhilaration of the clean and crisp air and found 'tongues in trees and books in running brooks'. The deep thinking done by them for years together, led them to believe: there is no duality; Man's self and elements of nature constituted the Cosmic Being – the mountains His bones, the earth His flesh, the sea His blood, the air His breath and the fire His energy. One of the earliest hymns the sages composed, about 4000 years ago, was addressed to the Earth with a sense of reverence and concern:

> *Whatever I dig of you, O Earth,*
> *May you of that have quick replenishment!*
> *O Purifying One, may my thrust never*
> *Reach right unto your vital points, your heart* !

What this prayer seeks for man is the good sense to respect the recouping capacities of the Earth and not to damage it irreversibly by over-drawing from its life-support system. The emphasis is on balance and harmony and treating the Earth as Mother.[6]

In the western countries, it is only in recent years that the organic entity and self-regulatory mechanism of the Earth's system has come to be recognized by a section of thinkers. In 1972, James Lovelock, the world famous ecologist, propounded the hypothesis of *Gaia*- a metaphor for the Earth's control system which 'does its own things' to remain in dynamic equilibrium and which requires that its constraints should be respected. If these constraints are exceeded, as they are being exceeded at present, disequilibrium would ensue and the system would be damaged.

Eulogising the deep rooted understanding of the true reality of the Universe by the ancient Indian thinkers, the great French scholar, Amaury de Reincourt, has rightly observed, "The wealth of the psychological insight revealed in Upanishads is based on the most profound study and understanding of nature ever achieved, one with which we twentieth-century Westerners, in spite of our vast present-day knowledge, have not yet fully caught up." In a similar line of thinking, Crispin Tickell, renowned British diplomat and environmentalist, has underlined "We have to look at life with respect and wonder. We need an ethical system in which the natural

[6]The attitude of treating earth as mother acted as a cultural constraint to exploit or harm it in any other way. "One does not", to borrow the evocative words of Carolyn Merchant, "readily slay a mother, dig into her entrails or mutilate her body."

world has value not just for human welfare but also for and in itself. The universe is something internal as well as external."[7]

Unfortunately, while a significant section of western leadership, in political, social and intellectual arenas, is becoming increasingly conscious of the need for maintaining balance and harmony in life and recognizing the wisdom of the Upanishadic sages, the contemporary Indian leadership, in almost all walks of life, has virtually forgotten the noble and insightful aspects of her ancient thought. Instead of recapturing and rekindling those aspects and synthesizing them with the new insights provided by modern science and technology, it has become a 'poor, wayward cousin' of the propagators of western materialism and consumerism, causing blighted cities, polluted rivers and 'surface and superficial greens'. In essence, India is now no more than a spiritual and cultural wasteland. Regeneration of this wasteland has, therefore, to precede, or at least go hand in hand, with the town planning venture of earmarking and developing green spaces and protecting them.

Unless attainment of a higher awareness, disciplining of inner self, learning the right kind of lessons from the sad chapters of her history, banishing of diffidence, divisions and desolation of the degenerated times, and determination to convert well-intentioned declarations into zeal-oriented deeds become integral constituents of India's culture, she would not be able to formulate a healthy and wholesome design of life for her people. Nor would she be able to muster courage, conviction and strong implementational will to realise this design in practice. India is badly in need of a strong and enduring philosophic pedestal, an all-pervasive renaissance, which would push her true tryst with destiny in an elevating orbit.

What could be the attributes of the regenerative and reformative forces, what course and colour could these forces take and in what manner could they creatively and constructively impact the overall scene, and how the intellectual, social and moral fibre of the nation

[7]Sir Crispin Tickell is the author of a noted book: *Climate Change and World Affairs*. He made the observations quoted here in his address at a Conference On the Earth: Our Destiny.

could be strengthened, have been discussed in the last chapter, titled:[8] *Need for Civitizational Regeneration and the Second Renaissance.* Here, I would restrict myself to indicating how inspirational tempo has been raised, how scores of vast urban greens have been developed and how elements of history, heritage, environment and clean civic life have been woven into them to create great assets of natural and cultural wealth. In the process, I would also show how new insights, new initiatives, new commitments and new styles of governance have been brought to bear on the multi-faceted problems to produce maximum results in minimum time at the lowest cost.

## Setting Up of Great Green National Cultural Hubs

Almost all the Clearance cum Resettlement cum Redevelopment Projects, the planning and execution of which has been narrated and analysed in the Chapters on Slums and Unauthorised Colonies[9], had an element of green-development inbuilt in them, and the character of this development was determined by the philosophic ideals outlined above in this section.

As briefly mentioned in Chapter I, the change of my portfolio from Urban Development had initially upset me but I soon collected myself, applied my mind creatively to the new circumstances and evolved, in my capacity as Tourism and Culture Minister, an all-India project of developing Great Green National Cultural Hubs for historically and culturally significant cities and sites spread over the country. The capital had its own share of these hubs. A detailed discussion about them[10] would show how multiple benefits of immense dimensions and permanent nature have accrued to Ninth Delhi.

---

[8]Since the issues of basic reforms and elevation of mind and soul of India are germane and common to quite a few propositions formulated in different sections of this book, they have been dealt with in a separate chapter, titled *Need for Civitizational Regeneration and the Second Renaissance*. This, I trust, would avoid repetition.

[9]The Chapter on slums is titled: *Slums—Physical and Mental*; and the Chapter on unauthorised colonies is titled as *Tragedy of A Self-Destructive Democracy.*

[10] To explain in depth and in historical context, I have taken up, for narration and analysis, four categories of Green Hubs in Delhi. One relates to the Red Fort Complex,

I would begin with the Red Fort complex which would provide a clear picture of the various components of the Hub Project and also show how these components were synthesised to create a Great Green National Cultural Hub in the heart of the city. To facilitate easy comprehension of what I had planned and how I had implemented the overall plan, I would split my discussions under the following five sub-heads, each dealing with a distinct but dovetailed component of the said plan:

(i) Rebirth of a Fort;

(ii) Removal of the squatters/slums from the area lying between Eastern wall of the Fort and the Ring Road and laying down of the *Delhi Chalo Park*; as a Memorial to Subhas Chandra Bose's call to the Indian National Army to reach Delhi and hoist Azad Hind flag on the Red Fort;

(iii) Development of the *August 15 Park* on the Western side of the Fort facing Chandni Chowk and Subhas Marg;

(iv) Ending the 146 year-old presence of the Army in the Fort; and

(v) Clearance of the heavily squatted upon middle part of the Yamuna embankment and its redevelopment as an elegant River Front in the vicinity of the Fort, the *Delhi Chalo Park* and the area covered by the national *Samadhis*.

### (i) Rebirth of a Fort

Fergusson, the celebrated historian of medieval art and architecture, has described Red Fort as "the most magnificent palace in the East – perhaps in the world."

By way of backdrop, it may be recapitulated that in 1638, the Mughal Emperor Shahjahan decided to shift his headquarters from

---

the second to the Humayun Tomb, the third to Lal Kot-Quila Rai-Pathora and the fourth to the combination of small scale hubs. Each has a distinct background and features of its own. But one basic element is common to them. They show how the Greens of Ninth Delhi have been spread over a larger canvas and how multiple objectives of local and national significance have been realised through them by placing them on a new philosophic pedestal.

Agra and build a new capital city on the bank of the Yamuna, near the old ruins of Firozabad, Delhi. A majestic Red Fort, with its mighty walls, gates, towers and battlements, was constructed in about eight years. Emperor Shahjahan lived in the Fort and ruled the empire from it. The Fort was a self-contained imperial township, with a population of about 5,000, including troops, royal staff and personal servants.

The layout of the Red Fort is unique. It is octagonal in conception. It has two long walls on the east and west and six smaller ones on the north and the south. It contains a number of remarkable buildings, including *Diwan-i-Am*, a hall for the public audience; *Diwan-i-Khas*, a hall where the high dignitaries met; *Rang Mahal*, justly famous for being "the crowning jewel of Shahjahan's seraglio"; and *Nahar-i-Bihist*, a branch of Ali Mardan's canal, which fed the fountains and chutes, etc.

The story of the Red Fort, however, does not lie merely in the grandeur of its building or its imperial tradition. Here, every stone, every column, every pavilion, painting and pathway constitutes some item or the other of a great human drama, which tells us how a great empire was built, how an unmatched splendour was injected into its brilliant buildings, how compassion and cruelty were simultaneously exercised, how an absolute power-structure ultimately became a victim of its own arrogance, indolence and delusion, and how it fell into the hands of a cool and calculating East India Company and eventually became an enmeshed item of the jewel in the British Crown.

Besides providing instructive lessons of history to the generations of post-1947 India – what pitfalls of intrigues, insinuations, indulgences, internal sabotage and corruption to avoid in building a democratic republic – the vast and varied heritage of the Red Fort and other great monuments of the country could have contributed, in a large measure, to the rapid growth of Indian economy and that, too, in a graceful and dignified way. The country could have earned substantial amount of foreign exchange by attracting daily thousands of foreign tourists to these monuments by conserving them and creating congenial environment around them.

India has 3606 protected monuments under the Ancient Monuments and Archaeological Sites and Remains Act. "For variety, extent, completeness and beauty, these monuments are unsurpassed, perhaps unequalled in the world. What is there that is not here". These were the observations made by a British Secretary of State in his communication to the Government of India in 1902, underlining its responsibility for preserving the ancient monuments.

For years together, particularly during the 18th and 19th centuries, the monuments of India remained in a state of neglect. It was Lord Curzon who rescued them. He wrote: "As a pilgrim at the shrine of beauty I have visited them, but as a priest in the temple of duty have I charged myself with their reverent custody and their studious repairs". He promulgated the Ancient Monument and Archaeological Sites and Remains Act of 1904 and laid the foundation of a scientific policy of protecting and preserving the archaeological assets of India. The country owes a deep debt to him. Jawaharlal Nehru, who was otherwise a bitter critic of Lord Curzon, said: "After every other Viceroy has been forgotten, Curzon will be remembered because he restored all that was beautiful in India."

By virtue of its great cultural and civilisational wealth, India could have succeeded in securing inclusion of a very large number of monuments and sites in the World Heritage List[11]. But on account of, poor maintenance, encroachments and degraded environment, only about a score of Indian monuments were included in the list of World Heritage sites. The other countries, much smaller in size and with less architectural wealth, got many more sites included. For example, the West European countries whose combined area is almost equal to that of India, were able to secure inclusion of as many as 153 sites in the list. Thus, India, on account of general neglect of its monuments, and presence of slums and squatters in their vicinity, lost heavily in both fame and fortune. Had it tapped its potential in this arena, it could have become the tourist destination

---

[11]From 1972, the UNESCO had started practice of listing World Heritage sites.

number one of the world. But it did not do so. Its apathy was appalling. Red Fort, which was rated by Fergusson, as the finest monument of the East, was not included by the UNESCO in its list of World Heritage Sites.

This sad reality, an inevitable outcome of a casual and routine-oriented machinery of governance, was known to me. But it impacted me sharply, when after taking over as Minister of Tourism and Culture, I went to have a look at the Red Fort and study in depth the conditions then prevailing.

I came across a number of shabby structures standing like sore thumbs, amidst grand buildings of medieval grace and charm. Ugly stalls and their clumsy signages, with loose and hanging electric wires, compounded the picture of disarray. Even a cobbler and a washerman had managed to sneak in. The broken 'Jharokas' on the walls fronting the river had been stuffed with bricks and rubble. The rampart and the bastion had innumerable black spots on them. The open ground, in the rear of the Fort-walls, along the Ring Road, had become nauseating slum, emitting foul smell. The staircase and the gates, which once opened to the water-front, were locked and their inner space filled with junk-stores. An old, worn out, building, which was used by the British army as a tea-house, had been turned into a huge heap of mud and garbage. The main entrance to the Fort and the open space between it and Chandni Chowk and Jama Masjid were cluttered with shacks, stalls, and stores, uglifying the entire landscape.

With regard to the area and buildings not under the control of the Army, there was a bewildering diffusion of responsibilities amongst the authorities concerned, viz. Archaeological Survey of India, the Department of Tourism, the Delhi Municipal Corporation, the Administration, Police and Land-owning Agencies in and around the complex. Nor had any sustained pressure, with cogent arguments, been put on the Army and Ministry of Defence to make them agree to move out of the Fort.

All in all, an uncoordinated maintenance of the Red Fort complex, in its entirety, showed the depth of sloth to which the working of the executive had been descending over the years. I was upset. But I kept the anger within myself. As was my wont, I did not shout at any officer; nor did I bewail the apathy of a particular department.

I was aware that, at the root of the crisis, lay the poor work-culture and shallow political and administrative values, which leadership at various levels of governance had been generating over the years. Most of the officers, by their own disposition, were not indifferent or lazy. In fact, most of them were well-meaning. But the overall atmosphere, contaminated by the unprincipled politics of the country, had undermined their potential and demoralised them, made them self-centred, prone to evasion of responsibility by taking cover under one rule or the other. What they needed was an inspiring leadership which would motivate them, share their problems, save them from machinations of politicians and petty elements within their own organisations, stand by them if any decision, taken *bonafide*, went amiss, make them proud about the worth of their contribution to the overall task and remind them, not by words, but by personal conduct, personal knowledge, personal insight and personal commitment and confidence that they all are, in one way or the other, worthy inheritors of the Upanishadic philosophic tradition which had given birth to the great ideal of *Karmayogi* and also of service to the man and environment being a worship of its own kind.

This belief of mine had been fortified by my experience of reforming Vaishno Devi Shrine Complex[12], where hosts of chronic problems had accumulated and where, in a short period, many objectives in managerial, environmental, social and cultural arenas were simultaneously achieved.

Here, in the Red Fort complex, too, I had to move in several directions, virtually at the same time. I spotted the right kind of officers from different departments, including those who were not directly under my Ministry's charge, and set up a team whose knowledge and animation were got upgraded, by way of repeated

---

[12]The reader, having interest in managerial, environmental, social and cultural improvements carried out in the Mata Vaishno Devi Complex, may go through my book, *Reforming Vaishno Devi and A Case for Reformed, Reawakened and Enlightened Hinduism*.

visits to the site. A contemporaneous report, appearing in the *Indian Express* of May 20, 2002, under the caption: *Jagmohan Tours Fort, Officials Turn Red,* had broadly captured the tempo of the activities generated. It bears reproduction here, as an evidence of result-oriented style of working:

> The common thought at Red Fort this evening was "On your toes. He knows everything and can quiz any body about anything he likes." Even worse for officials, Tourism and Culture Minister Jagmohan knows his history well. For over 90 minutes this evening, Red Fort was buzzing with 'official' activity.
>
> Jagmohan walked from one end of the Fort to the other, inspecting each dome, wall and even the vegetation in the campus. And as he walked, officials ran and leapt over fences and building material that came in the way. Nothing blocked them from taking notes.
>
> This is the third time in less than two months that the Minister took a round of the Fort. And Jagmohan made sure that he asked specific questions.
>
> While the Minister fired a volley of questions, officials had to come with sound, convincing arguments. Any hesitation, and Jagmohan would just say "one second....let me explain".
>
> From inquiries about "How many *jalees* have been ordered, how many have been put in the 17 *jharokas* and how much work remains?" to "progress on acquiring land from the Defence Ministry", Jagmohan knew the issue.
>
> When senior ASI officials said "kabaris employed by the Defence Ministry have been staying here for long now", the Minister retorted: "It doesn't matter how long they have been here. They have no business being here. Issue a letter in my name to the officers concerned, tell them we need to clear the land."
>
> Clear instructions about landscaping, restoring gardens and conservation were given. Details about new projects were discussed with officials and duties delegated.

> The Minister listened to conservation architects, asking them to coordinate with his officers.
>
> On his way back, the Minister again growled about security forces occupying areas inside the Fort "How does this fit into the ambience of the Red Fort?", he asked.
>
> When asked about his next visit to the Fort, he said, "anytime soon. Maybe next month or sooner." The surprise of the Minister's visits is becoming a worry for officials. A senior official said: "We are all on our toes. The Minister is very particular about things and knows what is happening. He asks tough questions."
>
> Perhaps the only one who was glowing from the visit was the senior most craftsman. When he said 'hello', Jagmohan grabbed him and said, "Please take my picture with him".

It was primarily due to a highly original, informed, all-pronged, ground-level, approach that extraordinary results were achieved, at all levels of the planning and implementation agencies. The entire surface of the Fort walls – 21,219 square metres – was thoroughly washed and chemically cleaned. 1.7 kilometres long moat, with massive slush accumulated over the years was cleared. About 23,000 cubic metres of debris, with a load of 3,500 trucks, was lifted from it. About 2,200 square metres of pathways which were of flag stones and were subsequently damaged and replaced by 'morram', were re-laid in accordance with the original design. The shell plaster on the walls of *Mumtaz Mahal, Rang Mahal, Hamam,* which had peeled off, was refixed. All the 23 red sandstone *Jali*-windows, which had broken, were remade. *Diwan-i-Khas, Khas Mahal, Naubat-Khana, Tehkhanna*, too were brought back to their old glory. The *Hayat Baksh Garden* with its fountains, channels and cascades was also restored. The old underground passage to the Yamuna River Front, under the Masamman Burj, was cleared and opened on the Ring Road side. Restoration of *Nahar-i-Bihist,* which seemed almost impossible, was also carried out.

A special treatment was accorded to a virtually unknown *baoli* – step-well. It had an indigenously designed bathing tank and a large courtyard, about 28 feet below the ground level, approachable through stairs. During the occupation by the British Army, the *baoli* fell into disuse and a good part of the courtyard was converted into prison cells, where the freedom-fighters, labelled dangerous prisoners by the British Intelligence, were brought for interrogation. After 1945, however, the *baoli* and the cells were closed. Later on, a lot of junk, garbage and building material got dumped here. Hundreds of truckloads of garbage were removed and the prison cells and the *baoli* exposed to the view, bringing to light quite a few hidden pages of history of India's freedom struggle.

It was truly an epic scale effort at conservation and restorative surgery that brought about a graceful rebirth of one of the most remarkable monuments of the medieval times. But there is history beyond the history of those times; quite a few momentous events of India's freedom struggle are associated with the Red Fort. I may now turn to them.

### (ii) Delhi Chalo Park

The *Delhi Chalo* Call, given by Subhas Chandra Bose, the Supreme Commander of the Indian National Army, to his officers and men, reverberated frequently within the premises of the Red Fort, where three senior commanders of the said Army, namely, Major-General Shah Nawaz Khan, Colonel Prem Sehgal and G.S. Dhillon were put to trial before a special Army Tribunal. Those were the days of intense fervour, passionate patriotism and fearless shouting of anti-British slogans[13], virtually in every nook and corner of India.

Never before had Indian emotions been so loudly and boldly expressed than at the time of INA Trials. With every passing day, the freedom wave rose higher and higher. But, regrettably, this revolutionary upsurge which the people, including those in the service of the Army and Civil Administration, experienced at that time has not been adequately reflected in the premises on which the history of India's success in winning freedom on August 15, 1947,

[13]The most popular slogan was : *Lal Quila Se Aye Awaz; Sehgal, Dhillon and Shah Nawaz.*

has been written. Did India get her freedom by merely turning the other cheek when slapped on one by her imperial master? Was the doctrine of non-violence, expressed through repeated *satyagrahas* and individual fasts, alone responsible for the colonial power to give up its most prized possession?

Undoubtedly, Gandhi's disposition to work as a saint and a statesman at the same time and his uncanny capacity to organise a mass movement by stirring the dormant spirituality of the common folks were the unique and dominant factors that brought India her freedom. But that should not make us forget the highly significant, valiant and inspiring part played by Subhas Chandra Bose and the example he set for the youth by performing one heroic deed after another.

In January 1941, Subhas gave a slip to the British-Indian Intelligence, undertook an extremely hazardous journey, via Afghanistan to Soviet Russia and Germany, from where, after two struggling years, he travelled to Japan on a German submarine, U-180, which had to transfer him, while remaining under the sea-waters, to a Japanese submarine, I-29. It foretold the fearless and indefatigable leadership which Subhas provided to the Indian National Army. He and his men fought even when it became clear that the Allied Powers were on the verge of victory. "When after four desperate months their attempt to break into India failed, they withdrew to the Irrawaddy where, though the British pursued them in overwhelming numbers and it was clear the war was lost, they fought again."[14]

When full facts about the undaunted leadership of Subhas Chandra Bose, the Indian National Army, and the *Delhi Chalo* call came to be known during the Red Fort trials, public opinion hardened against anything short of complete freedom. The surge of the masses, worked up by patriotic fury, could be handled, perhaps, only by the deployment of the British Indian Army. But Imperial rulers were no longer confident they could count on the Army as

[14] P.W. Fay: *The Forgotten Army*. p.9

they could before Subhas Chandra had injected a spirit of Azadi in its rank and file. If any confirmation of this phenomenon was needed, the same was provided by the mutiny of ratings of Royal Indian Navy in Bombay in February 1946 and also by the Army unit stationed at Jabalpur.

What the Indian National Army undertook was "a true war of independence, entitled, as such wars are, to our attention and respect. Historians may differ whether this war became the decisive agent of Britain's precipitate departure from India within two years of Red Fort trials. But something can be said with confidence at once. In India's pantheon there is space reserved, high, ample, and honourable space, for those men and women who, when certain accidents of time and place gave them the opportunity, seized it and went out to do battle for India's freedom[15]". To provide this 'high, ample and honourable space', and to keep the memory of the INA evergreen, what better location could be found than the vast area lying between the River and the eastern side of the Fort wall. I was also keen that history and heritage preservation of the Red Fort complex should not be restricted to the distant past. Equal, if not more, attention should be given to the recent past, especially the one connected with India's freedom struggle.

The aforesaid area was well spread out. During the Mughal times, river Yamuna, when flooded, came close to the eastern wall of the Red Fort. In the non-rainy season, the sprawling space was used for holding sports, such as elephant-fight, for the entertainment of the Emperor and members of the royalty. The Emperor used to watch the sports from the royal chamber, while the women-folk sat in their *jharokas.* After raising of the river embankment, Yamuna-Pushta, as it is now called, construction of the Ring Road and setting up *samadhis* of national leaders, the area got a distinct marking and well-defined boundaries. It had all the potential for becoming a new gem in the historical legacy of the period shortly before and also of the period shortly after August 15,1947, the era traversed by

---

[15]*Ibid.,* p.10

Gandhi, Nehru and Subhas Chandra Bose. But it remained uncared for.

Unfortunately, after the initial years of freedom, the political stage of the country came to be dominated by the leaders who showed little respect for history and little inclination to look beyond their narrow ends of power. They frequently misused the aforesaid area for parking of trucks, tempos, and even tractors on which they transported their supporters from outside Delhi for holding 'massive and impressive' rallies in the capital. Even temporary urinals were erected close to the wall, causing nuisance of dust and stink to the tourists who at that time happened to be around the eastern side of the Fort wall. A sprawling weekly market, nick-named, 'Chor-bazaar'[16], was also held in the area. The conditions were so messy that two pro-Pakistan terrorists managed to sneak in the Fort by scaling its rear wall, took the Army garrison by surprise and killed two soldiers.

As soon as the Department of Archaeology came under my charge, as Cultural Minister, I got all the misuses terminated and cleared the entire area of all squatters and 'Chor-bazaar' etc. Simultaneously, a blue-print of a large park, evoking the spirited steadfastness of *Delhi Chalo* call was formulated, and translated on the ground, with utmost speed and diligence; providing even an entry from the Park to the Fort by opening up a small and secret passage which Shahjahan had built as an escape route, through river-boats, in event of emergency caused by enemy action or internal revolt.

The transformation of the area was so rapid and radical that when, on invitation of Cultural Ministry, L.K. Advani, Deputy Prime Minister, came to inaugurate the *Delhi Chalo Park* on April 21, 2002 he could not, for a while, believe that he was on the same site which had become a byword for 'slums, stinks, shabbiness and security hazards'. And he said so in his inaugural speech.

---

16 'Chor-bazaar' literally means thief's market. It had become notorious for selling, at cheap rates, goods some of which were believed to have been stolen and then given a different form.

By a sheer quirk of the provisions of the Hub-Plan, the *Delhi Chalo Park,* designed to keep the memory of Subhas Chandra Bose evergreen, had come to occupy a place almost opposite *Shanti Van* and *Raj Ghat,* the national memorials of Nehru and Gandhi, who, in terms of political belief, were on other side of Bose. They had basic differences with regard to the manner of waging freedom struggle. Bose's militant nationalism and confrontational policies did not find favour with them. Gandhi once made it clear: "I am not equipped to issue an ultimatum to the Government. But Subhas Babu thinks we are ready for the struggle. My conception of *satyagraha* is not his. Is this difference of opinion not fundamental"? Jawaharlal Nehru, too, sometimes fulminated against Bose. In his characteristic paroxysm of anger, he, when provoked, once blurted out: "Hitler and Japan must go to hell. I shall fight them to the end and that is my policy. I shall also fight Subhas Chandra Bose and his party along with Japan if he comes to India. Hitler and Japan represent the reactionary forces and their victory means the victory of the reactionary forces in the world". Nevertheless, in his speech at the Red Fort on August 16, 1947 Nehru said:

> On this day we must remember those who have made sacrifices and suffered for the cause of independence. It is needless for me to name all of them but I cannot help mentioning Subhas Chandra Bose who left this country and formed the Indian National Army abroad and fought bravely for the freedom of the country. He hoisted this flag in foreign countries and when the day came for hoisting it on the Red Fort, he was not to see the dream fulfilled.

But after about 55 years of this day, an opportunity came, a thought came and this flag was virtually hoisted by Subhas Chandra Bosh in the form of the *Delhi Chalo Park*, which, I hope and trust, would keep flying for ever.

### (iii) August 15 Park

The area on the western side of Fort, extending up to Jama Masjid, had its own history of trials and tribulation, especially with regard to the series of tragic events that occurred around 1857. The forces of discontent against the British policy rallied round the aging Mughal Emperor, Bahadur Shah Zafar, and caused a violent upheaval. A lot of innocent blood was split. The native soldiers brutally killed Commissioner Fraser, Magistrate Hutchinson, and Head of Emperor's Bodyguard Douglas. About fifty civilians, including women and children, were also mercilessly put to death.

In September 1857, when the British Army entered Shahjahanabad from Kashmere Gate, the mood was of revenge and reprisal. Bahadur Shah Zafar was deposed and his sons treacherously murdered by an English Army Officer, Lt. Hodson, near Kotla Ferozeshah. The city itself was sacked by the British soldiers. "Our way", records Lord Roberts, "from Lahori Gate by Chandni Chowk led through a veritable city of the dead; not a sound was to be heard but the falling of our own footsteps, not a living creature was to be seen."

The British mood of the time can be judged from the fact that the City Magistrate Philip Edgerton proposed that "Jama Masjid should be used as a Christian Church and on each of its thousand compartments of the marble floor, the name of one of the Christian martyrs be inscribed." Another proposal made was to demolish the entire Jama Masjid and level the ground. It was only the good sense of Sir John Lawrence[17], the then Chief Commissioner of Punjab, which saved Shahjahanabad from such fantastic proposals. The Jama Masjid remained under the occupation of the British and Sikh troops. It was restored to the Muslim community in 1862 on payment of Rs. 2 lakhs and on the assurance that it would not be allowed to be used for any "disloyal activity".

To have a clear view from the Red Fort for the British artillery to bombard the city, in event of any future uprising, all the buildings within the radius of 448 yards of the rampart were razed to the ground and forfeited to the Estate. The vast open area that became

---

[17]Lawrence did much to save Shahjahanabad but even he was affected by the vindictive mood. He wrote of Bahadur Shah: "It is a great pity that the old rascal was not shot directly he was seen – I would not have taken him prisoner."

available, consequent to these demolitions and forfeitures, was extensively used by the British-Indian Army, stationed at the Fort, for drill-training and parades. After August 15-16, 1947 the area assumed national importance. It became a venue for annual function and for providing organised space to the people who came to witness the flag-hoisting ceremony and hear the Prime Minister's speech. Occasionally, a few other public functions of short duration were also allowed to be held.

But soon the epidemic of public-land encroachment, let loose by irresponsible civic leadership, spread to this area, particularly the lands in the vicinity of Jama Masjid. On the staircases of the historic monument alone, about 400 ramshackle commercial structures, including scrap material shops, small lathes and welding-machine-units, had been illegally set up, providing huge rental income to the powerful vested interests who claimed to be the custodians of the mosque. The parade ground fronting the Jama Masjid, too, had been encroached upon by all kinds of vendors, sooth-sayers, oil massagers.

I had all along planned to use the vast area lying between the Red Fort and Jama Masjid for spreading out a velvet of green between the two monuments. Master Plan itself prescribed that this area would be kept open. As Vice-Chairman of the Delhi Development Authority in early 1970s, I had set the ball rolling. A substantial progress was made. With the clearance of slums and squatters from the stair-cases and the resettlement of shopkeepers in newly constructed market named, 'Meena-bazaar', the Mosque wore a neat and imposing look.

Unfortunately, the vested interests, deeply entrenched as they are in India's social and political power structure, soon managed to entangle a straight-forward Master Plan project, into the Emergency-related controversies. With these controversies and their fallouts, I have dealt exhaustively in chapter IV, titled: *Slums: Physical and Mental.* Suffice here to indicate, the completion of a scintillating project was abruptly stalled. The dark side of the moon once again seized the horizon and has since remained so, giving opportunity to the 'marauder' to take advantage of darkness and reappear on the cleared area.

In view of the total sway of the regressive forces in the immediate vicinity of the Mosque, I thought it prudent to keep, at least for the first phase, the parameters of the *August 15 Park* Plan within the confines of western side of the Fort and the main road on the Chandni Chowk side. This area in itself was very large. Freed of encroachers, vendors, unauthorised parking of vehicles, shabby exhibition stalls and ugly hoardings, it could be developed as an impressive and elegant park, reflecting the buoyant spirit of freedom and urging, in silence, the nation to move on to actualise its true tryst with destiny. And this is precisely what I got done in a short time.

Prime Minister Atal Behari Vajpayee noted the spectacular transformation of the huge complex and hailed it in his message delivered to the nation on August 15, 2003 from the ramparts of the Fort. Referring to all round work carried out for the first time in Red Fort's history of 350 years, he said: "I would like you to emulate this example by undertaking such beautiful projects for conservation of heritage in your own village or town."

But all this transformation was in the physical realm, a mere transformation of lands, buildings and squatted upon areas. It was not likely to continue, if it was not accompanied by transformation of fundamental forces that govern the life of the nation. All along, during the last four decades or so of my public service, I had been wondering why any of our Prime Minister had not felt the urge for setting in motion, through his or her Independence Day message[18], those forces which would ignite a new spark in the nation, warm it up to values of discipline, dedication and dynamism and propel it into a higher orbit of creative, constructive soul stirring action.

---

[18] Most of the Independence Day's messages, delivered by successive Prime Ministers, read like Annual Administrative Reports which generally recount achievements of the Government in power and make populism-oriented declarations for the future. Practically, nothing is indicated to give expression to what Jawaharlal Nehru in his August 14-15 speech called 'The long suppressed soul of India'.

### (iv) Ending the 146 year-old presence of the Army in the Fort

When the British Army occupied the Red Fort in September 1857, the atmosphere, as already indicated in the section dealing with August 15 Park, was surcharged with bitterness and hatred against anything that was associated with Mughal princes and their way of life. Even before the brutal killings of English men and women in the course of bloody events of 1857, quite a few senior civil servants of the East India Company had nothing but contempt for what went on within the premises of the Fort. John Lawrence had labelled the Fort as the "sink of the city" where "slavery, polygamy, concubinage prevailed".

In the circumstances then prevailing, the architectural splendour of buildings, such as *Diwan-e-Khas*, *Mumtaz Mahal* and *Rang Mahal* or artistic and graceful lay-out of lawns and gardens, such as *Hayat Baksh*, elicited no respect. The military ruler of Delhi, Major General Archdale Wilson, set up his headquarters at *Diwan-e- Khas*. *Mumtaz Mahal* was first used as a detention centre and then as a Sergeant Mess. The lawns, which created harmony in the grand design of the Fort, were built upon.

While addressing the Asiatic Society of Bengal on February 7, 1900 Viceroy Lord Curzon spoke of "the horrors that had been perpetrated in the interests of the regimental barracks and messes and canteens in the fairy-like pavilions and courts and gardens of Shah Jahan." He declared that he regarded the conservation of ancient monuments as one of the primary obligations of Government.

It was under Lord Curzon's instructions that the portion of the Red Fort, covering Mughal palaces, was handed over by the Army to the Department of Archaeology for proper maintenance and restoration. However, it was only after the promulgation of the Ancient Monument and Archaeological Sites and Remains Act (1904) and the establishment of a separate institution of the Archaeological Survey of India that some worthwhile work for conservation of special buildings and gardens was carried out.

Following India's Independence in 1947, the British Army was replaced by the Indian Army. But there was no material change in the management and control system of the Red Fort, and the responsibilities between the Army and the Archaeological Survey of India remained divided. At that time, about 70 percent of the area (about 40 hectares) of the Fort was in possession of the Army. It put up additional barracks and flats to meet its increasing requirements.

Over the years, the presence of the Army in the Fort became a subject matter of public controversy. While a number of administrative ministries of the Government of India and a sizable section of non-official social and cultural organizations wanted the Army to vacate the premises, to enable the Archaeological Survey of India and local civic authorities to protect and preserve the monument and its environment, the Defence Ministry and the Army headquarters argued that the garrison-needs of the city and its internal security could not be overlooked, especially in the context of fool-proof arrangements to be made for the smooth and safe conduct of Independence-Day functions. In the early '70s Prime Minister Indira Gandhi herself initiated a proposal to transfer the management and control of the entire Red Fort to the Archaeological Survey of India, Department of Culture, but it did not materialize owing to the opposition of the Army.

The issue soon lost its steam. Later on, a few half-hearted attempts were made to resolve the issue. But the matter did not go beyond the blame–game between the Army and the Archaeological Survey of India. The former often berated the latter for not checking encroachments and other illegalities in the civilian area adjoining the walls of The Fort on its eastern, northern and southern sides. The senior officers of the Archaeological Survey of India, on the other hand, deplored what they called non-conforming use of the monument by the Army and its insensitivity in drilling holes in the ancient walls to instal air conditioners, lifts and other modern equipments.

In the above uncongenial backdrop of acrimony, it seemed well nigh impossible to make the Army and Defence Ministry change its long-held stand and agree to end its presence in the Red Fort. At the same time, however, I was acutely conscious of the fact that non-implementation of the fourth component of my Hub-Plan, that is, of securing transfer of control of the entire complex of the Red Fort to my Ministry, would severely undermine the overall project of creating Great Green National Cultural Hub in the heart of the Capital. After giving much thought to the vexed issue, I decided not to give up and adopt a new strategy, taking advantage of the positive public response to the vast improvement that had been brought about in the environment and upkeep of other monuments, such as Ajanta, Ellora and Mahabalipuram under similar Hub-Plan projects.

When I spoke to the Prime Minister about my efforts to take up once again the issue of transfer of the Red Fort, he doubted whether George Fernandes and Army Chief would ever agree. Nevertheless, he permitted me to make my video presentation to the Cabinet at its next meeting. The presentation had its impact. The dramatic improvements brought about at various important historical sites and monuments in the country received appreciation of my colleagues. Thereafter, I pursued my proposals, at personal level, with George Fernandes, held a couple of meetings in his office, apprised him, with the help of short notes, the salient components of my overall plan, and explained how their synchronised execution would bring huge economic and cultural benefits to the country, including the Red Fort's listing by the UNESCO as a World Heritage site.

I was aware of the difficulties which the Defence Ministry would have in asking the Army to end his 146 year old occupation of the Fort. But I was pinning my hope not only on George Fernandes' effective leadership of the Defence Ministry but also on the general regard which of late he had been showing to me and my stand on various contentious issues of public importance. In the meetings of the Union Cabinet, George Fernandes and I often found ourselves seated next to each other. I had been noticing a marked change in his attitude towards me. He was becoming more and more friendly and showed a lot more considerations to my points of view. Perhaps this was his way of making up for the hostility which he displayed against my firm stand in dealing with the ISI sponsored subversion and terrorism when I was sent to Kashmir for my second term as Governor in January 1990. His hostility was based on false assumptions. In more than one way, he was taken in by the diabolical network of disinformation and distortion which the ISI and its collaborators had spread in the Kashmir Valley and also in quite a few superficial segments of the opinion makers in the country. But, years later, particularly after he became Defence Minister, savage hands of terrorism, subversion and disinformation with all their hidden claws, were clearly seen by him. It was at that stage that he seemed to have fully realised how grievously had he wronged me and my efforts to pull out the Kashmir Valley from the jaws of Pakistan's sponsored terrorist organisations. Be that as it may, an impression persists with me that George Fernandes' accommodating attitude to my request for transfer of Red Fort from the Army's control to the control of Archaeological Survey of India had a subtle element of atonement for his wholly unfair criticism of my principled stand, consistent with grim ground-level realities, which frustrated Pakistan's design on Kashmir when most people had almost given up the situation as a lost cause[19].

Eventually, eighteen months of relentless pursuit at personal level and George Fernandes' considerate frame of mind bore fruit. On

---

[19]Reference here is to the Union Home Minister's statement made in Parliament on April 25, 1990. He said: "Jagmohan had to function in a vacuum, in a situation where there was no respect for the law or the authority of the state. He braved terrorists, instilled courage in government officials who had almost given up the situation as a lost cause." *My Frozen Turbulence in Kashmir (Tenth Edition).* Superficial and biased sections of the media and political parties had ignored the fact that I secured back the reins of the state power and authority without any tragedy like the Tiananmen Square massacre in China or Operation Blue Star in Punjab. Nor had any specific order of mine been cited, which could be described as repressive or devoid of human touch. Concocted stories were, of course, galore. All these concoctions and their dissemination have been narrated and analysed in my book, *My Frozen Turbulence of Kashmir,* particularly the two chapters, titled: *Nature and Pattern of Subversion and Terrorism in Kashmir* and *A Deluge of Disinformation and Distortion.*

December 5, 2003, a memorandum was circulated by the General Officer Commanding, Delhi Area, to all the authorities concerned, intimating that "the Red Fort would be handed over by the Army, on behalf of the Ministry of Defence, to the Archaeological Survey of India, on behalf of the Ministry of Tourism and Culture, on December 22, 2003 and that a ceremony, befitting the historic occasion, would be held on that day."

On the appointed day, after the Fourth Sikh Light Infantry, the last army unit, stationed at the Fort, presented a Guard of Honour to the Defence Minister, a stone plaque, bearing inscription of brief history of vacation of the Red Fort by the Indian Army was jointly unveiled by George Fernandes and I . The inscription, inter-alia, recorded: "...The Indian Army units continued to stay inside the Red Fort Garrison till it was vacated in national interest and handed over to the Ministry of Tourism and Culture to facilitate restoration work in December 2003. The Indian Army vacated the monument for reviving its old glory and presenting it is as an epitome of rich Indian architecture and history."

The mementos were also exchanged between the two Ministries, symbolising the transfer of control. On the occasion, in a dignified speech tinged with emotions, George Fernandes recalled 56 years[20] of association of the Indian Army with the Red Fort and the internal security that it had provided to the city and the state. He hoped that the Archaeological Survey of India would carry out its restorative and conservation work expeditiously and attract many more tourists than before. In my response, I warmly thanked the Defence Minister and Chief of Army Staff and said that it had not been an easy decision for them to take and end the Army's long attachment with the Fort. The country, especially its capital, would remain ever grateful to them for having shown the vision and decisiveness to recognise new priorities and look at the Army's own requirements in the larger framework of national development.

---

[20] The Red Fort was in occupation of the Army for a total period of 146 years (September 1857 to August 14-15, 1947), it was occupied by the British-Indian Army, and thereafter (August 14, 1947-December 22, 2003) by the Army of independent India.

### (v) Clearance and Redevelopment of the River Front in the vicinity of Red Fort

The fifth component of the Hub-Project pertained to the heavily squatted upon middle part of River Front, known in the common parlance as Pushta-Embankment, in whose vicinity stood The Red Fort, the City Wall, Salim Garh Fort, with remnants of Indraprastha in its premises and also the national *Samadhis* of the leaders of the post-1947 India. Over the years, on account of the ever increasing disposition of the political elements to build block-votes of squatters and slum-dwellers and extend patronage to all sorts of vested interests in commerce and industry, the Pushta cluster had gathered a huge mass. In size and complexity of composition, it was the second worst slum of Asia, next only to the *Dharvi Slum* of Mumbai. In addition to 62000 illegal units comprising shacks, it had a number of petty but polluting industries, scattered but sizeable cattle-farms.

In the process of implementation of this component of the Hub-Project, I had to face the combined onslaught of powerful vested interests in politics, bureaucracy and business. This onslaught was fiercer than that Dr. A.N. Jha and I had faced at the time of clearance of the Nigambodh Ghat-Kudesia Garden part of the River Front. In fact, my attempt in 2001, as Urban Development Minister, to bring the entire Yamuna Embankment under the master project of Clearance cum Resettlement cum Redevelopment was one of the unstated reasons of the vested interests to put pressure on the Prime Minister to change my portfolio. Though sorely disappointed by the change, the detail in respect of which have already been given in chapter I, I did not give up.

After the change of my portfolio to Tourism and Culture, neither the Ministry of Urban Development nor the Delhi Administration nor the Delhi Development Authority/Delhi Municipal Corporation took any action towards clearance of Pushta, despite firm directions given on March 3, 2003 by the Division Bench of the Delhi High Court, on a separate Public Interest Litigation case, to remove all encroachments from the Yamuna Bed and its embankment within a period of two months. The High Court order, *inter alia*, said:

> .......We, therefore, direct all the authorities concerned, forthwith to remove all the unauthorised structures, and jhuggis, from the embankment, within two months from today.

The Court orders, though specific and time bound, were flouted practically by all the authorities whom they were issued. What to speak of removal of all encroachments within two months, that is, by May 3, 2003, not an inch of squatted upon area, was cleared. This was especially frustrating for me. With other components, such as those relating to the Rebirth of the Red Fort and development of two Great Greens in its rear and front, the *Delhi Chalo Park* and *August 15 Park*, nearing completion, the compliance of the High Court directions with regard to Pushta-embankment would have enabled me to materialise on the ground, almost in toto, the Great Green National Cultural Hub in the heart of Ninth Delhi.

Upset by the intentional delay, I wrote, on December 11, 2003, to the Minister of State (Independent Charge) for Urban Development, drawing his personal attention to the project of clearing of Yamuna Pushta Embankment and its integrative-link with the other components of Great Green Hub-Project. Dwelling upon the significance of the Project, I underscored:

> Rarely would one find a complex in which so many national memorials, tourist spots and strands of ancient, medieval and modern Indian culture are present. I had synthesised all these elements and those of clean civic life and environment to create an inspiring symbol of the rekindled spirit of the post-1947 India. The items pertaining to Tourism and Culture Ministries have been implemented. But further progress to complete Hub Project is held up for want of action on the River Front/Pushta for which even the requisite cost was deposited with the Municipal Corporation of Delhi.

Since there was no response from the Ministry or other agencies to whom I had sent copies of my letter, I called a high-level meeting on January 3, 2004, in which, besides the two Ministers of State, Urban Development and Home, and their senior officers,

Lt. Governor, Delhi; Vice Chairman, Delhi Development Authority; and Commissioner, Municipal Corporation of Delhi, were present. I drew pointed attention of the participants to the fact that about 19,000 plots were available for resettlement of eligible squatters and yet the orders of the Delhi High Court regarding clearance of Yamuna River Front were not being implemented. This could cause serious consequences. After some discussions, it was unanimously decided that work of clearance and resettlement should commence by January 10, 2004.

The decision was specific. Even a date for commencement of the work of clearance and resettlement was fixed. Nevertheless, as on earlier such occasions, the decision was scuttled by devious means. The date of clearance was pushed further on one ground or the other. The role of a top functionary of the Delhi Administration was especially obstructive. In the meanwhile, to deter me from persisting with my efforts, a cleverly crafted campaign of disinformation was unleashed against me, propagating that I was out to remove the poor 'jhuggi'-dwellers to secure electoral advantage in the Lok Sabha Elections to be held after four months, intentionally side-tracking the fact that the implementation of the *Great Green Hub/River Front Project* had commenced years ago and the Division Bench of the Delhi High Court had passed firm orders for clearance of the Pushta-Embankment by May 2003.

The general apathy of the public and its lack of knowledge about vital facts was cynically exploited. Besides '*slum-dadas*', a few publicity hungry NGOs, whose expertise lay only in simulating sympathy for the poor and making wild allegations, without caring to offer any concrete and workable alternative plan, were roped in. Under the garb of protecting human rights, some of these NGOs did not hesitate to abuse the process of law, and approached different courts on one plea or the other, without disclosing what the Division Bench of the Delhi High Court had already ordered on March 3, 2003 and the scathing comments it had made on non-action by the authorities concerned.

The vested interests in politics, bureaucracy and business and my baiters, knew that I had been working for creating clean, elegant and soul-lifting water/river fronts at other important sites in the country as well. A sheer glance at the compendium of my tour-notes, which I recorded as Minister for Culture and Tourism, would show that I was proceeding, on similar lines, with regard to other culturally and environmentally significant Water Fronts. As an example, I have given in Appendix CIII-(i), relevant excerpts from my Tour note of April 14, 2003 in respect of Pandharpur complex.

I was outraged by the intentional falsehood that was being propagated against me, exploiting the politically surcharged atmosphere that prevailed on account of the Lok Sabha elections the date of which was unexpectedly advanced by about six months. The calculation of the vested interests was that I would be deterred by the electoral risks involved in persisting with my course. But they misread my mind; for me it was a matter of principles. Apart from betraying my favourite project of setting up a Great Green National Cultural Hub, I could not persuade my inner instinct to let falsehood prevail over truth.

I wrote a short booklet, titled: *Yamuna River Front: Undoing a Tragedy of Governance and Ushering in a New Dawn.* In this booklet, after giving a brief background of the struggle waged in the past, I published a few telling photographs to show how a substantial part of the 'Pushta-Embankment' had been parcelled out by the traders and industrialists, the 'kabaris', cattle-farm owners and *jhuggi-'dadas'*, how they were deriving huge pecuniary benefits from their illegal activities and how they were strangulating all our constitutional, environmental, cultural and civic values. Here, by way of examples, I reproduce four such sets of photographs, with suitable questions posed in the captions. The answers to the questions would provide a peep into the savage ground reality with which most political elements and some NGO play to attain their ends of power, position and publicity.

When the aforesaid booklet, with photographs, came to the notice of the High Court/Supreme Court, in the context of the overall plan of synthesizing elements of culture, tourism, environment and clean civic life, all obstructive tactics stood exposed and firm and final orders were issued for clearance of the entire Pushta-Embankment. But all this took a long time. And the coalition of disinformers was able to extract its pound of flesh by piercing the weak spots of India's body-politics. I had to pay very heavy price. Contrary to all earlier expectations and after being in Parliament for about fourteen years, I lost my seat by a narrow margin primarily because my opponents and other vested interest had joined hands to strain every nerve to hide the truth and paint me as anti-poor. But the unhappy tale did not end in Delhi. It extended to scores of projects, which were nearing completion at other culturally significant sites and cities all over the country under the umbrella of Great Green National Cultural Hub Project. I was sad–doubly so, because it was a section of the leaders of the National Democratic Alliance that took the decision to advance that date of elections by about six months. Had the elections been held, as scheduled, in October 2004, all my key projects would have been implemented almost *in toto*, and a complete model of my blue-print, translated on the ground would have been seen by the nation.

## Humayun's Tomb Green Cultural Hub

The plan of setting up of a Great Green National Cultural Hub in the Humayun's Tomb Complex assumed, in the process of implementation, a different shape and colour. Its experience confirmed my belief that, in the current governance set up in India and its ethos, the authorities who concern themselves with only the soft crust of a complex and chronic problem, usually succeed in claiming all the credit, especially when accompanied by a clever publicity blitz; while those who attempt to break its hard crust and solve the problem lock stock and barrel, get all the brick bats and run the risk of being fatally injured in the process, both at the personal and political level.

As a Union Minister, my first date with the Humayun Tomb Complex occurred when, as in charge of Urban Development, I undertook a surprise visit of Nizamuddin residential colony on May 3, 2001. I noticed that in the vicinity of the area of my visit, there was a large cluster of slums and squatters which extended into the Archaeological Survey of India's protected and prestigious monuments of the Humayun Tomb and Neela Gumbud. I decided to move into the complex. The following excerpts from the report of *The Hindu* of May 4, 2001, regarding my visit, would provide a broad idea of the conditions prevailing and the impunity with which the provisions of The Ancient Monument and Archaeological Sites and Remains Act were being violated:

> During his unannounced visit, which took tourists visiting the monuments and residents by surprise, the Minister came across several blatant violation of rules and regulations and is reported to have expressed shock over the 'filthy' state of the area. As Jagmohan walked along the back of the monument, the condition was still worse. The Jhuggi jhomparis residents had broken up the fencing around Humayun's Tomb and were using it as open toilet. There were also jhuggis surrounding the once prestigious and now utterly neglected 'Neela Gumbad'.

*The Hindu* and other national dailies also highlighted quite a few other serious violations of law in the complex. A gas agency had set up an illegal godown, and semi-permanent structures had come up on the land between the twin monuments of '*Bare Batashe Wala*' and '*Chote Batashe Wala*'. At the main entry of the Humayun's Tomb itself, shabby stalls had been put up under a notoriously corrupt system of municipal patronage, known as *Tehbazari*[21], and all sorts of heavy vehicles, which had no concern with the monument, were allowed, *albeit* illegally, to occupy open spaces. On the Neela Gumbad side was a huge citadel of India's vote bank politics. Here, thousands of slum dwellers were kept by an influential section of political leadership to serve virtually as 'bonded voters' during the elections to the Municipal Corporation, State Legislature and

---

[21] '*Tehbazari*' means a short duration licence to occupy a small space for selling a few items, usually in the festival season, such as Diwali, Dussehra and Eid. In actual practice, on account of corruption, it is turned into a permanent shop, covering much more space than licensed.

Parliament. The environment of the Dargah of Hazrat Nizamuddin Auliya had also been savagely degraded. The holy tank had become a huge cess pool of stinking slush. To prevent any mishap, the police had locked its entry-gate.

Since all these violations and connected issues pertained primarily to the Department of Archaeology and Ministry of Culture, I suggested to the senior officers of the Department and Ministry to discharge their obligations effectively and bring the matter, in its entirety, to the notice of their Minister. Their response was positive but they hesitantly murmured a number of obstacles that they had to face on the ground due to the interference of political elements and other vested interests. I could understand their predicament. They could hardly go beyond issuing notices or operating in an arena where only easy action was called for. Even when, in 1997, the Aga Khan Trust for Culture and the Archaeological Survey of India entered in the public private partnership, the Trust chose to restrict its items of work which involved soft action only.

In the meanwhile, in the circumstances already discussed in chapter I, my portfolio was changed from Urban Development to Tourism and Culture in September 2001. It now devolved upon me to take effective action to deal with plethora of vested interests, and secure meaningful and lasting results.

By way of historical backdrop, I may underline that the Humayun Tomb reflects the synthesis of some of the finest architectural traditions of India, Persia and Central Asia. As has been rightly observed by SAA Naqvi in text of the Archaeological Survey of India, the Humayun Tomb marks "the end of the sombre style of early Indo-Islamic architecture and laid the foundation of the ornate style that characterised the mature Indo-Islamic architecture and culminated in the Taj Mahal. The rigid main lines of the building are diversified by *chattris* or pavilions, essentially Hindu in origin and without impairing the strength of the design, give it a coherence foreign to its Persian prototypes."

Humayun's Tomb has also within its complex a number of monuments, including the house where the great Sufi saint

Nizamuddin Auliya lived. In fact, one of the reasons for selection of the site for Humayun's burial was its close proximity to the Dargah of the holy preacher. The other notable sites and buildings that fall in this complex are: Arab-ki-Sarai, Bu Halima Tomb, Barber Tomb, Tomb of Isa Khan and grave of Dara Shikoh etc. and also graves of two wives of Humayun, Haji Begum and Hamida Begum (Mother of Akbar). No other mausoleum contains so many distinguished dead of the Mughal dynasty. The Mughal rule virtually ended here, when the last King, Bahadur Shah II and his three sons, who had hidden themselves in this complex, after the failure of 1857 uprising, were arrested by Lieutenant Hodson.

In view of the close links between the Humayun's Tomb complex and the area of Hazrat Nizamuddin Auliya's Dargah, and the commonalty of the problems, of squatting, slums and commercial encroachments, I decided to treat them as a single unit for the purpose of creating a Great Green Cultural Hub in which the elements of history, heritage, environment and clean civic life could be synthesised to cause a wholesome impact from the Neela Gumbad in the north to the southern extremity of the Nizamuddin Basti.

To actualise this Hub plan on the ground in a short time, I set up, under my chairmanship, an implementation team comprising senior officers of the Slums department of the Municipal Corporation and heads of Engineering and Horticulture wings of the Delhi Development Authority and the Central Public Works Departments. Wherever necessary, the representatives of other organisations were requested to join, especially at the time of visit to the sites, which were quite frequent. As a result of these efforts, all the slums and squatters were cleared and resettled in appropriate colonies.

On the cleared sites, green spaces and parks were developed through the agencies of the Delhi Development Authority and Central Public Works Department. The land owning agencies were activated to secure eviction of transport companies, and other commercial establishments, including stalls and petty repair workshops for scooter and cars, from Arab-Ki-Sarai and '*Chote Batashewala*' and '*Bare Batashewala*' areas. Unauthorised and idle parking of buses and other vehicles, along the walls, was also curbed with a firm hand. On the extremities of the Tomb-complex, two new boulevards were laid out, one leading to the historic Gurudwara, Dum-Duma Sahib, and other to Nizam-ud-Din Railway Station along the Barapullah Nallah, thereby making the whole area of monuments noise and air-pollution free.

On the Dargah side, the holy tank was thoroughly cleaned perhaps, for the first time in living memory, by using high-pressure technology. The centuries old slush which filled scores of huge tankers, was sucked out. The important monuments in the neighbourhood, like Chausath Khamba, Bara Khamba and Mirza Ghalib Mazaar were also extensively cleaned up and restored by the Archaeological Survey of India/Delhi Development Authority/Central Public Works Department/Slum Department Teams.

What especially interested me, while executing improvement plans for this complex, was the fulfillment of my long cherished desire to give a memorial park to Dara Shikoh whose grave is located in this complex, almost unknown and unattended. He was the eldest son of Shahjahan and the most learned, the most enlightened and also the most tragic figure of the Mughal History. He was an eclectic soul who wrote two invaluable treaties, *Majma-ul-Bahrain* (Unity of Two Seas) and *Sarr-i-Asran* (Secret of Secrets), underlining the common strands of Hinduism and Islam, and who held promise of being another Akbar. This noble prince, whose ascendency to the Mughal throne, instead of Aurangzeb, could have turned the course of Indian history in the direction of peace, harmony and brotherhood certainly deserved a memorial park to keep alive his memory as well as the story of his tragic end at the hands of his younger brother.

For carrying out the above plans, programmes and projects and a few other works, about 14 crore were spent by the Archaeological Survey of India and the Ministry of Culture and Tourism and other public authorities involved in evictions, clearance and resettlement. Separately, about Rs. Three crore had earlier been assigned by the Aga Khan Trust For Culture, under the Public Private Partnership

Agreement executed in 1997, to restore Chahar-Bagh–the four part park paradise garden surrounding the main Tomb.

The Trust repaired the old water channels, reset the internal pathways, regrassed the internal lawns and installed rain water harvesting system. It was an admirable contribution and warmly acknowledged by me on April 16, 2003 at a function jointly organised by the Aga Khan Trust for Culture and Ministry of Culture to mark the completion of the first phase of restoration work. As an internationally renowned champion of conserving "spaces embodying historic realities", Aga Khan's interest in preserving the architectural legacy of Humayun's Tomb was especially lauded. I also took the opportunity, provided by the function, to acquaint the public of the main features of the Hub Plan and also of the scores of the restoration and improvement works that the Ministry of Culture and Tourism and the Archaeological Survey of India were themselves executing in the entire area covered by the Hub. A broad idea about the nature of these works can be formed from the following report which appeared subsequently in *The Statesman* of August 9, 2003:

> In an unprecedented operation, the Archaeological Survey of India is engaged in cleaning up the $14^{th}$ century baoli (pond) in the Nizamuddin Dargah complex in a comprehensive manner. The ASI is also trying to give a new lease of life to the tomb of Mirza Ghalib, the great $19^{th}$ century Urdu poet, as well as other neighbouring monuments like Urs Mahal and Chaunsath Khamba in the Nizamuddin area of the Capital.
>
> The Union Minister of Culture and Tourism, Mr. Jagmohan, yesterday visited the sites of Hazrat Nizamuddin Dargah complex and the adjoining monuments to assess the ASI's restoration work. He was accompanied by top ASI officials.
>
> The desilting of the baoli in the Dargah complex for the first time ever, is bound to benefit devotees from the country and abroad who use its water to clean themselves. Hundreds of tonnes of silt and effluents have already been removed from the pond. The desilting was done manually in the beginning

> up to a depth of 30 feet following which it was taken up through "eco-friendly super sucker machines".
>
> The desilting has been carried out up to a depth of 50 feet so far. The Rs. 15-lakh project is likely to be completed next week. The stagnated, unhygienic water will be sucked out completely from the pond to be replenished with treated water. Mr. Jagmohan asked the Dargah attendants to check the dumping of waste materials into the pond. Mazare-e-Ghalib has been refurbished and illuminated. Its old flooring has been replaced with new sand stone surface and its boundary wall secured with grill fencing.
>
> The ASI is also undertaking restoration and illumination of Urs Mahal and Chaunsath Khamba. These are part of 24 monuments in the Nizamuddin area whose conservation and restoration work is being handled by the ASI.

Most of the works, involving 24 monuments and costing about Rs. 14 crore, had either been completed, or were very near completion, when the National Democratic Alliance Government went out of office in May 2004. By that time, a dramatic improvement in the overall environment of Humayun's Tomb Complex had been brought about. The hard crust of the chronic problems, created by non-action against the vested interests, had been broken up and a smooth road for further restoration and greening of historical memory laid down.

Acknowledging and appreciating all this, Dr. M.S. Usmani, Vice-Chairman, National Commission for Minorities, wrote to me, on August 13, 2003, as follows:

> It gives me immense pleasure to inform you that the devotees, tourists and people belonging to Muslim Community have been praising the initiatives taken by you after assuming charge as Union Minister of Tourism & Culture, Government of India, towards renovation, beautification, development of surroundings and upkeep of the following important places of special concern to Muslims of our country and those visiting

> from outside:- Baoli of Dargah Hazrat Nizamuddin Auliya; Mirza Ghalib Ka Mazaar; Barakhamba; 64 Khamba; Urs Mahal and Humayun Tomb. The efforts and initiative taken by you, for the first time since Independence, are really praise worthy.

I have mentioned all this and reproduced the contemporaneous press reports and letters not to eulogize the most difficult works done by the Archaeological Survey of India and the Ministry but to keep the records straight and not to allow partial truths to prevail. Because, later on, months after I left office, it was noticed that in all the publicity material, circulated by the Aga Khan Trust for Culture and the exhibitions it organised at different venues, there was, regrettably, not a single word about the most politically explosive tasks performed by my Ministry in teeth of bitter opposition of a number of entrenched vested interests. Nor was there any indication of the massive administrative work done to overcome years of inertia which had seized almost all the organs of the state and non-state bodies.

The Aga Khan Trust for Culture, as indicated earlier, has successfully performed the tasks of restoring water channels and regrassing of the internal lawns etc. But all these tasks were comparatively easy. They, by and large, involved engagements of some conservation architects, award of a few contracts and arrangement of adequate funds. Far more difficult, on the other hand, were the task of clearance of slums and clusters of residential and commercial squatters; of development of resettlement colonies and allotment of alternative plots therein; of facing troublesome litigation and defending trumped up charges of being anti-poor; and of warding off the combined onslaught of vested interest in politics, business and bureaucracy.

All these onerous, challenging and risky tasks, as particularised above in this section, were successfully performed by my Ministry and Archaeological Survey of India. A sea of trouble was virtually swum through. And yet nothing is now being said about any of the items of pioneering work that was done by the Ministry at that time in respect of clearance, laying down of lawns, building of roads, improvement of environment, restoration of 24 small but significant monuments, and giving practical shape to the idea of developing a Great Green Cultural Hub comprising both the Humayun Tomb and Nizamuddin Dargah Complex. What is equally unfortunate, in certain arenas, reverse gear has been clutched. Since no one is now concerned with tackling the hard crust of the problem and everybody is resting on its laurels in the lap of soft arenas, the land and building mafia and other vested interests in local politics have reappeared on the scene with vengeance. Hundreds of new illegal constructions and encroachments have come up, and are continuing with impunity in the Nizam-u-Din Basti Complex. On the Humayun Tomb side, in the green area between Delhi Public School and the restored wall, a huge new cluster of slums and squatters has grown unchecked. Earlier, you could see the open area from the Oberoi Hotel Fly-over. Now you would see an ever expanding group of shacks, shops and stores.

### Lal Kot- Quila Rai Pathora Green Cultural Hub

The hitherto little known, and even much less noticed area, Lal Kot–Quila Rai Pathora, provides the simplest and the most telling example of achieving multiple objectives, under the Great Green National Cultural Hub Project, by synthesising elements of history, heritage, public health, environment and clean civic life. There is also an instructive background to it.

Colonel James Todd, in his classic work, *Annals and Antiquities of Rajasthan*, has insightfully observed: "Rajasthan exhibits the sole example in the history of mankind of a people withstanding every outrage barbarity can inflict or human nature sustain.....yet rising buoyantly from the pressure and making calamity a whetstone to courage." Unfortunately, all these qualities of unmatched perseverance and valour were of little avail to the Rajput-clans in face of their internal broils and chronic discords and divisions. They suffered one bloody discomfiture after another. But they refused to recognise and get rid of their fatal flaw: disunity.

This tragic leaf from the book of Indian history lay buried in the ruins of Lal Kot- Quila Rai Pathora, the first of the seven historic medieval cities of Delhi. By the end of the eleventh century, the Tomar Rajputs had extended their hegemony north-westward and established their regional headquarter at Suraj Kund. Their chief, Anang Pal, built a citadel, named Lal Kot, about ten kilometres west of Suraj Kund. In the early twelfth century, Vigrar Chauhan defeated the Tomar King and brought his territory, including Lal Kot, under Chauhan's control. When Prithvi Raj Chauhan, also known as Rai Pathora, became the King, he built a massive fort as an extension of Lal Kot. In the strict sense, it is the Lal Kot- Quila Rai Pathora, and not Lal Kot as a separate entity, which is the first historic city of Delhi. Both the Tomars and Chauhans built several temples within the Lal Kot. A four-armed stone image of Lord Vishnu dated about 1147 was found recently and is now exhibited in the National Museum.

Prithvi Raj Chauhan was a powerful and chivalrous king, having vast territories of Ajmer and Delhi under his control. He defeated Shibab-ud-din Mohammad Gori in the first battle of Turin in 1192 and saved India from invaders. But due to bitter feud between him and Jai Chand, king of Gohadwala Rajputs of Kanauj, Mohammad Gori came out victorious, when he undertook invasion for the second time and established foreign rule in a large part of North India. The discord between the local kings, which was taken full advantage of by a foreign invader, has since become proverbial. It has often been cited as one of the basic reasons for a series of discomfitures which the country had to suffer at the hands of its adversaries. Dr. Ambedkar, in his memorable speech made at the time of adoption of the Indian Constitution, reflected:

> ....What would happen to India's independence? Will she maintain her independence or will she lose it again? This is the first thought that comes to my mind. It is not that India was never an independent country. The point is that she once lost the independence she had. Will she lose it a second time? It is this thought which makes me most anxious for the future. What

> perturbs me greatly is the fact that not only India has once before lost her independence, but she lost it by the *infidelity and treachery* of some of her own people. In the invasion of Sind by Mahommed bin Kasim, the military commanders of King Dahar accepted bribes from the agents of Mahommed bin Kasim and refused to fight on the side of their king. It was Jai Chand who invited Mahommed Gori to invade India and fight against Prithvi Raj and promised him the help of himself and the Solanki kings.....Will history repeat itself? It is this thought that fills me with anxiety.....

If India does not want the tragic chapters of her history to get repeated, in one form or the other, she must seize every opportunity to etch on the mind of the present and future generations the need to learn effective and lasting lessons from the betrayals and blunders arising out of her internal disputes and dissensions. What better opportunity in this regard, I thought, could be found than the mound underneath which lay the buried remnants of the first historic city of Delhi associated with Prithvi Raj Chauhan.

It speaks volumes of the current public culture of indifference and Delhi's citizens' general lack of interest in learning the right kind of lessons from the tragic chapters of their civic history that hardly any one was aware that the sprawling mound, near the newly developed residential colonies of Saket and Press Enclave, was none other than the site where once the first city of Delhi stood. Over the years, a sizable part of the mound had been squatted upon. Most of the squatters were using the unoccupied portion as an open defecation ground, causing unhygienic conditions not only in their own clusters but also in the new residential colonies in the neighbourhood.

I set my eyes on this mound as soon as I took over as Union Urban Development Minister. I drew up an integrated plan which could simultaneously serve a number of public causes and help in creating another Great Green National Cultural Hub in the Capital. Besides eliminating health hazards to the thousands of inhabitants in the vicinity, I was eager to bring out before the public the historic significance of the site and the warning signals it could send in perpetuity to the present and future generations of India not to repeat the fatal error of placing personal, party, clan and caste animosities above the interests of national unity and freedom.

I took the Senior officers of the Delhi Development Authority and Archaeological Survey of India on the board, set up joint teams, visited the site with them on a number of occasions, assigned specific tasks to the officers and issued instructions for speedy and systematic execution of the overall work.

The activisation of the DDA machinery resulted in clearance of the site, allotment of alternative plots to the genuine squatters in the resettlement colonies, development of a green buffer upto Sri Aurobindo Marg and construction of an elegant information cum conservation centre with a special section on the March of Indian Civilisation.

The Archaeological Survey of India started excavations in the portion of the 'cleared area' which already stood 'protected'. This area was very small. When my portfolio was changed to Tourism and Culture, which included the Department of Archaeology, I saw to it that the entire mound, underneath which lay buried the citadel of Lal Kot- Quila Rai Pathora, including the walls and ramparts, was brought under the legal protection of the Ancient Monuments and Archaeological Sites and Remains Act and also arranged for its extensive excavations. The results were spectacular.

By the time the project was completed in 2003, one could see the excavated ramparts and walls, in all their 'ruined magnificence' whose charm was enhanced manifold at night when the monument was lighted. The newly built Information cum Documentation cum Conservation Centre, with a splendid statue of Prithvi Raj Chauhan standing upon it, and development of green park, on all its sides, had become a glorious example not only of meaningful restoration but also of weaving history, heritage and greenery in India's urban fabric and producing freshness and buoyancy in the highly congested and fast expanding cities. About 5000 persons from the neighbouring residential colonies started using the Hub daily for morning and evening walks. Many other visitors availed of the facilities provided by the Information cum Cultural and Conservation centre.

The Union Home Minister, L.K. Advani, who was requested to inaugurate the project, lauded the initiative of linking such conservation plans with *Quami Ekta Week* (National Unity Week). In my speech, at the function, I dwelt upon the need to learn from our past omissions and emphasised: "Herein, history speaks through bricks and battered stones; heritage stares in our eyes through heavy but broken and sunken walls; herein can also be heard voices and warnings for the future. If we do not become concerned, cohesive and committed individuals and inject civic consciousness in the society, then things could go wrong again."

## Small Scale Green National Cultural Hubs

In the process of creating Great Green National Cultural Hubs, such as around Red Fort, Humayun's Tomb, Quila Rai Pathora, most of the items pertaining to the overall Project of Clearance cum Resettlement cum Redevelopment got implemented as adjuncts. But this Project, as delineated in the Chapter, titled: *Slums- Physical and Mental,* had other objectives in view. These were: enforcing urban discipline; inculcating respect in the citizenry for the Master Plan; safeguarding the interests of the common citizens in arena of public health; ensuring regular resettlement in *bonafide* cases of squatters and slum dwellers in appropriate colonies with basic civic facilities; and undertaking simultaneous redevelopment of the cleared site in accordance with the prescribed land-use. And if the land-use was green, as was the position in most cases, the cleared site could be redeveloped as a park or a garden in memory of a national hero whose services could act as a perennial source of inspiration, particularly to the younger generation, and help in ushering an era of social and cultural awakening which, in turn, could give birth to a well-ordered city run by a set of conscientious and committed civil servants and political leaders. Let me elucidate.

A huge mound of garbage and junk, with scores of shanties, tin-sheds, 'kabari' stores etc., with crows and stray dogs hovering all

# PHOTOGRAPHS

The thinking that had gone into the conceptualization of the Ninth-Delhi Greens, the struggle that had to be waged in translating the new concepts into concrete reality and in attaining multiple objectives by way of synthesizing positive elements, have been narrated and commented upon in the text of different sections of Chapter III. The reader, I hope, would note that, while every Hub/Sub Hub Plan and every specific Project/Sub-Project, had its own historical back-drop and called for a different set of initiatives, the ultimate goal sought was to disseminate cultural fragrance in the society, after filtering it through the lessons of history, and building a powerful urge to propel the Indian polity to a higher and healthier orbit of thought and action and for creating a new civilization which would synthesize the best in the Indian heritage and the best that was available to it from modern advances in science and technology.

The photographs cover four main categories of the Green-Hubs. One relates to the Red Fort Complex, the second to the Humanyun Tomb, the third to Lal Kot-Quila Rai-Pathora and the fourth to the combination of small scale Hubs. They show how Greens of Ninth Delhi have been spread over a larger canvas and how multiple objectives of local and national significance have been realized through them.

*Red Fort Reborn*: After a massive cleanup drive in and around the complex and subjecting it to an all-pronged restorative surgery, a 'reborn red fort' emerged on the scene, and soon found its way to the list of world Heritage Site, which had earlier been denied to it on account of extensive encroachments.

(Reference: Section captioned Rebirth of a Fort; pages 106-113).

*Red Fort Reborn* (contd.): Clearing the clogged passage in the rear of the Fort and opening it towards the River Front and green vistas.

(Reference: Pages 106-113)

*Delhi Chalo Park*: A memorial to Subas Chandra Bose's call to the Indian National Army to reach Delhi and hoist the Azad Hind flag on the Red Fort. By way of the provisions of Hub-Plan, the Park has come to occupy a place almost opposite to *Shanti Van* and *Raj Ghat,* the national memorials of Nehru and Gandhi who, in terms of political beliefs, were on the other side of Bose.

(Reference : Section with the same caption; pages 113-117).

*August 15 Park*: As an important component of the Hub-Plan, the large area lying between the western side of The Red Fort and the main road on the Chandni Chowk side, was developed as an elegant park, reflecting the buoyant spirit of freedom. Prime Minister Atal Behari Vajpayee noted the spectacular transformation of the huge complex and hailed it in his message delivered to the nation on August 15, 2003 from the rampart of the Fort.

(Reference: Section with the same caption; pages 117-120).

*Ending the 146 year old presence of the Army in the Fort:* Defence Minister George Fernandes handing over to the author the symbolic plaque at the time of transfer ceremony held at the Fort premises on December 22, 2003.

(Reference: Section with the same caption; pages 121-125).

*Lal Kot-Quila Rai-Pathora*: With its excavated ramparts and walls, in all their 'ruined magnificence', Quila Rai-Pathora has now become an outstanding example not only of meaningful restoration but also of weaving history, heritage and greenery in India's urban fabric.

(Reference: Section with the same caption; pages 138-142).

*Ajay Ahuja Memorial Park*: A case of 'the small scale green cultural hub,' by way of which multiple liabilities of slums in the vicinity of Pragati Vihar Complex were converted into multiple assets. It also served as an excellent specimen for creating soul-lifting and instructive pieces of historical memory, after clearance of large slums-clusters, in 39 other colonies of public servants.

(Reference: Section with the same caption: Small Scale Green National Cultural Hub; pages 142-151).

*Deen Dayal Upadhyay Park:* An example of small scale cultural hub which was set up to reflect the philosophy of integral humanism on one of the 39 cleared sites after resettling the squatters from the Government Servant Colonies. The philosophy underlines the need to integrate, in a harmonious pattern, the elements of body, mind intellect and soul.

*Vivekanand Park:* Another case of small-scale cultural hub developed on the cleared site, to serve multiple objectives of attaining both external and internal cleanliness.

The photographs, published in this part, with the questions posed in the notes below, would show how a variety of vested interests resort to disinformation campaign, under the garb of human rights protection, to prevent clearance and secure their political, pecuniary and publicity ends.

(Reference: Section Captioned: Clearance of the River Front facing the eastern side of the Red Fort).

Are these electroplating industries discharging daily all sorts of pollutants in the river and injecting heavy puffs of poison in the lungs of the poor workers, not being run for providing monetary gains to a section of politically influential city-traders in stainless-steel-utensils? Whose human rights are being protected and by whom? (page 129).

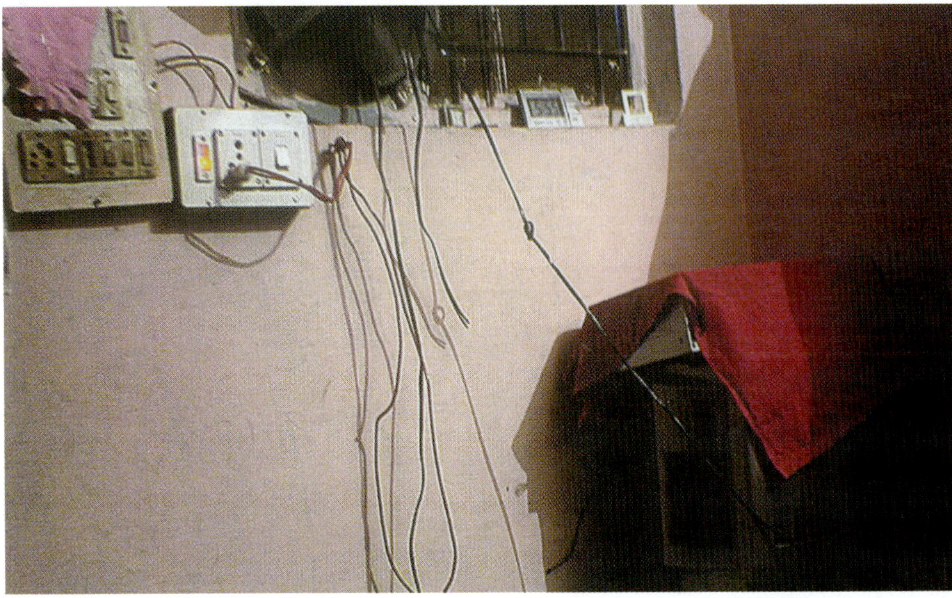

Are the houses of this category built by the 'poor'? (page 129).

How is it that the drama of encroachments and illegal constructions has no end? Is proliferation the way of attaining goals set out under the National River Water Conservation Mission? (page 129).

Who are these Kabaris and other commercial elements doing business, running into several lakhs, and securing huge pecuniary benefits by illegally occupying public lands and that, too, on the embankment of holy Yamuna? (page 129).

*Cleaning up Humanyun Tomb and Nizamuddin Dargah Complex:* At a function jointly organized by the Ministry of Culture and Tourism and the Aga Khan Trust for Culture, on April 16, 2003, the author apprised the public of the initiative that the Ministry itself had taken to break the hard crust of the 'politically explosive' problem of non-action against vested interests of different categories. The 'Baoli' of the Dargah was got cleaned through the DDA with modern mechanical equipment, after 350 years, and other parts of the Complex were rid of unauthorized structures and encroachments.

(Reference: Section with the caption: Humanyun's Tomb's Green Cultural Complex; pages 130-138)

*Samaj Sadan at Narela*

*Composite School at Narela*

*Real Service to the poor squatter:* One of the resettlement colonies where squatters from 39 clusters, and Yamuna Pushta were accommodated was Narela. As in the case of 41 – resettlement colonies set up in the earlier phase of development, emphasis was on provisions of small shelter units, with secure tenure, healthy environment and facilities for good schools, parks and play-grounds.

*A view of Trilokpuri Re-settlement Colony:* With organized layouts, paved roads, drainage, parks, schools, dispensaries and other community and environmental facilities, 41 such resettlement colonies, housing a population of about 7 lakh, were set up. The future of poor *jhuggi-walas* was assured with permanent allotment and the whole process of migration of the poor from the rural to urban was made a planned one and skill and productivity-oriented.

(Reference: Pages 201-204)

Another item of community and public health facility for Resettlement Colonies.

*Indraprastha Park.* Created after years of efforts of filling and consolidating the vast dumping pit, this park served as an excellent example of converting multiple liabilities into multiple assets. Incidentally, it also came with the line of vision of Humayun Tomb and Gurdwara Dum Duma Sahib, the two monuments, whose preservation had been separately strengthened by providing two bypass-roads, one to Nizam-u-din Railway Station along the Barapulla Nallah and other to the Gurdwara etc. In the northern extremity of the Indraprastha Park, an elegant stupa and surrounded by green areas came up.

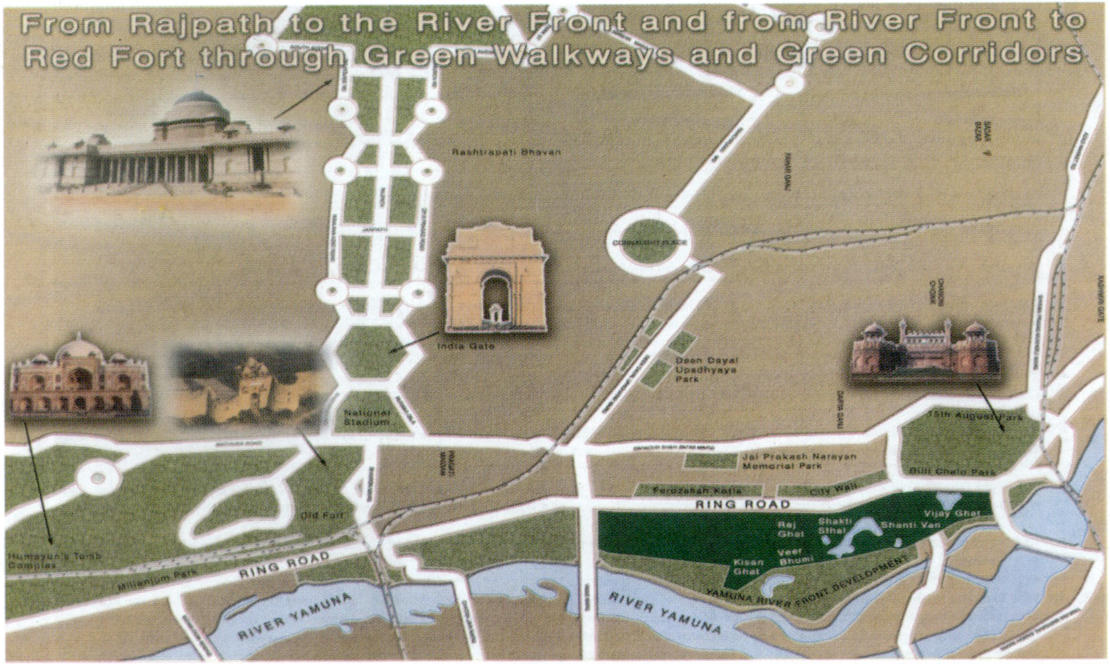


*Great Green Vista to prop up Regeneration of City's Mindscape:* In connection with what was known as the India Gate Canopy (Chhatri) / Gandhi Statue Controversy, the context and the contents of which have been given in Appendix Special, I placed before the Lok Sabha, in July 1997, a plan which not only resolved the controversy but also provided a vision to inject inner energy in Delhi-city and, through it, to the Indian Republic and the Indian Civilization. The above rough sketch of the concept plan, titled: From Rajpath to the River Front and from River Front to Red Fort through the Green Walkway and Green Corridors.

Reference: Appendix Special (pages 316-318)

around, had come into being near Pragati Vihar, on the public land lying between the Nehru Stadium and the newly built office complex of National Building and Construction Corporation. The residents of the dozens of government servants' colonies in the neighbourhood were bitterly aggrieved by the nuisance of flies, mosquitoes and general insanitary conditions. But, thanks to the prevailing work culture of casualness, no agency or authority did anything to relieve them of their distress. Even the squatters and slum dwellers on the mound, whose needs were *bonafide* and who would have moved out, if alternative site had been offered to them in a migrant or resettlement colony, continued to suffer. A little bit of concern to enforce urban discipline and a little bit of creative and constructive approach could have ended the miserable conditions, and converted a deplorable civic liability into a valuable asset for the city. A small scale green cultural hub, reflecting the splendour of the best in the Indian spirit, could be set up, thereby making a contribution, howsoever tiny it may look on the surface, to the refertilization and regeneration of the nobility-oriented value in the philosophic heritage of India.

And this is exactly what I proceeded to do, in respect of the above mentioned Pragati Vihar slum-cluster and 39 other similar clusters, on the green spaces in or around the Government Servant Residential Colonies, which had come to my notice during my public hearings and frequent visits to the sites.[22]

Amplifying my proposition by referring to the specific case of Pragati Vihar, I may indicate that on the day of my visit to the slum mound, I had read in the morning newspaper, before leaving my residence, the tragic story of Sqn. Leader Ajay Ahuja's supreme sacrifice in a daring air-operation to locate specific areas of Pakistan's treacherous intrusion in Kargil. I was sad and sullen. I wondered whether the loss of a young and valorous officer was not attributable

[22] The details in respect of public hearings and site-visits, which I undertook after becoming Urban Development Minister, and the first-hand assessment done as a result thereof, have been given in Chapter II. These may be glanced through, while studying the position and proposition enunciated here.

to the soft, superficial, and, in certain cases, selfish attitude of successive Union Government leadership in dealing with Pakistan and its separatist collaborators in Jammu and Kashmir. The leadership had shown itself incapable of learning from history. Appeasement of both external and internal foes, I thought, must be abandoned. An awakened and insightful sense of history accompanied by a determined attempt to strengthen the fibre of national leadership, was what the country urgently needed; otherwise, the Kargil type of tragedies would continue to occur.

With such agonising thoughts weighing upon my mind, I reached the spot. Surveying the scene, it occurred to me that the best that I could do, in the totality of circumstances confronting me, was to suggest redevelopment of the site, after its clearance, as an elegant park with the twin objective of keeping Ajay Ahuja's memory evergreen and of signaling to the nation to "resolve that the dead shall not have died in vain." The members of various deputations, who had gathered to present their points of view, had no hesitation in accepting the suggestion, especially because, in *bonafide* cases of poor squatters, I had offered alternative allotments of plots in resettlement colonies. Soon thereafter, the formal orders were issued and various components of the project got executed expeditiously.

Within a year of laying down his life for the country, a lush green public park, named Ajay Ahuja Memorial Park, emerged at the site where once a stinking slum had existed. It has an elegant fencing, a long walkway, a children corner, sweet smelling flower beds and shrubs and fast growing trees. It is a fine specimen of the small-scale green cultural hub, the multiple objectives of which have been outlined in paragraph I of this section.

At the 'dedication function', held on June 10, 2000, Ajay Ahuja's young widow and 5-year old son were honoured. In my speech, I recalled the events leading to the supreme sacrifice[23] of Ajay Ahuja–

---

[23] This is what General (Rtd.) V.P. Malik, Indian Chief of Army Staff at the time of Kargil Operation, has recorded about Ajay Ahuja's virtual murder by Pakistanis in his book, *Kargil: From Surprise to Victory* (p.131).: "One MiG-27 was lost over the Batalik sector on May 27, 1999 at about 1100 hours due to an engine flameout. The pilot,

how concerned was he about the fate of his colleague, what risks he undertook in pursuance of that concern, and how Pakistani Armed Forces dishonoured themselves by killing him, instead of taking him prisoner.

I also explained how Ajay Ahuja Memorial Park would provide a valuable cultural infrastructure to the several Government Servant Colonies in the vicinity, how an instructive piece of contemporary Indian history would get imprinted on the national memory, how a large segment of public would read the contours of Pakistan's recurring machinations and help in ensuring by drawing appropriate lessons, that in future the country's destiny was shaped by selfless and sound leadership and not by the one that remained prisoner of its softness or superficiality or short term political or personal gains.

Since the dedication function was attended by a very large number of Government servants from colonies in the neighbourhood of the Memorial Park, I especially spelt out in my speech, many other planning, civic and environmental positives that had been attained. The land-use provisions of the Master Plan had been enforced, and the grievances of thousands of residents, in respect of insanitary conditions caused by the slums and encroachments, were redressed. In cases of poverty-compelled squatting, simultaneous resettlement was carried out at pre-planned sites. In short, a multi-pronged plan to achieve multiple objectives of ensuring clean civic life, of integrating the squatters in the emerging urban pattern in an orderly way, and of preserving instructive and inspiring pieces of historical memory through a Small Scale Green National Cultural Hub, was successfully implemented.

I have considered it necessary to indicate at length the principles and pattern on which Pragati-Vihar-Ajay Ahuja Memorial Park was conceived and created, as it typifies the approach that I followed with regard to 39 other large slums and squatters' clusters existing

Flight Lieutenant Nachiketa Rao, was able to bail out. He landed inside Pakistan territory and was captured by the Pakistanis. His colleague, Squadron Leader Ajay Ahuja, flying a MiG-21, tried to ascertain Nachiketa's location and the wreckage of the MiG-27. In the process, his aircraft was shot down by a surface-to-air missile. He also bailed out and was captured. But his captors, instead of making him a prisoner of war, killed him."

in the residential colonies. The only difference was the name of national hero, statesman or reformer or philosopher or a notable public figure whose memory was sought to be kept evergreen.

The sites vacated by the squatters and slum-dwellers, consequent to their resettlement, were rapidly redeveloped and turned into elegant and elevating Memorial Parks. These included -Vivekananda Memorial Park, Andrews Ganj; Aurobindo Memorial Park, Sadiq Nagar; Tyagaraja Memorial Park, Prem Nagar; Sankara Memorial Park, Lodhi Colony; Maharishi Valmiki Memorial Park, Mandir Marg; Indraprastha Park, Ring Road; Karmayogi Park, Udyan Marg; Dara Shiko's Park, Humayun's Tomb complex, etc.

Each of the Memorial Park of this genre now serves as a Small-Scale Green National Cultural Hub, and assumes, in the unison with such other hubs, an elevating role and keep the citizens, at least some of them, in touch with the best that was thought and preached by the great philosopher and reformer of India. For example, a morning walker-resident of Sadiq Nagar, even with a moderately receptive mind, is most likely to pick up self confidence, when he and his family members confront practically every day a plaque in the Vivekanand Park, with the message: "Lift up your head. For each one of you carries God within. Be worthy of Him...There are no weak; you are weak because you wish to be. First have faith in yourselves." Likewise, the Karmayogi Park transmits the message of a noble philosophy of work in this simple and meaningful engraving on the ornamental wall-tablet: "What is required is not only physical and mental efficiency but also spiritual and character efficiency. And this requirement would be fulfilled only if the ideal of 'karma yogi' is taken as a guiding star. Pursuit of this ideal alone uplifts a knowledgeable and intelligent person to a wise and perceptive one and a casual and negative mind to a creative and positive one."

In a number of other areas, huge clusters in the neighbourhood, were cleared on similar patterns, and large parks, reflecting soul-lifting values of ancient Indian philosophy, were developed. Astha Kunj, covering about 81 hectares, in the vicinity of Nehru Place, Bahai Temple and Iskon Temple, is a fine example of this category of Parks. Indraprastha Park (34 hectares), is another.

There were many other massive Greens which were created, in the form of city-forests, woodlands, district and community parks, play-grounds and sports complexes, on the lands acquired for the planned development of Delhi. In every sense, these Greens were treasures of environmental wealth and included such flag posts of ecological balance as city-forests/ woodlands/ parks of Hauz Khas (250 hectares); Tuglakabad (300 hectares); Jahapanah (50 hectares); Rohini Swarna Jayanti Park (101 hectares); Ashoka Garden, Ashok Vihar (32 hectares) etc. By and large, the yard-stick followed was to provide a city forest/ woodland of 100 hectares for every one million population; a district park of 25 hectares for every 5 lakh habitants; a five hectares Community Park for every one lakh people and a neighbourhood park of 1 hectare for every 10,000 residential group. All in all, in addition to the Greens provided in the urban extensions of Rohini, Dwarka and Narela and the Aravali[24] mountainous ridge of 7,777 hectares gifted by nature, 29 city-forests/Regional woodlands, 111 District Parks and 225 neighbourhood Parks and scores of Sports-complex and stadia have so far come up in Ninth Delhi. But that was not all. Spirited action, if it had to continue, required an inspirational will at the national level. And I took necessary initiative in this regard, when an opportunity came my way.

---

[24]Aravali mountainous ridge, which divides Ninth Delhi practically in two equal parts, is the most significant feature of its geography and invaluable gift to its environment. Soon after the independence and influx of displaced persons, a few patches of the continuous line got urbanized. It did not receive the attention of the authorities that it deserved. When I was appointed Lieutenant-Governor of Delhi in February, 1980 and took residence at Raj Nivas, which is located on the foot of the Northern Ridge, I made it a practice to combine my morning walks with my efforts to improve Ridge's maintenance and protect it from vandals and eliminate traffic and noise pollution. This interest, together with the concern shown by the other authorities and Non-Government Organisations, eventually led to legal protection of the entire ridge of 7,777 hectares, under the Central Forest Act and Delhi Development Act. Presently, it exists in three large and distinct stretches- Northern Ridge which moves along the Delhi University and Bara Hindu Rao; Central Ridge, which extends from Jhandewalan and western Paharganj to Talkatora to Dhaula Kuan; and Southern Ridge which extends broadly from the West of newly developed colonies, such as Vasant Vihar, Vasant Kunj and Mehrauli-Badarpur complex.

As I have underlined in para 4 of this chapter, no act of reform, regeneration and dissemination of cultural fragrance, taken at the city level, can bear full fruit and yield lasting results, if it is not accompanied by an overall urge for such a reform, regeneration and dissemination of cultural fragrance in the society in general and system of governance in particular. To help in creation of this urge and its continued augmentation, I formulated, soon after I took charge of the Ministry of Culture and Tourism, an all India project, named- *New Initiative Programme*. Under this Programme, some of the finest, but now fading signposts[25] , created during the long march of Indian Civilization, were taken up for restoration and also for provision of facilities and infra-structure which would not only preserve them in a more scientific way but also make them easily accessible to more and more tourists, both domestic and foreign.

Overall, my effort was to remove the dust and dross of time as well as imprints of the soft state from the great cultural assets of India, present them in their true glory, use them for promoting healthy tourism, securing integrated and inclusive development and also for projecting a civilisational image of the country that was clean, orderly, vigorous and alive to the new realities of the modern and fast globalizing world. I undertook extensive tours of the most culturally significant cities and sites, in company of the officers concerned, recorded my impressions and decisions and got them implemented in a short time. I took particular care of the 'protected monuments' by clearing encroachments, laying green buffers around them, and creating great hubs of culture. The motivation was to

---

[25]In addition to the Great Green National Cultural Hubs discussed in the main text of this chapter and its related appendices, the network of such Hubs, covered many other nerve-centres of India's cultural and architectural heritage. These included: Dholavira, Somnath and Modhera in Gujarat; Chittaurgarh, Ajmer-Sharief and Pushkar in Rajasthan; Bhimbetka, Khajuraho, Gwalior and Shivpuri in Madhya Pradesh; Ajanta, Ellora, Pandharpur and Sindhu Durg in Maharashtra; Hampi and Chitradurga in Karnataka; Mahabalipuram, Kanyakumari and Kanchipuram in Tamil Nadu; Nagarjuna Konda in Andhra Pradesh; Manali, Keylong and Kaza in Himachal Pradesh; Varanasi and Agra in Uttar Pradesh; Amritsar in Punjab; Bodhgaya, Nalanda and Vaishali in Bihar; Udaigiri, Konark and Puri in Orissa.

ensure that 'the silent voices of history and heritage', emanating from them, were heard in perpetuity and in serene environment.

How all this was done would be outside the scope of the book on Delhi. But to bring home to the reader how sparks of new inspiration were ignited in the system as a whole through the New Initiative Programme, I have given in Appendix CIII (ii), a brief account of what was done, with regard to a few representative cases of each category, to set-up Great Green National Cultural Hubs at the national level, such as Ajanta, Ellora, Mahabalipuram, Kumbalgarh. In yet another category of cases (Part II of the Appendix), such as Taj Mahal and Agra Fort, irreparable damage to the country's heritage was averted by taking a principled stand against the politics of populism and profiteering.

It was, in fact, the creation of vast network of Great Green National Cultural Hubs, at the all-India level, that caught the attention of the enlightened sections of the media and Parliament, won me their warm applause[26] and enabled me to accomplish a good part of my mission in Delhi, despite no holds barred opposition of a number of vested interests. Here, it may not be out of place to share with the readers what was said by non-ruling party Members of Parliament on my contribution in this regard:

> On July 25, 2003 Fali S. Nariman, eminent jurist and Member of Rajya Sabha, said, "Jagmohan is not only a Minister, but also a cultural gem and pride to our heritage and our Government. He is the sort of spirit we need today…"
>
> Janardhana Poojary, Congress Member of Rajya Sabha from Karnataka, observed on July 30, 2002: "We must appreciate the approach of the Minister. His knowledge is superb. The

[26]There were other recognitions as well. On January 15, 2003, the South Asia Travel and Exchange Association declared me as Man of the Year and said: "With single minded determination and almost single handedly, he has reshaped the way we look upon our tourism." Likewise, the citation of the INTACH STATE Award for Heritage Tourism Conferred on March 27, 2003, said: "The contribution of Shri Jagmohan towards making us aware of this rich heritage and his efforts to preserve the same, for the present and future generations, is sure to become part of our folklore."

House should be grateful to him. It will do a great good to the Nation if the response of all the Ministers was like that of Jagmohan."

Addressing, on July 25, 2003, Congress Member of Rajya Sabha and noted Poet, Shri Bal Kavi Bairagi, said: "The country will remember you (Jagmohan) at least for two things. Firstly, you have done a great work in Vaishno Devi and, all over India, people take your name along with Mata's name. Secondly, you are the only Minister whose name is associated with the fact that while Shahjahan made Taj Mahal, you have saved Taj Mahal. The maker of Taj Mahal is no longer in the world, but its protector is before us and we can say with confidence that we have seen you and your work with our own eyes."

Speaking about the radical improvements brought about in the realm of cultural heritage of Rajasthan, Congress Member of Lok Sabha, Shri Vijayendra Pal Singh from Rajasthan, said: "I would like to put it on record that during the last 55 years of independent India, nobody has taken so much care as Jagmohan has done to Rajasthan monuments. We must pay a tribute to him. We, in Rajasthan are very happy about Chittorgarh, Ranthambhore, and Maharana Pratap's Foundations, and the wonderful work he has done in a short time."

Simranjit Singh Mann, Akali Dal Member of Lok Sabha from Sangrur, Punjab, said on March 3, 2003: "I want to congratulate the Minister for Culture (Jagmohan) for being our best Culture Minister since 1947."

On July 23, 2003, Mulayam Singh Yadav, Leader of Samajvadi Party in Lok Sabha, congratulated me for the historic act of saving Taj Mahal and for doing reformative and upgradation work on epic scale in and around Vaishno Devi Shrine.

Earlier, speaking about clearance-cum-resettlement-cum-development work pertaining to slums, Chandra Shekhar, former Prime Minister, said in Lok Sabha on July 25, 2000: "The Minister (Jagmohan) is doing laudable job and he would be acclaimed by our future generations."

On a morally parched national soil and amidst ever increasing contamination of social and political climate, the creation of Green National Cultural Hubs and their linkages with the long march of Indian Civilization would, undoubtedly, be reckoned as an act of triumph for the capital of the nascent Republic. But would not this act he soon overshadowed by the accelerated negativity that is being witnessed daily in many other arenas of public life? I have my fears.

CHAPTER IV

# SLUMS – PHYSICAL AND MENTAL

*To cleanse the dirt of the city is quite different from cleansing the dirt of politics. From the former, you get a good night's rest, while the latter keep you worried and you lose sleep.*

— Sardar Vallabhbhai Patel[1]

*I believe in no argument, economic or other, which is based upon creation of slums. I have a horror of slums. I do not mind a person living in open like a vagabond or a gypsy. But I do mind slums in cities. I have often said if you cannot provide building, for those living in slums, give them open space to live in and provide them social services like water and sanitation. The rest would follow.*

— Jawaharlal Nehru[2]

*To me, who has been a long distance walker in the slums and whose tired and aching limbs and smoke and dust filled eyes, have refused to surrender before the forces unleashed by the mental slums in the society and the state-power structure, the agonizing reality is far more menacing and messy than perceived so far by the national leadership.*

— Author[3]

In 1919, when the Secretary of State for India, Edwin Montague, who was known for his liberal views, wrote to Lord Lyde, the then Governor of Bombay, to take measures to improve the housing and

---

[1]These remarks were made by Sardar Patel, in reply to the civic address presented to him by the Bombay Municipal Corporation in 1948. He was referring to the inner happiness which he experienced while serving the common citizens of Ahmedabad. Selfless service to the needy is virtually an act of godliness; its cathartic impact purifies the human soul.

[2] This view was expressed by Jawaharlal Nehru at a public function, held at Bangalore on October 6, 1955.

[3] Author's reflections, as penned, in one form or the other, on the *Slums of India* in national dailies, journals, memorial lectures.

sanitation in the city, the latter examined the problem and threw up his hands in despair. He wrote back to Edwin Montague, bewailing that sanitation and housing are 'really a nightmare'.

With the rise of national movement and emergence of public spirited leaders in the civic arena, nightmarish conditions began to be attended to by the leaders of eminence. In this regard, it is instructive to recall what Sardar Patel did for the city of Ahmedabad, first as a Chairman of the Sanitary Committee (1917-22) and then as President of the Municipal Board (1924-28). He showed how an inner impulse to serve the city and its people could make up for many other constraints.

Sardar Patel's work as a functionary of the Ahmedabad Municipal Board commenced in 1917, when bubonic plague struck the city in an epidemic form. There was so much of scare that the schools and courts were closed, and people started fleeing to villages. But Sardar faced the calamity with his characteristic courage and composure. He said: "I know what it is to be attacked by bubonic plague. I was a victim when I lived in Godhra in 1900. In any case, I prefer to die serving the people than live in safety."

Patel's approach was direct and dynamic. He often combined his morning walks with the inspection tours of the city. In the company of G.V. Mavalankar and civic officers, he moved into the narrow streets, ascertained the problems from the people and took prompt remedial measures. Several limitations notwithstanding, he constructed a model which solved many of the acute problems of sanitation, health, water supply, waste disposal and traffic. Sometimes, Sardar Patel himself appeared on the streets, leading the sanitary team. He drew immense satisfaction in having become an effective instrument of service to the people in matters which affect them most in day-to-day life. Years later, in 1948, speaking at a civic reception, organized in his honour by the Bombay Municipal Corporation, he said: "I had unalloyed happiness in the tasks which I performed. After all, to all of us, to serve our own city must give unmitigated pleasure and satisfaction which I cannot get in any other sphere."

Sardar Patel never hesitated to call a spade a spade. He frequently chided the people for their lack of civic consciousness. To facilitate expansion of the city, he, despite bitter opposition of the vested interests, got the old wall punctured. He refused to be browbeaten by the charge of being anti-Muslim.

Jawaharlal Nehru worked as President of the Allahabad Municipal Board, and Dr. Rajendra Prasad of Patna. Both of them left, finding themselves helpless against the tactics of the bureaucracy. Dr. Rajendra Prasad, in his autobiography, has recorded: "Finding ourselves in helpless position, we tendered our resignation after a year's experience."

Sardar Patel, however, was made of a different stuff. He used to say: "Goody, goody, is not my style." He virtually bulldozed the negativity of the bureaucrats, and did not hesitate to measure his strength against the "mighty ICS commissioners, such as John Shilidy, G.F. Partt and Alfred Master. His steadfastness won him applause even from his adversaries. Alfred Master, for example, said: "I remember Patel as a most efficient chairman of the sanitary committee, who stood aloof from the domestic and political intrigues in which some of his fellow councilors indulged."

Sardar Patel's intimate association with Ahmedabad Municipal Board had other dimensions, too. It was here that his administrative skill and organizing capacity found deeper expression. It was here that his tenacity of purpose was sharpened. It was here that he became an "iron man with a melting heart". It was here, again, that he came in intimate contact with the grim reality of India and learnt the practical lessons of dealing with it. For a perceptive mind, there is no greater teacher than the experience of traversing the lanes and bylanes of a metropolis, moving into its slums and shacks and coming in touch with its other facets.

The shining example, set by Sardar Patel in Ahmedabad, was not seen in any other city of India. Even his efforts, though heroic, could not produce a lasting impact on the problems of shelter, sanitation and slums in his own city. But he showed what the Indian cities and their leadership needed most: a sense of discipline, dedication and dynamism; a strong disposition to be in touch with ground-level conditions; an inflexible will to stand against the vested interests and exploiters of religion; and an urge to develop a frame of mind which seeks inner peace and pride, through selfless service to the needy. Patel's great contribution lay, in fact, in pointing out the right way to mentally reorient the civic leadership and the citizens to attain the best results, within the resources and legal set-up available at a given time.

The new animation for solid work was the outcome of Patel's powerful personality and great organizational ability. The moment he disappeared from the Ahmedabad stage, the negative forces in the society asserted themselves and undermined his impact on the overall scene, both at the local and national levels. He himself was deeply disappointed. In his last Independence Day message, four months before his death (December 15, 1950), Patel had lamented: "Our public life seems to be degenerating into a fen of stagnant waters; our conscience is troubled with doubts and despair about the possibilities of improvement. We do not seem to be profiting either from history or experience. We appear helplessly to be watching the sickle of time taking away the rich corn, leaving behind the bare and withered stalks."

India, at the fateful turning point of her history, needed a Great Helmsman. Sardar Patel seemed to fulfil that need. But India also needed a Great Inspiration to churn the stagnant pools of the Indian society. In absence of the inspiration, the constructive urges and service-oriented trends, set in motion by Patel, could not be sustained. And the bureaucratic and political culture of casualness re-established its sway on the civic stage.

Prime Minister Jawaharlal Nehru's approach to the problems of slums, shelter and sanitation was of different kind. It was more poetic than practical. In 1954, during his visit to the walled city of Delhi, he was so anguished by the spectacle of the dilapidated, dangerous, congested and insanitary buildings of Turkman Gate slums that he involuntarily shouted at the local leaders and officers accompanying him: "Burn them". But such paroxysm of moral restlessness could not alter the miserable conditions which Marshall Clinnard, a noted American scholar and sociologist, after visiting the same locality, in late 1950's, had described as follows:

> Houses are one and two storey, so close together that no sun comes through; everything is damp and this makes the odours of filth and urine all the more noticeable. There is an awful stench everywhere. The area was covered with hordes of flies. Children use the gutter. Saw a man eating his lunch in front of his house a yard away from flies and offal in the gutter. I almost threw up, and the educated Indians with me put their handkerchief over their faces. The children have only one small place to play, and it is in bad condition.... As we drove away I kept the widows up so that the hordes of flies would not get inside. I couldn't eat my lunch that day.... Had a feeling as though I had seen enough and wanted to forget the misery.[4]

In all earnestness, Nehru wanted to see slum-free cities within a short span of time. He pinned his faith in central socialist planning and set up a powerful Planning Commission.

It was mainly on account of Jawaharlal Nehru's views on slums that the following provision was made in India's First Five-Year Plan (1951-56):

> These slums are a disgrace to the country and it is a matter of regret that governments, both Central and State, have so far paid little attention to this acute problem. No city can be considered healthy which tolerates within itself the existence of a highly congested area. Slums are a national problem. From the national point of view, it is better to pay for the cost of clearing slums than to continue to pay the mounting cost of slums and suffer destructive effects upon human lives and property indefinitely.

But, after about six decades of government declaration of its intent and completion of eleven Five-Year Plans, what is the ground-level

[4]Marshall B. Clinnard, *Slums and Community Development*, p.74.

reality? In Bengaluru, where Jawaharlal Nehru gave poetic expression to his perception of slum-problem in India and where a thriving software and computer service industry has since brought an unimaginable prosperity to a section of the inhabitants, there are now over 1000 slums in which about two million people live in hideous environment.

In almost all the cities, particularly the metropolitan ones, the slums have proliferated and living conditions have deteriorated. Mumbai is now derisively labeled as global capital of slum dwelling. The feelings of Marshall Clinnard, quoted earlier, are, in essence, echoed by all sensitive visitors to Mumbai slums, such as UNICEF Chief, Cecilio Adrona, who recently observed: "Racing away from me as I drove out of my hotel, the slums of Mumbai moved me beyond words. They left a lasting impression on my mind. I took it to my heart".

According to the most recent data, released by the Census Commissioner in March 2014, about 64 million urban Indians live in 'unsanitary slums that are unfit for human habitation'. In the capital of the Republic, at least 35 per cent of its citizens live in slum-settlements the hallmarks of which are 'dirt, decay, disease, danger and despair'.

The U.N. Millennium Development Goals Report[5], 2014, also speaks poorly of India's performance in improving the lives of slum dwellers. All this is tragic in itself. But what is far more tragic is the ever increasing domination of the politics of slums which prop up regressive forces in the society, add to their crudities and inhumanities and threaten to convert a very large part of our cities into 'slums, semi-slums and super slums.

---

[5] While releasing the U.N. Millennium Development Goals Report, on July 16, 2014, Lisa Grande, resident coordinator, Delhi, bemoaned: "The Development Goals cannot be met globally if they are not reached in India". Largely, slum-living is an integral part of poverty. In India, poverty reduction has been sluggish, while it has come down from 49.4 per cent in 1994 to 42 per cent in 2005 and 32.7 per cent in 2010; in the case of China, it has come down from 60 per cent in 1994 to 16 per cent in 2005 and 12 per cent in 2010.

History has recorded the birth and growth of many awful slums. The earliest slums, the Jewish ghettos, were labelled as 'nauseous and deadly'; the Irish and Chinese slums earned the notoriety of being 'most fearful'; and the English slums of the 19$^{th}$ century were called 'frowzy dens' by Charles Dickens. In quite a number of city-slums of today's India, the living conditions approximate to those obtaining in the 'fearful', 'frowsy', and 'deadly' slums of the ages gone by. No site is too slushy, too filthy and too dangerous for the precarious huddle of huts to be put up and for human beings to dwell in them.

Lest the reader should think that I am exaggerating or resorting to poetic licence, let me draw his attention to the report of March 28, 2014 of the national daily, *The Hindu*, about the Indira Camp Slums of South Delhi, which has 1600 'jhuggis' and 6000 inhabitants. The report says:

> In order to reach the stinking slum, one has to wade through a bumpy, uneven passage with massive heaps of garbage on both sides. "It's not only garbage," a young boy said, "it is a marshland filled with human and animal excreta, coming from two overflowing government toilets close to the water pipe. These are the only toilets for the inhabitants here".
>
> The slush pools also have parents in these slums worried for more reasons. We have lost count of small children who have died by slipping into this filth," said Dilshad Mohammad, a resident, adding, "when it rains, we pick our kids on our shoulder to take them to their schools and bring them back the same way."
>
> A resident, Sushila, lost her aunt Shanti Devi when rain water flooded her Jhuggi in 2008. "She was trying to pull her trunk to save medical documents of her hospitalized husband. She fell into water that had reached her waistline. We found her body only when we saw her clothes floating a few days later," Sushila recalled.

Why do such inhuman conditions exist? Why have the spectacles of 'disease' and 'horror' that slums in 1950's had evoked in the top leadership of the country not only remained but also engulfed a larger number of people?

To provide an answer, in all its depth and dimensions, to this key question, let me take the reader on my long and eventful journey through the slums of Delhi. In the process, I hope, to show how the 'resolute practicality of Sardar Patel, or the poetic and humanitarian passion of Jawaharlal Nehru, or the principles and provisions of the Delhi Master Plan, or the enhanced allocations under the National Five Year Plans, alone were not sufficient; and how a few triumphs of transforming slums of darkness and despair into settlements of light and hope could be more than off-set by the mental slums of the Indian polity.

The first slum-related event of note was the special census, conducted in June-July 1960, of the Jhuggi-families who were occupying public land in Urban Delhi. The data revealed that there were 34,000 such families. They were declared eligible for alternative accommodation. Simultaneously, it was declared by the government that those who occupied the public land after that date were to be treated as 'ineligible' and evicted summarily. All these decisions were taken in accordance with a scheme approved by the Union Cabinet, and christened as 'Jhuggi-Jhompris Removal Scheme'.

The salient feature of the scheme, as originally sanctioned, was to allot 80 sq. yds. of plot to each eligible squatter family on a 99-year lease. The plot was to be provided with a latrine, a water tap, and a plinth on which the lessee could build a hut or a house according to his need. The implementation of the scheme which was to be financed by the Central Government, was entrusted to the Delhi Municipal Corporation.

As soon as the above provisions were translated on the ground, it was noticed that almost all the allottees, transferred physical possession of their plots, on monetary considerations, to comparatively well-to-do persons and squatted upon some other piece of public land. On account of the wide-spread corruption and other malpractices, which were seen as a consequence of permanent allotment of larger sizes of plots, the scheme was revised, with the approval of the Union Cabinet.

The revised scheme eliminated the element of ownership and provided for allotment of open developed plots or small tenements on rent, with common facilities for water and sanitation. Further, since the 'eligible' and 'ineligible' Jhuggi-families were existing virtually side by side and the area could not be freed without removing both the categories, it was provided that allotment of camping site of 25 sq. yards each would also be made to the 'ineligible Jhuggi-units' but only in far-off colonies and on payment of full rent, instead of the subsidized rent payable by the eligible families. The thinking of the decision-makers was that this would discourage fresh squatting on public land. But the modified provisions met with the same fate as the original ones. The misuses, pertaining to transfer of plot and tenements and illegal occupation of public land at some other site, continued with impunity. Clearly, the malady was misdiagnosed.

The core shortcoming was not in the provisions of the scheme but in the absence of discipline, honesty and other healthy values in the society. It was this shortcoming that the top leadership showed no inclination to spot, much less to remove. The allottee, the transferee, and a sizable segment of municipal bureaucracy, and elected elements in the Municipal Corporation did not feel even the slightest prick of conscience in doing one wrong thing after another. Instead of attending to the dross in the mental slums of the society, the Government of India undertook another revision of the Scheme.

A high-level Study Group, under the Chairmanship of the Minister of Works and Housing, Jagan Nath Rao, was appointed. The other members of the Group were the Lieutenant-Governor, Delhi, and senior leaders of the political parties represented in the Metropolitan Council.

As was the general practice with most representatives of the political parties, they castigated the municipal bureaucracy for being negligent and corrupt, glossing over the murky role of their own party-men in the field. Nevertheless, during the deliberations, the Study Group adopted two main recommendations unanimously.

First, the problem of squatting and slums should be treated as 'non-political', and no member of any political party should interfere at the ground-level in the process of 'implementation'. Secondly, in view of the ever swelling tide of slums and squatters in the capital, unauthorized occupation of public land should be made a cognizable offence, punishable with imprisonment upto three years.

Both the above unanimous recommendations of the Study Group were accepted by the Government. While issuing the formal orders, the Government of India let it be known that it was unhappy over the manner in which the Municipal Corporation had handled the scheme. Despite substantial allocation of the central funds, the problems of slums, squatting and sanitation, and the accompanying malpractices, had mounted. Even the public lands, got cleared earlier by providing alterative accommodation, had been reoccupied, either by the new squatter or by one of the family-members of the old squatters. The execution of the scheme was, therefore, transferred from the Delhi Municipal Corporation to the Delhi Development Authority. By the time of transfer, the number of Jhuggi-family units, occupying public lands, had increased to about one lakh.

It was in this background and emerging scenario that I was assigned, as Commissioner, Delhi Development Authority, the task of securing effective implementation of the Government of India's Scheme, named somewhat inappropriately, I suppose, as Slums and Squatters' Removal Scheme.

As briefly indicated in Chapter I, titled: *City and its Leadership and Civilisational Contours,* a path-breaking venture was undertaken at the Nigambodh Ghat-Yamuna Bazaar, in the area between the river and the Kudesia Garden. The initial inspiration for the venture came from Lieutenant-Governor, Dr. A.N. Jha, an eminent scholar of ancient Indian Philosophy and Sanskrit literature. At the field level, I provided a new thrust by linking the elements of clearance, resettlement and redevelopment and treating them as a part of one and the same chain of action.

Nigambodh Ghat is associated with the core Vedic belief in the imperishability of the human soul and in the inseparability of the process of creation and destruction, of every beginning having an end and every end having its own beginning. It is at this spot that Yamuna, sister of Yama, 'king of death', who had caused loss of memory to Brahma, the Lord of creation, threw back, during the course of a heavy flood, the Vedas, containing all the knowledge and wisdom about the human existence in the universe. Thus, the pious and merciful sister, Yamuna, became an instrument in making available again to humankind true knowledge about its station in life. In view of the sacred character of the site, Prince Yudhisthira, performed, according to Puranic mythology, the 'Asvamadha Yagya' here, around 1500 B.C., when Indraprastha, the present site of Purana Quila, was the capital of the Pandava kingdom.

Despite its association with the centuries-old traditions and its unquestioned cultural significance and also its prescribed green land-use in the Master Plan, the hallowed site of Nigambodh Ghat and the area around had remained in an utter state of neglect. It had become a huge slum, with about 6,000 squatters' families, scores of cattle dairies and about 700 petty non-conforming industries, godowns and fodder cutting machines. The land was slushy, uneven, and floodable with hardly any drainage, latrines and clean water supply. It was incapable of being serviced, even at a very heavy cost.

The agonized embarrassment which President Rajendra Prasad had to undergo at the time of his elder sister's cremation at Nigambodh Ghat has already been narrated in Chapter I.[6] Nothing could have damaged the cultural image of the nation more than this nauseating slum. Yet the vested interests, political as well as pecuniary, prevented its clearance and resettlement of about 20,000 of its inhabitants in healthier environment, with organized layouts and basic municipal services. All this was done in the name of human considerations. Politics could not have traded in human misery in worse form.

---

[6]The reader may find it rewarding to refresh his / her memory by glancing at the first sixteen paras, particularly paras 10 to 15, of Chapter I, titled: *City and Its Leadership and Civilisational Contours.*

By way of backdrop, I may indicate that, soon after the transfer of the scheme to the Delhi Development Authority from the Municipal Corporation, I undertook extensive visits to various slums and squatters' clusters and selected sites, where the inhabitants of these clusters could be re-settled within regular lay-outs and with secure titles on the plots allotted. The selected sites were subjected to rudimentary development and provided with basic, civic amenities, with scope for improvement and augmentation in the future. In popular parlance, they came to be known as resettlement colonies.

In line with the same organized approach, I got prepared regular redevelopment plans, and also got them sanctioned from the competent authority before undertaking clearance of the squatted upon slum-clusters. The objective was to ensure that the work of redevelopment was commenced immediately after the clearance. I was confident that this simple innovation of dovetailing processes of clearance, resettlement and redevelopment would not only facilitate execution of the Master Plan projects with extraordinary speed but also eliminate the risk of re-squatting and other malpractices built therein.

With the above pattern of new thinking in mind, I drew up an integrated plan of action with regard to the Nigambodh Ghat Slums and Squatters' Clusters and explained it to Dr. Jha. I was surprised to note that, though he was anxious to secure help for me from other departments of the Delhi Administration, he was not interested in knowing the details of my ground-level plan or programme. He reposed full confidence in me. After discussions with him, I was left with no doubt that if I succeeded I would be applauded and given full credit, and if I failed, I would be sympathized with and protected. Such was the attitude of our great civil servants like Dr. A.N. Jha, Bhagwan Sahay, Dharma Vira, and Vishwanathan.

I spoke to the squatters direct. I explained to them the long-term advantages of moving to Seelampur and Seemapuri, where resettlement colonies had been planned and developed with basic civic facilities. Some responded favourably, some were sceptical, and a few others, particularly those who were generally called *dadas,* were hostile. I avoided the political element to the extent I could.

On 17th June, 1967 the clearance and connected works commenced. Disregarding the solemn pledge taken by all the political parties, during the deliberations of the Study Group, that the issue of removal of squatters and slums from public land would be kept above party politics, the Congress Party, which was then in opposition in the Delhi Metropolitan Council, organized a protest march to the site. It was led by the senior leaders of the Delhi unit, including Santokh Singh, Member Parliament, and Shiv Charan Gupta and other members of the Metropolitan Council. They demanded stoppage of all work. I politely refused, and reminded them of the unanimous resolution adopted by all the political parties in the Study Group and Government of India's policy declarations on the subject.

But they brushed aside every argument of mine. Since they and their supporters in the procession persisted with their loud slogans, they were arrested, taken away and released after a few hours. Thereafter, every item of the pre-planned action was carried out within the pre-planned time-frame. About 300 trucks were made available to the squatters for moving to the new site with their luggage. The entire chain of clearance cum resettlement was completed in a short period of three days.

On the cleared site, bull-dozers were immediately pressed into service to remove the debris and level the land to undertake redevelopment works in accordance with the overall project of Nigambodh Ghat-Yamuna Bazaar area. Thus, the processes of clearance, resettlement and redevelopment were effectively synchronized, leaving no scope either for re-squatting or for continuance of the political agitation, A team of landscape architects, planners, engineers and horticulturists who were well-versed in the ancient Indian mythology associated with water, greenery and life's cycle, was selected and motivated to complete the project in a record time.

In the political arena, however, serious trouble was brewing for Dr. A.N. Jha and I. We were caught in the cross-fire of the two main political parties who remained prisoners of their narrow outlook. The Delhi units of these parties started blaming each other 'for being up-rooter of the poor' though neither had any hand in formulating or executing the specific project of Nigambodh Ghat-Yamuna Bazaar.

A statement issued on June 20, 1967 by the Delhi Pradesh Congress insinuated: "Yamuna Bazaar was a Congress stronghold and the Administration's action was aimed at embarrassing the Congress Party and its supporters"[7]. Not to be left behind, on the same day, the Jan Sangh Party retorted: "The local Congress leaders are shedding crocodile tears. The Lieutenant Governor had acted under the orders of the Central Government which was being ruled by the Congress Party". Two days later, on June 22, the blame-game was played in the Lok Sabha, when Congress M.P. Bibhuti Mishra criticized Jan Sangh administration. Kanwal Lal Gupta and Hardayal Devgun, Jan Sangh Members of Parliament, accused the Congressmen of picking up a row, not because shacks were cleared from Yamuna Bazaar, but because the unauthorized godowns of the erstwhile Congress Mayor were demolished by the Delhi Development Authority. The makers of such statements knew that these were either false or based upon hearsay. And yet they were made with reckless abandon, from the platforms of what were supposed to be prestigious institutions or high public offices.

What was worse, no attempt, howsoever, boorish or indecent, was spared to browbeat or demoralize the senior functionaries of the implementational agencies. On July 27, 1967, the Delhi unit of the Congress Party took out another big and highly offensive procession. At the terminal point of this procession, Dr. A.N. Jha's effigy, 'complete with goggles and a pipe', was beaten with 'shoes' and 'lathis' and then burnt. I was aghast at the low level of criticism to which Dr. Jha was being subjected, and cursed myself for having assured him that the project could be successfully executed.

---

[7] Little did the Congress Party realize that by describing the slums and squatters' settlement, in the vicinity of Nigambodh Ghat, as their stronghold, they were admitting that they had a vested interest in its continuance, and it were they or their supporters who were benefiting, directly or indirectly, from illegal occupation of public land and setting up there on as many 700 non-conforming industries and godown.

Clearly, I had underestimated the thickness of the mental slums of the Indian polity. But Dr. Jha's equanimity and sense of humour never deserted him. When, after a few days of the ugly procession, Mir Mustaq Ahmed, senior leader of the Congress, rang up to ask for appointment, Dr. Jha replied: "Mir Sahib, you have to come to hell because your friends have already sent me there."

Dr. Jha's generous and cheerful disposition notwithstanding, he was saddened by the politics of deceit and hypocrisy, as would be clear from the letter which he wrote to the Home Minister, Y. B. Chavan: "To me the attitude of ambivalence on the part of the political parties has been to say the least most disappointing.... I must, in the end, confess to a feeling of having been personally let down by everyone and shown up as one who has been acting arbitrarily and tyrannically – the only person lacking in sympathy while everyone else has been falling over each other to be human and helpful and generous."

With such a demoralizing and disgusting environment around and with Dr. A.N. Jha entering a poor phase of health, the implementation machinery found the going tough. But, somehow or the other, it managed to get the project completed.

In its simplicity and in the background of its association with the cultural heritage of India, the Nigambodh Ghat, after redevelopment, appeared to have emerged from the ancient soil as truly as folk music springs up from the soul of a nation.

An inexpensive and rugged mural, created at the entrance of the gate-wall of the redeveloped Nigambodh Ghat, depicts the central belief of our philosophic thought: the immortality of the soul. It reminds us that death is nothing but a signpost of rebirth; that the whole cycle of construction, destruction and reconstruction would go on; and that we have been existing eternally, and would continue to do so.

My special endeavour, therefore, was to create a clean and elevating atmosphere which would whisper to the departing soul: "Be upward and divine. There is no power that could undo your existence. You are an inextricable part of the all-pervasive Divinity who is invisible, undying and formless and whom no sword could pierce, no fire could burn and no water could drown. You have not come out of zero, and you would not go back to zero."

That my endeavour was not pointless dawned upon me, when, shortly after the completion of the project, a case of an alleged illegal removal by the Delhi Development Authority of a noxious industry in the area, set up by an influential politician, came up for hearing before the Delhi High Court. The Advocate of the complainant started a harangue against me. The presiding Judge of the Court interrupted him gently, and remarked, *albeit* off the record, "He has done an amazing service in transforming the area. Now, I would not be very unhappy when death comes; at least, my soul would pass through a clean, open and elevating park, and not a smoke-laden and filthy slum."

As the implementation of the project, both in its planning and cultural contents, got completed and its fall-outs settled down, I was haunted by a strange sense of fear and frustration. This happened not because A.N. Jha and I were unfairly treated, but because the huge mounds of nation's 'mental' slums, with all the contaminated stuff filled in between their layers, were visible to me, far more clearly than ever before. Everything around looked daunting, oppressive. The slum-dwellers had themselves been dehumanized. Instead of asking even for a small but semi-developed space, within a serviced and organized lay-out, to build a sunny future for themselves and their families, they could be trapped by the agents of the vote-banks politics and other vested interests into believing, that their employment was feasible only in or near their savage and frightful slums. But what could I do?

The exploiter and the exploited had been possessed, in their own way, by the mental slums of the contemporary Indian society. Unless the removal of mental slums was given priority, or at least these were simultaneously tackled, clearance or containment of physical slum would continue to present all kinds of challenges to the authorities operating at the ground level. As an officer, I could hardly do anything in this regard, except write articles in the national dailies and magazines or expound my views in the seminars and symposia. Whether my attempt to educate the public on the fundamental need to tackle the mental slums had even the slightest element of success or not, I cannot say. But it certainly helped me in overcoming my sense of dejection and despondency and getting into a frame of mind which, later on, found expression in one of my poems in these words:

> *And yet*
> *With all millstones*
> *Around my neck*
> *I stand erect*
> *Willing to fight*
> *Willing to dream* *

A large number of slums and squatters' clusters were, thereafter, taken up, and subjected to the same pattern of clearance, resettlement and redevelopment as was followed in the case of Nigambodh Ghat-Yamuna Bazaar. These included massive clusters of 'Kela-godams' Pahar Ganj; 'Quarry-Pits', Prasad Nagar; Jhuggis, petty workshop, stores, cattle dairies in and around the complexes of 'Nizam-u-din Basti', 'Jat-ki-Pahari - Motia Khan' *Idgah;* Kotla Feroze Shah; Darya Gunj Ghata Masjid; Tilak Bridge; Patel-Nagar Hillock; and New Delhi Hanuman Temple area.

In every case, the reaction pattern of the local political elements and other vested interests was practically the same – the same hypocrisy, the same disposition to resort to distortion and, sometimes to unabashed concoctions, the same unscrupulous attempt to brow-beat the head of the implementing agency and to hide their own political, and often pecuniary, interests behind their posture of being saviours of the poor squatters and slum dwellers. But, after the bitter experience of Nigambodh Ghat-Yamuna Bazaar case and long brooding over the existence of mental slums in the Indian society, I had accepted the harsh reality and decided not to get perturbed by the campaign of calculated disinformation and to keep my composure

---

* *Rebuilding Shahjahanabad*: Epilogue; 'This Battered Child of Shahjahan'.

as well as firmness. This, in the ultimate analysis, enabled me to see all my projects through.

The obstructions were, however, galore. More often than not, long delays were caused in the execution of individual projects by the local political elements by approaching their senior leaders in the central government. The senior leader, to ingratiate himself or herself with his or her local party elements, generally resorted to the temporary expediency of getting the work stopped. Little did any one of them realize that by doing so, not only huge time and cost overruns of various redevelopment projects were being caused but also the collective uncertainty of the squatter and slum dweller was being prolonged. Clearly, the phenomenon, was nothing but an exercise in posturing; and it merely resulted in enlarging the hold of soft, selfish and superficial elements in the society and state.

The above phenomenon, especially its range, could be better understood if I give here, as specimens, case histories, in brief, of three significant types of clearance cum resettlement cum redevelopment projects.

The first type would elaborate how the local politically influential leaders, aided and abetted by the 'slum-dadas',* were able to mislead a section of senior leadership, both in the Union Cabinet and Union Parliament and at the same time goad slum dwellers to stay put, even when better alternatives were available. The second type of cases would illustrate how most of the custodians and functionaries of Darghas, mosques and grave-yards played the card of religion and manufactured a sense of minority victimhood to protect illegal gains by misusing the premises under their charge and also by unauthorizedly occupying public lands in the immediate vicinity. The third type of cases would show how a many splendoured cultural and historical legacy was being mutilated for want of courage and commitment on the part of the authorities concerned.

---

* The term is commonly used for 'musclemen', 'bosses', 'god-fathers' etc. who often resort to criminal intimidation to secure obedience to their fiat. They occupy large area unauthorizedly, parcel it and collect large sums as illegal rent from the slum and shack-dweller. Their aggressive disposition and hold over their 'allottees' make them influential with the political parties.

For the first type, I would take up the case of Prasad Nagar area. Here, in early 1960s, a huge slums and shacks' cluster had come about on government land from which stones were once quarried for construction of buildings in New Delhi. The abandoned pits were interspersed over a large area. For most part of the year, these pits remained filled with stagnant rain-water and garbage thrown from the 'Jhuggi-Jhompris' and petty shops, set up on their edges. The area was wholly unsuitable for human habitation. It caused a number of air and water borne diseases, not only to its inhabitants but also to those living in the neighbouring rehabilitation colonies of Patel Nagar and Rajinder Nagar. A substantial part of the area was also needed for execution of important development projects, envisaged in the Master Plan. These projects included laying down of new network of roads and circulation spaces and construction of a District Commercial Centre to serve as a counter magnet to the Connaught Place. The area also afforded an excellent opportunity for converting huge disease-ridden liabilities of pits into environmentally valuable assets in the form of a clean-water lake, encircled by green shrubs, trees and walkways.

Though a large number of 'Jhuggi'/shack-dwellers had shown willingness to get themselves resettled at the newly developed colony of Madipur in West Delhi, a few influential leaders, having a strong vested interest in politics of Prasad Nagar and also under pressure from the 'slum dadas', were able to stall the project, for over a year, by painting a false picture before senior political executive and legislative functionaries of Central government. Even after I had crossed all hurdles and implemented successfully clearance cum resettlement component of the project, within three days, from November 17 to 19, 1968, concocted and calculated allegations were levelled against me and my staff. While asking Parliament Questions No.534-537 in January, 1969, reference was made to "the forcible demolition of 10,000 houses in Prasad Nagar and Amrit Kaur Puri and bulldozing of the locked premises". A death under the bulldozer was also alleged. No particulars, however, of the 'dead individual' or 'locked premises' or its 'owner' was ever given.

All such false allegations, coined out of reckless rumours, intentionally spread by hostile parties, which got wide publicity after they were mentioned in Parliament, were designed to defame my drive and hound me out of office. There was, however, a sizeable section of the people who, warmly but silently, commended my commitment to secure the planned development of the Delhi, numerous obstacles notwithstanding. Unfortunately, in our society, knowledgeable and enlightened persons seldom speak in public. They usually content themselves by talking in their drawing rooms, while strongly entrenched vested interests resort to vicious and prolonged propaganda.

With regard to the second type of cases, I would briefly unfold my experience of dealing with the slums and squatters' clusters in and around the complexes of Nizam-ud-din Dargah; Motia Khan Jat-ki-Pahari *Idgah*; Darya Gunj Ghata Masjid; and Mir Dard Road tomb of Shah Wali Ullah.

In the complex of Hazarat Nizamuddin Dargah, there are a number of historical monuments and old grave-yards. The functionaries, associated with these monuments and grave-yards, had abetted in the growth of vast slums on the spaces meant for circulation and community facilities. Large areas of government land in the vicinity were also unathorizedly occupied and made part of the slums. These functionaries and their agents had been collecting huge amounts as 'rent', *albeit illegally,* from hundreds of closely built Jhuggis, motor mechanic shops, cattle dairies and 'kabari' godowns.

When all these savage and stinking slums were cleared in 1969 for widening of link roads, construction of public sector undertakings, offices and flyover, and bonafide residential squatters, who were staying here out of compulsion of poverty, were allotted alternative plots in what is now known as Sunlight Colony, an attempt was made by the beneficiaries of illegal collections to whip up communal passions and start an aggressive agitation to reoccupy the sites. While allotments of valuable plots in the Sunlight Colony were hardly mentioned, cooked up and communally coloured allegations were repeatedly made with shrillness similar to the one raised, at the end of emergency, with regard to Turkman Gate slum clearance scheme.

The stratagem was to drown the voice of truth and deflect the gaze from the plethora of old documents. The agitators were even able to get the support of Fakhruddin Ali Ahmed, Union Minister, by misrepresenting that the old graves, including the grave of Sheikh Abdullah's mother, had been 'bulldozed' by the Delhi Development Authority. The fact was that, before the clearance, motor-mechanic workshops and cattle dairies were located on and around the graves and had caused considerable damage to them. To undo the damage, the DDA had fenced, cleaned, and grassed the area around the graves and other old monuments, thus saving them from extinction.

Nevertheless, Prime Minister Indira Gandhi was persuaded by Fakhruddin Ali Ahmed to meet a delegation of the 'aggrieved parties', led by him. I was asked by Prime Minister's office to be present at the meeting. The allegations, earlier propagated vociferously, through the press, were repeated, though in a subdued tone. I placed before the Prime Minister a few photographs taken by the officials prior to the commencement of clearance work. I also referred to land-records existing since the days of British Administration of Delhi. Prime Minister did not react. The delegation skirted the issue of records but put extraordinary emphasis on their allegations about the demolition of the old mosque. Fakhruddin Ali Ahmed, apparently misinformed, read a few lines from an Urdu publication of 1910s. These lines indicated that if one travelled from the north-east side towards the Dargah, one would first come across an old mosque. I gently took the book from him. After having a hurried look, I returned the book to him. I kept quiet. After the delegation had left, I spoke briefly to the Prime Minister about what had been read over to her and what had been omitted. The words preceding the word mosque described it as 'abandoned and in ruins'. Indira Gandhi was surprised that I knew Urdu so well. But what she appreciated more was that I had not confronted the Minster with the 'omitted words' in the meeting, as this could have vitiated the atmosphere and made it difficult for her to let the 'worked-up protesters' lose their steam in due course.

Soon thereafter, an elegant lawn and row of little trees and shrubs emerged all along the widened link-road, besides Nizam-ud-din flyover, Public Undertakings Office Complex, Cultural and Educational Institutions etc. In course of time, all these Master Plan landmarks won warm admiration of the public. But the irony of the admiration was never lost on me. When I undertook to discharge my obligation to the law, to the Master Plan and to the future of Delhi, I was made to feel as if I had done something terribly wrong and those who had ravaged the Dargah environment and violated every law, rules and regulations on the subject, could act as my tormentor, and go right upto the Prime Minister. Tragically, though secularism is constitutionally mandated, the misuse of religion in India has become the most potent weapon to protect and advance one's personal, pecuniary and political interests.

The above phenomenon of blatant misuse of historic mosques and no holds barred harassment of those who dared to set the matter right, had once again to be faced by me while clearing the slum-clusters in and around 'Jat-ki-Pahari'-Motia Khan *Idgah* in Central Delhi. This mosque has its own significance. It was here that the Mughal emperor, Aurangzeb, and President Fakruddin Ali Ahmed offered their Id prayers.

Over the years, highly congested slum-clusters, comprising godowns, 'kabari'-stores, workshops, Jhuggis-Jhompris etc. had grown along the walls of the *Idgah*, puncturing and damaging them at a number of points. The mosque was hardly visible from the main road. A few self-styled 'Mutawalis' claimed the public land in the vicinity as *Idgah* land. They had been collecting huge sum of money as rent and pocketing it themselves. When clearance was carried out, they made every effort to exploit the religious sentiments and accused me and the officials of the DDA of severely damaging the historic mosque. In fact, the boot was on the other leg. It were the self-styled 'Mutawalis' and their collaborators who had virtually clogged the monument. Contrary to the canard fed to the 'high-ups' in the political circles, the DDA had developed a beautiful garden which enhanced the architectural simplicity of the monument, upgraded its environment, and provided the much needed 'patch of green' to the suffocating population of the residential localities around.

The bonafide squatters, including 'kabaris' and motor mechanic and spare part dealers, were offered alternative sites in the conforming areas that had been newly developed in the West Delhi, such as Mayapuri and Naraina. Those who accepted the offer are now doing roaring business and living in clean and well-serviced colonies, while those, mostly poor Muslims, who were taken in by the false propaganda, are still hopping from one miserable slum to another, mostly around Dargahs, graveyards etc.

Similar conditions and similar reaction were encountered when the slum-clusters in the compound and along the walls of Ghata Masjid, Darya Gunj, were cleared on September 15-16, 1967. The special features of these clusters was that they were predominantly in the form of commercial go-downs and workshops, showing a disposition among the custodians and functionaries to extract maximum monetary gains from misuse of mosque's premises and unauthorized occupation of public land in the neighborhood. In another case of clearance on 30 June, 1967, 30 trucks load of tents had to be lifted from the *tomb* of much revered muslim saint, Shah Wali Ulhah Mahaddis, on Mirdard Road.

For the specimen of the third type of cases, mentioned earlier in this section, the case of Purana Quila Complex would be most appropriate. This Quila is one of the most precious items in the treasure-house of Delhi's history and heritage. The site on which it was built was once a part of the mythological city of Indraprastha, founded by the Pandava prince Yudhishthira. Its 'bastioned ramparts, massively constructed of rubble masonry, are marvels of strength', and its three gates are the first manifestation of harmonious synthesis of Hindu and Muslim styles of architecture.

Despite being a valuable cultural asset, Purana Quila was not taken care of for about two decades in post-1947 Delhi. A temporary 'refugee camp' was set up in the large open space inside the Quila. Even after the camp was closed, consequent to the rehabilitation of the displaced persons in regular colonies, a few commercial establishments, such as timber stores, coal depots and furniture shops continued to stay along the outer walls of the fort. Over the years, under political patronage, these establishments grew in size and many new ones were also added. The area between the walls and the moat was jam-packed. With every passing day, the walls were being damaged and disfigured, and the moat was being filled with rubbish and refuse. The site had become an eye-sore in the city, transmitting a very poor impression about the capacity of the Indian Republic to manage its affairs properly. Hardly any tourist, foreign or local, visited the Purana Quila.

With no action being taken by any authority, the venture of squatting for commercial purposes became highly profitable. It extended to the legendary Bhairon Mandir* along the eastern wall of the Quila and also to the shrine of Matka Pir in the vicinity. On the other side of the road, the grave of the famous Persian poet, Bidel (1642-1720), too, had been encroached upon by the motor mechanics who had set up repair workshops in the small garden, known as Bagh-e-Bidel, around the grave.

To end this sorry spectacle and pave the way for a land-mark development and environmental upgradation of the entire complex, the slums and squatters were cleared from all the above sites. The timber depots were relocated in the conforming area of Mayapuri, semi-industrial units in Naraina industrial area and shack-dwellers in the resettlement colony of their choice in West Delhi. The cleared areas were redeveloped in accordance with their original designs and their surroundings were radically improved with provision of community greens. In place of muddy and garbage-ridden moat, a

* The core of the ancient Bhairon Mandir, according to the legend, was built during the Pandava Kingdom of Indraprastha and Bheem offered his prayer in this temple. The nearby shrine of the famous Sufi saint, Hazrat Ahmed Sheikh, whose blessing are associated with the simple offering of a pitcher (Matka) containing peas (Mattar) is especially popular with the poor devotees, both Muslim and Hindus. On the annual 'Urs', first offering to the shrine of the Sheikh is traditionally made by the 'Mahant' of the Bhairon Mandir.

delightful water-body of substantial length and breadth was created between the wall of Quila and the main road.

From the analysis of case-histories of all the three type of above cases, it should be clear that, finally, every public cause was admirably served. The squatters soon realized the immense long-term benefits that had accrued to them. The city-scape wore a more organized and elegant look. The only losers were the 'slum-dadas'; exploiters of religions, and propagators and patrons of the vote-bank politics. But in such poor health has been our state and society that they could carry on with their nefarious activities for a long time and bully and defame those who dared to do the right thing in the service of the city.

While I continued to execute projects of this genre with undiminished determination, I did not relax my efforts to expound my views through newspapers' articles, essays and discussions in seminars etc. I had hoped that this would draw attention at least of the intelligentsia and the enlightened leadership in politics and bureaucracy to the deeper issues involved. It is neither possible nor necessary to provide details of these writings here. It would suffice if the central thrust of my main propositions is given, in brief, as follows:

> The more I have been associated with it, the stronger has become my conviction that the seeds of the problem of the slums and squatters lie buried in the womb of an indifferent and superficial society—a society which has substituted empty rhetoric for significant content and from which real humanism is absent.
>
> On August 15, 1947 we had our tryst with destiny. But were we clear about the type of destiny that we wanted to have for ourselves, our children and grandchildren? Had we an inspired and clear vision, we would have perceived that the pre-eminent issue that confronted us at that time was civilisational and cultural. We should have first decided what was the nature of the civilisation that we wanted to build and what cultural values, what motivation and what frame of mind would be needed to create and sustain that civilisation. The fundamental question was of evolving a new design for life, distinctly our own, and a

new style of living, born out of our new needs and new aspirations.

A powerful, creative and constructive mind should have been our main instrument in building a new civilisation, a new culture. The edifice of the new India should have been erected on the soil and in the climate created by that civilisation and culture. The bricks of this edifice should have been baked with the fire of new spirituality and cemented together with the values of compassion, commitment, balance, harmony, justice and truth. The hands that should have gone to work should have been those of Karma Yogis.

It is time that we set our mooring right and recreate the best in our ancient tradition and culture and adopt 'priorities for future', and not 'priorities for self-centred short-termism'. We must begin to measure the greatness of our cities by the extent they enable their inhabitants to lead a clean life and build social, economic, intellectual and moral capacities for themselves and their children.

My persistence with the campaign, both in the realm of ideas and the realm of implementation, did not go unnoticed, particularly by the senior members of the Indian Civil Service who had been trained in the tradition of respecting discipline. Prime Minister Indira Gandhi's natural instinct, too, was in favour of orderly and planned development of the capital. Occasionally, she spoke of the DDA as being the pace-setter for other large cities of the country. And the President of India did me the honour of conferring Padma Shri Award on January 26, 1971 for what the citation described as "significant contribution in the formulation and implementation of Delhi Master Plan and for playing a pioneer role in Planning and Implementation of Projects."

Apart from the personal encouragement that the national recognition gave to me, the Padma Award opened wider avenues for me to provide to the public in general and political and bureaucratic authorities in particular, deeper insight into the darker and destructive reality that hovered around the squatters and slums of urban India. There was a virtual spate of write-ups in the press on the subject. Almost all the national dailies sought my personal interviews and gave large coverage to the central points of my propositions.

Here, as specimen, I give excerpts from two such press interviews – one from the *Statesman* of October 6, 1971 and other from the *Hindustan Times* of October 7, 1971. The former had reported:

> For Jagmohan, Vice-Chairman of the Delhi Development Authority, who received the Padma Shri on Tuesday, "the challenge of our cities is of crucial importance to the future of our country. It is time that we attend to this challenge seriously and formulate a long-term public policy suited to our soil and conditions and not imitative of the Western models. If we continue to neglect the challenge, we will soon be overwhelmed by it", he said in an interview after the investiture ceremony at Rashtrapati Bhavan.
>
> The young DDA official who has been instrumental in giving a face-lift to the capital, continued: "The real improvement of our cities can take place when we remove not only the physical slums but also the mental slums – the forces of decay and decadence in our society. It is only the inner force of social, cultural and spiritual rejuvenation that can wipe out the infected and stinking spots beneath the glittering super-structure."

The interview of the *Hindustan Times* ran as under:

> Jagmohan, the young Vice-Chairman of the Delhi Development Authority, who was among the 123 recipients of this year's national awards on Tuesday, was in a rather poetic and pensive mood.

Jagmohan believes the role an individual can play in improving the city's environs is of limited significance. Real and lasting improvement can come if we remove not only the physical but also the mental slums – the 'slums of human faith,' the degenerated values that dominate the social arena. He quotes from his poem on Delhi:

*In your slums of human faiths,*
*Mighty minds come and go;*
*But your dirty lanes remain,*
*And your stinking drains flow.*

He elaborates: "The basic problem is not taking the people out of slums but taking slums out of the people. And this can be accomplished by a band of dedicated social and cultural reformers our cities must produce to find peace, progress and inner as well as outer cleanliness. Imbecile urban institutions are a major handicap. Some time back, when I was asked to take charge of the Jhuggi-Jhompri removal scheme and resettle the squatters, I tried to list in my mind the various difficulties which had to be faced. Almost involuntarily, I jotted down the following lines:

*My city is thousand years old,*
*It has four million souls,*
*Some live in mansions.*
*Most in holes;*
*But will you and I,*
*With slender thread and broken poles,*
*Bring these mansions close to holes?*

Can we ever hope to bring about inner harmony and balance in our cities and solve their massive problems arising out of urbanization and abysmal poverty with weak instruments – 'slender thread' and 'broken poles'? We must evolve new urban institutions, strong and dynamic.

Lest I should appear to be striking a pessimistic note, let me refer to a short success story: Some time in the year 1963, while roaming on the bank of the river and watching the huge, sprawling slums of Yamuna Bazaar, certain thoughts surged and tormented my mind. On my return home, I included the following passage in my poem on Delhi:

*In these soul-less domes of humanity,*
*In these cemeteries of our living men;*
*Ghosts of future progress walk,*
*While we indulge in our fashionable talk.*
*Of doing this and that.*

Well, as you see now, we have not been merely talking all these years. We have been able to eliminate the slums of Yamuna Bazaar, Tilak Bridge and Nizamuddin – the 'soul-less domes of humanity', and 'cemeteries of our living men.' Instead, we have smiling flowers and swinging trees, flowing fountains and streams, and soon there would be woods, dark and green. This shows that, in spite of various impediments, something worthwhile can be achieved.

Apart from underscoring the need for according priority to the task of cleaning up of the mental garbage of the degenerated times, I wrote several essays and articles, arguing that the Indian city must evolve its own pattern of Human Settlements. In the *Hindustan Times*: Sunday World, of May 14, 1972, I wrote a comprehensive essay which was published under the title: *A New Human Settlement*. Since the rationale and feature of this Settlement have been discussed, in the context of the connected issues, in a subsequent Chapter, it does not seem necessary to say anything more here than to underline that haphazard migration and unchecked squatting is most injurious to every element involved. It is injurious to the squatter, the society, the city, the state and the civilization itself.

CHAPTER V

# IN HOT AND DUSTY WINDS

*If a society is not in reasonable health, democracy can not only be risky but disastrous.*

— Robert Kaplan*

*Truth is the best of tactics because it excludes tactics.*

— Ivan Svitak**

The overall picture that emerged by 1971 was more reassuring than the one obtaining at the time of execution of the Nigambodh Ghat Project. A number of important Master Plan Schemes, though often obstructed and delayed by all sorts of devious means, could not escape implementation at the hands of a determined set-up which had been fired by a sense of mission. At the intellectual level, the constructive propositions, advocated by me, were getting published in the national press by way of essays, articles and interviews, and attracting attention of the thinking class. The words of appreciation were also becoming warmer and more frequent. But the general polity and administration was nowhere near ridding itself of its deeply infected ethos and attitudes.

The infected stuff continued to cause occasional sickness in the body-**politic** remained vulnerable to relapses and to additional infections. Any unfavourable circumstance could suddenly halt the progress, even reverse it. And this, tragically, was not long in coming.

Dr. A.N. Jha who had been keeping indifferent health for quite some time passed away on January 19, 1972. According to the family

---

* Robert Kaplan is a noted American journalist and writer of travel-books. He is known for his penetrating observations on the current global reality.

** Ivan Svitak was a celebrated Czech poet and philosopher of the twentieth century, who sought to humanize politics.

custom, he was cremated not at the Nigambodh Ghat but at a site little away on the bank of the river. As an expression of gratitude for the services rendered by him to the Delhi Administration, a small and simple memorial, *a little green hermitage*, was proposed to be set up at his cremation site. A special meeting of the Executive Council of the Delhi Metropolitan Council was held, under the chairmanship of Acting Lieutenant Governor, M.G. Pimputkar. It resolved to accept the proposal.

The above resolution was not implemented, primarily because of the swollen ego of Baleshwar Prasad who took over as Lieutenant Governor in April 1972. When I drew his attention to the Council's Resolution of January and suggested its translation on the ground, he cut me short by saying: "Why are you bothered about the dead?" I was appalled not only because of the crude way in which he spoke but also because he betrayed traits which appeared to render him unsuitable for a high level sensitive assignment in Delhi.

Personally and as a general rule, I was not in favour of setting up of any memorial by using government funds. But in this case, a family Trust had volunteered to meet the expenditure which in any case was insubstantial. Only a small, elegant, green space, in the ancient Indian tradition was intended to be carved out. But Baleshwar Prasad's reaction was not actuated any consideration that he thought was of public interest. He left me in no doubt that he was too jealous, too supercilious, to see Dr. A.N. Jha, his predecessor in office, being put on high pedestal.

Pretentious to the core, Baleshwar Prasad did not have the patience to even go through the Master Plan, or otherwise understand the multi-faceted challenges that the expanding metropolis of Delhi was facing. Nor did he show any inclination to acquaint himself with the ground-level conditions by visiting any slums or squatter-settlement. He was one of those civil servants who believed in exercising authority for authority's sake. He tended to be self-centred and short-sighted in taking decisions which required 'enlarged views' to be entertained.

Baleshwar Prasad soon collected like-minded officers in his office. Without comprehending the rationale of various land development and housing schemes, and without respecting the precedents, they went about securing plots for themselves, their family members and friends. Fortunately, their misadventure did not last long. While hearing writ-petition No. 340 of 1972, the Supreme Court discovered their malfeasance in what came to be known as VIP Land Grab Scandal[1] and cancelled all the allotments.

Following angry outburst in Parliament with regard to their unseemly conduct, they had to leave the scene. But in the two-year period they stayed in office, they had caused damage all around.

Atmosphere had been contaminated; initiative had been stifled and dynamic coordination and cohesiveness amongst the departments concerned had been brought to a halt.

From the above, however, it should not be inferred that no clearance cum resettlement cum redevelopment project or any other linked scheme of the Master Plan was carried out, during January 1972 to June 1975[2], by the implementing agency of the DDA. Adopting the same principle, pattern and procedure, as were followed earlier, some[3] projects and plans of this genre were put through in the said period.

But the zest for creative and constructive work had gone. Petty pin-pricking of Baleshwar Prasad's coterie had proved fatal to it. Realizing that entering into any argument with this coterie over matters of great vision for Delhi would result in nothing but irritation and waste of time, I started spending my non- office hours in Sapru House Library and other centres of intellectual and cultural activities

---

[1]To avoid repetition, the detail pertaining to the VIP Land Grab case, the unbecoming role played by Lt. Governor Baleshwar Prasad and his Special Assistant R.C. Jain, the verdict of the Supreme Court in Writ Petitions and the severe criticism to which the misconduct of the two aforesaid functionaries of Delhi was subjected to in Parliament, are not being discussed here. All these and connected matters have been dealt with, in a more relevant context, in a subsequent section of this Chapter.

[2]After the removal of Baleshwar Prasad, in the wake of the Supreme Court's observations in the VIP land-scandal case, Kishan Chand took over as Lieutenant Governor.

[3]These plans and projects covered areas of Rampur, Shahjada Bagh, Sheikh Sarai, Chirag Delhi, Jhandewalan, Najafgarh Road, Dr. Krishna Road, Tihar, INA area, Pandav Nagar, etc.

for acquiring new knowledge, new insight, that was being provided by scholarly and data-based reports of the United Nations' Commissions and Committees, with regard to the subjects which were fast changing the social, economic and political architecture of the contemporary world and putting the national and international institutions of governance to the most awesome test in human history.

I devoted special attention to the problems of old and historic cities. In the case of Delhi, I also undertook extensive walks to its interior. The idea was to supplement the latest theoretical knowledge by the latest personal insight attained by studying street-level reality. Eventually, this, led me to write my first book in 1973-74, titled: *Rebuilding Shahjahanabad; the Walled City of Delhi*. A few excerpts from its Preface, reproduced below, would speak for themselves:

> Shahjahanabad has always cast a strange spell on me. I have sometimes been repelled by its congestion, its slums, its overgrown trade, and its apparent lack of pride. I have often grieved over the fate of about half a million people, jam-packed in its two square miles of area. Yet I have been charmed by its vast and strange antithesis, by the romance and tragedy of its past, by its milling crowds, by the pulsation and vigour of its life in the day time, and by the poetry of its broken silence in the midnight. Its numerous monuments, old buildings, *chhattas,* colonnades, and its street patterns have excited and stimulated my imagination, and brought to me the vision of the old life—its style, charm and grace.
>
> Haunted by the romantic as well as tragic face of Shahjahanabad, I have always had the inner urge to do something for it. But the urge remained incipient, hazy, till I got the opportunity to voice my views in the two articles, published in the *Hindustan Times* (Sunday World) in October 1973. These articles evoked considerable interest and friends suggested that these should be expanded into a book form. But the suggestion of the friends is only a secondary reason for this book.

My primary reason for the book is my emotional attachment with Shahjahanabad and the urge within me to focus public attention on its fate, to unravel its cultural treasure, its way of life, which has been submerged by the sand-storm of its history, to bring light and hope to its half a million inhabitants, and to outline a bold new programme, a blueprint of action, of reform and regeneration.

There is a larger purpose, too. "Show me your cities and I will tell you about the cultural aims of its population." Looking at the present-day Shahjahanabad, what impression of our cultural pursuits can be formed, what inner strength for the nation can be claimed? A sick, shattered, and dismembered city like Shahjahanabad can neither inspire nor be inspiring. It can only be a symbol of national shame and diffidence, a readymade material for our critics and denigrators. If, on the other hand, we are able, with sustained efforts, imagination, and courage, to eliminate what is cruel and clumsy in the existing Shahjahanabad, preserve what is healthy and beautiful, bring about creative regeneration of the old and new, and make Shahjahanabad a new cultural magnet, it could become a symbol of national pride and resurgence. What is needed is courage and faith, love and confidence, sweat and tears, ability to comprehend the situation in depth, and seize the opportunity that history affords us.

Rebuilding of cities is not an act of isolated civic reform; it involves the vaster task of restructuring the fundamental forces which govern the life of the people. The efforts to rebuild Shahjahanabad should, therefore, not be viewed in isolation but in the overall context of the need to rebuild India. Sustained efforts and success in such a venture can bring about a healthy change of mind and spirit—a silent revolution which might ultimately enable us to rebuild India in a new social, cultural, and intellectual mould.

Will we be able to do that? Can we rebuild and rejuvenate Shahjahanabad? Can we restore its healthy past, and blend it artistically and creatively in our current urban needs and requirements? Can we reorganize and refashion its dismembered threads and make Shahjahanabad, within the wider metropolitan context of Delhi, a new cultural and commercial magnet with a vigour and buoyancy of its own? Can we provide a new meaning direction, and significance to it? Can we melt down the old and forge it into a new steel?

The book, a product of painstaking study both at the intellectual and ground levels, was hailed as first of its kind to be published in India. Positive comments were galore. An example, which would be even otherwise instructive, when viewed from another angle of great public interest, may be given. In its issue of April 1975, the India International Centre's Quarterly, expressed its warm appreciation in these words:

> Jagmohan's concept of rebuilding Shahjahanabad is thought-provoking. It brings out his deep understanding and emotional involvement in a matter concerning human settlement. He has eloquently underlined the historic, cultural and socio-economic significance of Shahjahanabad. There are certain striking features which come to light when one goes through the pages of the book: (i) While identifying the manifold problems of Shahjahanabad, feasible solutions have also been put forth. (ii) Probably, for the first time, an idea has emerged to rebuild the Walled City in an Indian style and scale and not in the form of a westernized imitation. (iii) Public opinion has been focused on this issue and people now talk in terms of Shahjahanabad rather than referring to the area as Old Delhi or Walled City. (iv) The thread of an imaginative approach runs all through the book. There is a balanced emphasis on the need for preserving the rich heritage and discarding what is unbecoming or burden-some.
>
> So far, practical experience has shown that Shahjahanabad was left neglected, to be reduced to a veritable slum over the years. Is the government keen to take steps for the improvement

> of slums of which the Walled City comprises a sprawling area?... ....Words are not being matched by deeds. With this attitude, the slum areas will continue to grow. The Master Plan was paid scant attention to Shahjahanabad. Even the Delhi-Ajmeri Gate scheme has remained on paper during the last 25 years.
>
> ....There can be no two opinions on the issue of decongesting Shahjahanabad. The traffic hazards, unauthorized structures and activities, noxious industries and obnoxious trade, all should be contained and then eliminated. Similarly, there need not be any controversy on the proposal that a rebuilt Shahjahanabad should be a city for pedestrians. Other ideas such as the setting up a small university, a new civic centre, provision for sports, educational, recreational and cultural centres with T.V. sets, if given a practical shape, will serve the long denied needs of the people.

Like this write-up, there were other pieces which eulogised many of my formulations and key items of my blue-print. But when it came to doing anything on the ground, howsoever small or insignificant, one spanner or the other would be thrown in the wheel by a visionless authority in a higher position, or by a jealous bureaucracy holding a position of influence, or by a political leader used to changing colours to suit his narrow ends.

The scattering, and somewhat desultory, experience of these uneven and irritating months, merely served to strengthen my growing belief: "We, as a nation, have generally not realised that the great questions of the day are not settled by speeches and slogans but by sound and solid action. Ideas are important; but it is the constructive work alone that can 'inject meaning into the veins' of history and civilisation."

Separately, at the national plane, the most serious omission, on the part of the post-1947 leadership, in the arena of nation-building, was manifesting itself in disruptive and divisive activities. Forgetting that an essential pre-requisite for a successful democratic governance was the character of its people and moral health of the society, the top political leadership of practically all hues and colour found itself trapped in a net of its own making, and lost sight of the constitutional goal of building a fair and just state by fair and just means. With increasing depletion of constitutional morality from the national environment, different segments of the political power structure started chaining a fairly liberal constitution with their own grammar of selfishness, which was bound to give birth, sooner or later, to the governance pattern in the form of 'democratic dictatorship' or 'functioning anarchy'.

The declaration of Emergency on June 25-26, 1975, its duration of about 19 months,* the happenings in the three years' period preceding its declaration and in the three years' period following its lifting, all prove the above proposition to the hilt. They have exposed the deep chinks in the armoury of the Indian democracy and the weak metal with which it had been mostly **fabricated.** The common lesson, which the working of the governance-machinery of these three otherwise distinct periods, is: 'if a society is not in a reasonable health, democracy can not only be risky but disastrous.'

In 1971-72, Mrs. Indira Gandhi won the general elections on the populist wave of *Garibi Hatao*: 'Remove Poverty'. In its wake came the spectacular success of the Bangladesh Operations. She was hailed as the incarnation of goddess Durga by no other person than Atal Behari Vajpayee. Had she mustered more courage and developed an inspired vision of the type that India's true destiny called for, she would have taken the initiative to involve senior and respected leaders, such as Jayaprakash Narayan, Atal Behari Vajpayee and Morarji Desai, and created a movement for social and cultural reforms to underpin the purity of politics. But that, unfortunately, was not to be. On the other hand, in the next three years, the gap between the promises and performance,[4] between the declarations and deeds and between

*The three periods that have been referred here are: (i) June 26, 1972 to June 26, 1975, leading to the declaration of Emergency on June 26 1975; (ii) 19 months duration of Emergency till January 1977 and three years period from September 1977 following the lifting of Emergency.

[4] Let alone the promised removal of poverty, the government failed to control prices and the Fourth Five Year Plan proved a failure.

the provisions of the Constitution and Laws, and their actual working on the ground,[5] increased to an unprecedented width. Any attempt to jump over such a gap was bound to prove disastrous, especially when the 'jumper' had no constitutional morality to pin up his or her strength.

At this juncture, Jayaprakash Narayan gave a call for 'total revolution'[6]. The ideology of total revolution was, undoubtedly, a noble one, but the call for it came at a time – mid August 1974 – when it could be misinterpreted as confrontationist and disruptive.

To the tense environment then prevailing, the spark for the crisis was provided on June 12, 1975, by the Allahabad High Court judgement which, taking a highly narrow view[7] of two technical lapses on the part of a few officials, set aside Indira Gandhi's 1971 election to the Lok Sabha and declared her ineligible to hold any elective office for six years. The single Vacation Judge of the Supreme Court was no less restrictive in his views, and granted her only a conditional stay. On Indira Gandhi's refusal to resign, massive protest rallies were organised, and an impassioned call was given to the nation on June 25, 1975, from Delhi's Ram Lila ground, by Jayaprakash Narayan to commence an All-India agitation to bring down the government. The Army, the Police and other officials were asked not to obey any illegal order. The following day, early morning, Emergency was declared!

What does the above chain of events of about three years before the Emergency reveal? It clearly shows the fatal flaws of the

---

[5] Public Order could not be properly handled by the government. In the violent agitation, launched by Nav Nirman Samiti an organization of Gujrat students, 180 persons were killed. In the atmosphere vitiated by violence, Railway Minister L.N. Mishra was assassinated, and a bomb was thrown at Chief Justice A.N. Ray.

[6] The term 'total revolution' was first used by Karl Marx in his book *The Poverty of Philosophy*. The ideology was implicit in the works of Gandhi and Vinoba who wanted a basic change in the ethos of the individual and the society.

[7] The judgement went against Indira Gandhi on petty technical points. Commenting upon the issue, the Baltimore Sun, a leading US daily, observed: 'In America, such transgression might cost some civil servants their jobs, but would never threaten the tenure of even the lowest candidate of elected office'. In the same strain, James Cameron, a noted political analyst of the time, remarked, 'It is as though a head of government should go to the block for a parking ticket.'

governance machinery – no constructive and imaginative leadership to prevent a crisis, no ability to rise above the short-term gains, no hesitation to disregard true norms of democracy, and resort to extra-constitutional means and no inclination on the part of judiciary to be dynamic in its interpretation of the law and go by the intrinsic merit of the case rather than by its technicality.

The Emergency was a tragedy! Its imposition led to a large number of unjustified arrests[8] and caused many other aberrations.

All that is well-known and need not be restated. What, however, must be underlined here is that the issue had much larger depth and dimensions than is generally assumed. It extended to the poor social and moral health of India's overall system of governance and its principal actors – the political leaders, the bureaucrats, the judges, the pressmen etc.

Was it Mrs. Indira Gandhi or her son, Sanjay Gandhi or few of her advisors who alone were responsible for the imposition of Emergency and what happened during it? What about the judges[9]

---

[8]The persons detained during the emergency under Maintenance of Internal Security Act (MISA) fell in the four categories (i) members of political parties; (ii) members of banned organisations; (iii) habitual criminals; and (iv) economic offenders, such as smugglers and black-marketeers. The total number of persons belonging to political parties and banned organisations, that is category (i) and category (ii), detained under MISA during the Emergency was 13,000. To inflate the figures of detenus, quite a few critics of Mrs. Indira Gandhi include even those who were arrested on charges of habitual smuggling, black-marketeering and serious criminal offences. For instance, in UP where the maximum number of persons were detained under MISA, 80 per cent of the detenus were hardened criminals, bootleggers and smugglers.

[9]S.P. Sathe, in his book, *Constitutional Amendments*, has remarked: Many crimes committed during the Emergency seemed to be a natural consequence of total self-negation by the judiciary. Justice H.R. Khanna, in his minority judgement, as summarized in Granville Austin's book. 'Working of Democratic Constitution' had argued "Article 21 cannot be considered to be the sole repository of the right to life and personal liberty; rights created by the statutes, being not fundamental rights, can be enforced during the period of Emergency despite the Presidential order: Article 226 of the Constitution (empowering High Courts to issue writs) is an integral part of the Constitution, and this power cannot be bypassed by the Presidential order in question; and there is no antithesis between the power to detain a person under preventive detention and the power of the court to examine the legality of detention."

who despite their high constitutional status, not only held that the declaration of Emergency was valid but also refused to safeguard even elementary liberties, the denial of which would reduce the individual citizens to a 'state of utter rightlessness'? What about the pressmen who,[10] 'started crawling when they were asked only to bend?' What about both the Houses of Parliament which endorsed the Emergency by an overwhelming majority – 336 to 39 in Lok Sabha and 136 to 33 in Rajya Sabha? What about those who adopted an excessively agitational approach to attain Jayaprakash Narayan's nobly conceived ideal of Total Revolution but started wrecking, as Chaudhry Charan Singh[11] did, the new government from inside to realise personal ambitions? And what about the people themselves, who just 'melted away' as soon as the Emergency was declared? Noting the absence of the 'angry voices', the 'Guardian', London observed: "India's State of Emergency is almost three months old now, and rapidly becoming the Mystery of the Missing Opposition."

Clearly, the Indian Republic, its institutions and its basic constituent, the people, were in moral disarray. So was its capital, Delhi. With regard to its pre-Emergency days, beginning from September 1, 1962, the date of enforcement of statutory Master Plan, I have already brought out, in the preceding Chapters, how a number of wielders of political power, especially at the local level, are made of insubstantial clay; how they suffer no prick of conscience in abandoning their pledges, declarations and even laws passed with their approval; and how they resort to falsehood, concoct stories, spread rumours and impute motive to those who are conscientiously concerned about the fate and future of Delhi and who are committed to the rationale of its planned and purposive development.

Since the poor elements of Delhi's social and political structure, and the moral rot that it had been undergoing, continued in the

---

[10] Shortly after formation of the Janata Government L.K. Advani, Minister of Information and Broadcasting, remarked to the Press: "When you are asked only to bend, you were willing to crawl." – from *The People Betrayed*.

[11] L.K. Advani, in his book, *The People Betrayed*, gives a detailed account of what Chaudhry Charan Singh did to his ambition.

post-Emergency period of the Janta regime, these years saw their own type of unprincipled politics, their own type of lies and vengeful acts and their own type of atmosphere of fear and intimidation. The modus operandi changed. The substance, in outcome, remained the same.

There was a spate of Inquiry Commissions and Committees. These agencies were set up with the main objective of painting everything that happened during the Emergency as black and put the blame on Indira Gandhi, Sanjay Gandhi and the handful of supporters that they were left with. The officers and erstwhile political colleagues of the Gandhis were subjected to all sorts of pressures and threats and made to say before these Commissions and Committees that whatever 'wrong' they did was done at the behest of Indira Gandhi, Sanjay Gandhi and their coterie, no matter what the written records indicated. Most of them, in fact, were themselves inclined to follow the dictum: 'Let us lay all the evils on the Friar and rid ourselves of them all'.

In the vanguard of the Commissions and Committees was what came to be known as Shah Commission[12]. It was a single man Commission set up, under the Commission of Inquiry Act, 1952 to inquire into 'subversion of lawful processes and well-established conventions, administrative procedures and practices, abuse of authority, misuse of powers, excess and/or malpractices committed during the Emergency.' Terms of reference of the Commission were tailored. So were the pieces of evidence which were mostly hearsay.

Ironically, as if to prove that the nation was in the thick of all round moral collapse, the Shah Commission initiated its work by abusing its position and virtually transforming the Commission of Inquiry Act into the law for lampooning through the mass media. Its approach was pronouncedly one-sided and grossly unfair. Partisan

---

[12] Justice J.C. Shah was a retired Judge of the Supreme Court. His bias against Indira Gandhi was known. And yet, on May 28, 1977, he was appointed as a single-man Commission. I was roped in, mainly because I had made it clear to all concerned that the so called demolitions in Delhi during the Emergency were not demolitions but a part of the resettlement cum redevelopment scheme which had been in operation since early 1960s and nothing new, either in procedure or practice had been done.

case summaries were prepared by the Commission's staff by doctoring documents and isolating events from their context. These summaries were highlighted on television, radio and in the press. Yet they were given to the persons concerned only at the time of commencement of the proceedings. The intention was to surprise, confuse and pressurize witnesses and extract incriminating material. In the examination of witnesses, a pre-designed pattern was followed. Those who said anything to denigrate the so-called demolitions in Delhi during Emergency were encouraged, humoured, and even applauded. These obliging witnesses were not stopped by the Commission even when their statements clearly contradicted the written records. On the other hand, those who tried to stick to the truth were jeered, taunted, insulted, even asked to shut up.

The manner in which the erstwhile Ministers and Civil Servants were induced or intimidated to make totally false statements would be clear from an example. After approving and answering a number of questions in Parliament on clearances of squatters from haphazard clusters and their resettlement in new colonies, after presiding over the meetings of the Parliamentary Consultative Committee in which the issue was repeatedly discussed, after visiting the resettlement colonies, and after getting the squatter settlement, in the rear of his own bungalow, cleared, K. Raghuramaiah, the erstwhile Minister of Works, Housing and Parliamentary Affairs, told the Shah Commission, in reply to its questions, that he was hearing for the first time about the slum and squatter clearance and resettlement programme. Instead of confronting Raghuramaiah with the written records, the Shah Commission gleefully accepted his deposition. Nor would he allow cross examination of such a witness at what he called the 'First Stage of Inquiry'.

My own case provides another example of the Shah Commissions' shockingly unjust approach to the matter. I was appointed as Vice-Chairman[13] of Delhi Development Authority in January 1971.

---

[13]Being an officer primarily concerned with the planning and development of Delhi, I had nothing to do with the imposition of Emergency. In fact, at that time, I was in Australia in connection with a Cultural award given to me by the Australian Government. Nor had I been given any new assignment during the Emergency.

Earlier, I had worked as Commissioners for Implementation of Delhi Master Plan and given the Padma Shri Award by the President of India for what the citation of the said award described as a 'significant contribution to the formulation and implementation of Delhi Master Plan and for playing a pioneering role in planning and implementation of projects'. Thus, my commitment to the concept of planned development of Delhi was nationally known and recognized. I had a passionate urge to make our Capital one of the cleanest and most well-organised and disciplined cities in the world. I was dead against encroachments and illegal construction on public lands, a phenomenon which was encouraged by selfish politicians to create vote-banks in their constituencies.

In the early days of Emergency, I was not even in India. I was away to Australia in connection with a cultural award which had been given to me in May 1975 for my book, *Rebuilding Shahjahanabad: The Walled City of Delhi.* Nor, as an executive head of the city's planning and development agency, was I even remotely concerned with any issue or event which led to the declaration of Emergency on June 25, 1975. After my return from Australia, I carried out the same scheme of Clearance cum Resettlement cum Redevelopment as I was carrying out before the Emergency. The policy, procedures and mode of implementation, which I have narrated and analysed with regard to Nigambodh Ghat, Hauz Khas, Hazrat Nizamuddin Complex, Purana Quila, Prasad Nagar, Idgah and Kela Godown – New Delhi Railway Station etc. were not in any way different from those that pertained to the period of Emergency.

All these stark facts which were, knowingly and intentionally, biased out of consideration by the Shah Commission and the politico-bureaucrat caucus of the Home Ministry, which had maneuvered to get itself attached to the Commission for all practical purposes. The furious hostility of the caucus was compounded in my case by the craftiness of a few unprincipled bureaucrats, such as R.C. Jain, who had sneaked into the said caucus to settle personal scores on account of the ignominy which they had to face in the VIP Land Grab Scandal.[14]

My conscience was clear. My commitment to the principles and procedures of securing planned development of Delhi, was of the same nature in the period of Emergency[15] as had been shown by me in the pre-Emergency times. It remained so even afterwards. It was based not on loyalty to any political leader but on intellectual convictions imbibed after a thorough study of the highly complex social, economic and political architecture of contemporary India and also of other developing countries. And, over the years, this commitment had been painstakingly strengthened and sharpened by extensive practical experience at the ground level.

I had come to the firm conclusion that 'free for all' squatting was harmful, practically to all aspects of city's life. It gravely undermined the civic set-up and escalated the cost of infrastructural projects. It irritated the law-abiding citizens and weakened their resolve to make positive contribution to the orderly growth and upkeep of the metropolis. It bred diseases, put extra pressure on health services and lowered the overall productivity of the city's economy. It was also not in the interest of the squatter himself. His migration which had a great potential for acquisition of modern skills and modern social and cultural norms, had assumed a huge negative connotation. He was made to live in extreme congestion, exploited politically and compelled to bribe petty officials of the police and civic bodies. He was left with little option but to learn quickly the art of crookery and corruption. The fallouts of squatting, in short, were destructive of both civic and moral fabric of the city. It sent wrong signals to other cities and lowered the overall quality of contemporary India's culture and civilization.

---

[14] The VIP Land Grab case has been briefly mentioned, while discussing Lt. Governor Baleshwar Prasad's attitude towards Delhi's development. Its detailed particulars would be found in the subsequent part of this chapter and also in chapter VI Tilted: *Clearance of Turkman Gate Slums: Facing an Inexhaustible Arsenal of Lies.*

[15] I had also underscored that I was in no position to say anything about the justification or otherwise of the Emergency-declaration or several arrests made under the Maintenance of Internal Security Act, as all such matters were not germane to my office or functions.

Further, since most of the squatted upon lands were required for public utility projects or were situated on the embankments or on the beds of open *nullahs,* no investment was practically made by any public authority to provide even basic amenities like latrines. On the plea of human considerations, which the vested interests or ill-informed persons advanced, the squatters were made to live in health-shattering locations with extraordinary high densities and with stink of human excrement and urine all around.

In view of above considerations, I thought that the best way to deal with this hugely complex problem of city's governance and to contribute to the building of a healthy, humane and politically clean, economically forward looking society and civilization was to resettle the existing clusters on permanent sites and to ensure that future migration took place in a planned and purposive way and the process of migration was made skill and productivity-oriented, and not restricted to petty jobs or business in which poor virtually competed with one another. And I launched an all-embracing 'clearance-cum-redevelopment-cum-resettlement' project.

It did not seem odd or self-contradictory to the Shah Commission and the politico-bureaucrat caucus of the Home Ministry to find fault with the project for which, in 1971, that is four years before Emergency, Padma award was conferred on me by the President of India. They refused to open their eyes on all relevant documents. Like cruel dusty winds, scattering and kicking pale and innocent leaves on the ground, they would, with a sneering look and in intimidatory tone, reject, albeit orally, all request for summoning certain witnesses and asking them to support their evidence by way of sworn affidavits.

I was left with no doubt that they were merely fishing out evidence, mostly by unethical and unfair means, to provide some credence, to their pre-determined findings, and anyone who did not abet their unsavory venture would be taught a lesson of his life. It was beyond their sphere of thinking that there could be an officer who, while being in the good books of the Prime-Minister and not averse to listening to the views of other public men had stuck to the same policies, procedures and norms of rectitude which he had been observing before the Emergency. Why did not they ask for sworn affidavits from the complainants as well as the officer complained against? Had they done so, they would have found out in no time what the 'well-established' procedure were in this regard? And who was violating them – the Commission, or the Home Ministry caucus, or the Defendant?

In essence, my only 'fault' was that I happened to occupy a particular post at a particular time, and was not prepared to step out of my 'island of truth' and pose like a traitor and self-condemned criminal, throw mud on others, and hypocritically condemn a programme and policy which had been formulated with the concurrence of leading political parties and the implementation of which was totally in public interest. Subtle hints were given to me that I should become a sort of "approver" and pass on the "blame" to others. I marvelled at the lack of morality and the ignorance of the persons who gave such suggestions. Was clearance of some of the most inhuman slums or allotment of 1,000 hectares of developed land with market value of over thousands of crore or disbursement of building loans at only 4 per cent rate of interest, or creation of stable and development-oriented avenues of employment, preservation of historical legacy, or general environmental up-gradation of the city, an "excess" for which one should feel ashamed?

Perversion of values and dominance of superficial thinking was, indeed, appalling. Clearly, the injustices and excesses perpetrated by a small but crafty and vengeful section of the Home Ministry's caucus of Janta Regime were no less reprehensible, morally and administratively, than those that occurred during the Emergency with regard to hundreds of unwarranted arrests of political opponents of Mrs. Indira Gandhi and Sanjay Gandhi under MISA.

To expose the entire diabolical venture and the accompanying false propaganda, I prepared a comprehensive statement and submitted the same to the Shah Commission. During the course of the proceedings, I wanted to read my statement. But Justice J.C. Shah would not allow it, having found that the statement would tear the false picture desired to be painted by him and the Home Ministry's politico-bureaucrat caucus, attached to the Commission for all practical purposes. Every time I said I would like to read my statement, Justice J.C. Shah would say, "We would do so later". When on the subsequent days, I repeated my request, he would say: "I have given the statement to my officers. They will mark some portions. Then we would have the statement read out." In the meanwhile, lies after lies, half-truths after half-truth, and one tendentious report after another, were fed to the media – national dailies, radio and television. The objective was to lower my standing in the public eye and shatter my self-confidence. When I made another request to Justice Shah for allowing me to read my statement, drawing specific attention to the false propaganda that was going on against me in the press, I got the same reply. Justice Shah went on saying so till the proceeding ended.

More unfairly I was treated, more determined I became to fight against the net-work of injustice, woven so clumsily and crudely around me. With the intention of leaving a documented record for the times to come, I started writing a book, titled: *Island of Truth.* It was published in early 1978. The following two paras extracted from its preface, set out the long-term objective that was intended to be achieved:

> When the autumn is gone, the storm blown over, and the dust and haze of ignorance and prejudice settled down, the true faces of those guilty of falsifying history will stand exposed. Today, by their own queer logic of slant and slander, they may paint a false picture. But what will be the verdict of history? How will they escape the terrible consequences of their falsehood? Will not their murky soul stifle and destroy them? Truth can be hid, but not for all times.
>
> Truth annoys power, because it is stronger than power and it takes time to demonstrate its strength. More often than not persons with good intentions have been overwhelmed by the forces of their time. The more attached they are to the basic truth, the worse are they likely to be treated by their compatriots.

In the introduction, addressing the reader, I had said:

> Mine is an island of truth – truth in its essence, truth in its basic frame work. I intend to take you to this island. But for reaching this island, we have to pass through a turbulent sea of falsehood. The island, too, is desolate and deserted. Of late, it has been visited by marauders and systematically pillaged and shorn of its greenery. The sentinels themselves have been terrorized. They are silent. And:
>
> *That silence roars on my behalf*
> *Silence tear my ears*
> *All know it and are silent*
> *Their mouths are stifled by fear.*
>
> Notwithstanding the silence and sullenness that has gripped this once buoyant and thriving island, I hope to show you a few spots from which the reality would emerge, and you would be able to see true reflections even in a cracked mirror.

This book was filed as an affidavit[16] by me on November 7, 1977 in the special court of Justice M.L. Jain, Judge, Delhi High Court, because it was the only way I could put my documented facts, sworn on oath, on the official record, and simultaneously show how completely overtaken was Justice J.C. Shah and the Home-Ministry caucus by their extra-ordinary bias and hostility. I was confident that no one from the Home Ministry or any other authority would file a counter-affidavit because such a counter affidavit would not be able to reconcile true facts and documents, including document relating to Parliamentary questions, with the false and tutored oral evidence procured or manipulated by the Shah Commission and the Home Ministry caucus, during the proceedings. My confidence

[16]The affidavit was filed in the Court of Justice M.L. Jain, Judge, Delhi High Court, where Mrs. Indira Gandhi and others were being proceeded against on the complaints/findings of the Shah Commission. The contention was that these complaints/findings were a nullity on account of the unmitigated bias and legal lapses on the part of Justice J.C. Shah.

was not belied. No one from any public authority or member of the public dared to file a counter-affidavit, so much of solid and unalloyed truth my assertions contained.

Since the aforesaid affidavit is of great significance not only from the point of view of my stand and the extensive physical and moral damage that the Ninth Delhi had suffered at the hands of ravagers of their own kind, but also from the point of view of assessing the general health of the society and the political and administrative ethos of the times, I have considered it necessary to quote from it extensively, highlighting sworn assertions in their context. While reproducing excerpts from my affidavit of November 7, 1977, all the sworn facts have been kept intact; only slight editing has been done to facilitate continuity and clarity of composition. Here are excerpts from introductory assertions which expose Shri J.C. Shah's wholly unfair and non-judicial approach:

> Even before the commencement of the proceedings, the Commission demonstrated that it was merely looking to statements and documents which could fit into its pre-conceived conclusions. An instance of this phenomenon is the public pronouncement made on behalf of Shri J.C. Shah that those officers who pointed to the source from which the orders emanated would not be adversely commented upon. In other words, Shri J.C. Shah induced officers to make statements against the source of authority and thus buy immunity from adverse comment or action. A hysterical atmosphere of fear and intimidation was simultaneously built up by subtle management of the press and public media like Television and Radio. In the context of its atmosphere of fear and open declaration of a presiding officer of one-man Commission, most officers and witnesses accepted the inducement with open arms.
>
> Shri J.C. Shah publicly declared that he would conduct inquiry in two stages. If a witness was an obliging witness, and helped in painting the desired picture, he was let off. His lapses were not only ignored but also rationalized. Remarks like 'I could well imagine you were helpless' were frequently made.

> Even when such a witness spoke a patent lie, he was not questioned and no adverse comment was made. If, on the other hand, the witness turned out to be un-obliging, he was picked for second stage, and the whole evidence was tailored to hold him guilty. Leading questions were put to other witnesses to extract evidence against the un-obliging witness.

To bring home to the reader the extent to which suppression, distortion and intimidation was resorted to by the Shah Commission and the Home Ministry's caucus, I reproduce below another set of excerpts from the same affidavit:

> The basic objectives and intentions with which I proceeded should be evident from the fact that before clearance cum resettlement cum redevelopment projects were undertaken on a large scale, there were about 1,400 haphazard, ill-planned, clusters, scattered all over the city in unsuitable and unhealthy sites. About 78 per cent of the squatter households were living beyond 6.5 km of the centre of the city (Connaught Place). About 71.8 per cent of these 1,400 settlements were not having any water taps. 58.31 per cent had no hand-pumps, 68.9 per cent no lavatory seats, 65.1 per cent no brick pavements or pucca streets, 68.9 per cent no storm water drains and 63.1 per cent no street lighting. With extreme congestion and irregular and shapeless structures, with only 4 per cent of pucca shacks, with unstable families and low sex ratio (730 females : 1000 males), the environmental degradation could not be worse.
>
> It was from these sub-human conditions that the squatters were relieved and accommodated in the 41 resettlement colonies. Extraordinary hard work was put in to provide maximum facilities to the largest number in the shortest time. In about a year or so, about 1,45,000 residential and 10,000 shop plots were developed, and 200 km of main drains, 400 km of small drains, 650 culverts, 60 tube-wells, 4,000 hand-pumps, 2,500 public hydrants, 80 km of water supply lines, 200 km of metalled roads, and 14,000 permanent lavatory seats

were constructed. About 500 parks were developed, besides planting 5 lakh trees, Ten new higher secondary school buildings, 23 new dispensaries, 60 TV sheds were also constructed. In some colonies, facilities of super-bazars, community halls, adult literacy centers, milk-bars, "balbaries", etc., were provided. In addition to the employment opportunities existing in the neighbourhood of the resettlement colonies, a large number of new employment opportunities were provided. During the peak period, about 12,000 persons were employed every day. About 250 trucks, 25 road-rollers, and 20 bulldozers were engaged per day. About 5 lakh bags of cement and 50,000 truck-loads of bricks were consumed in the development work of the resettlement colonies. As compared to almost cent per cent construction (excepting small lanes) in pre-resettlement sites, the resettlement colonies were planned and developed with only 32 per cent of the area as residential, 13 per cent was earmarked for metalled roads, 15 per cent for paths, 16 per cent for parks, 4 per cent for shops, and 20 per cent for community facilities.

What has been done, and this has either escaped the notice of superficial observers or deliberately ignored by critics and self-styled experts, is that not only residential population has been disbursed but also industries, the commerce, and numerous other avenues of employment. Have not the wholesale fruit and vegetable market, iron merchant market, the "kabari" markets, the spare part machinery market, truck-terminals, etc., been shifted to the outlying areas? Are not thousands of new industries, new housing complexes, cattle resettlement farms, and milk dairies fast coming up in these areas? There is an overall development pattern in which the resettlement colonies fit. They do not exist in isolation.

Take, for instance, the resettlement colony of Shakurpur. Here, about 10,000 families, comprising a population of about 50,000, have been resettled. The colony is located right on the Ring Road, opposite one of the most thriving industrial colony of Lawrence Road. In Delhi Development Authority's residential colony of Paschimpuri, which is about two to three miles away from the city than the resettlement colony of Shakurpur, residential plots have been selling at the rate of about Rs.300 per sq. yd. Likewise, the Mangolpuri resettlement site is opposite the Paschim-puri residential colony. It has a population of about one lakh, and covers valuable lands. If market value of these lands are calculated, the extent of the benefit given to the re-settlers, who have an option to keep the plot on nominal rent or purchase it on nominal price or hire-purchase basis, would become self-evident.

And has any one cared to reply the obvious questions: where are the nearby areas where permanent resettlement of about 1,20,000 squatter families, involving a population of about 700,000 could be carried out? Which are the sites available near the heart of the city – Ramlila Ground, area around Red Fort and samadhis, India Gate or Purana Quila? Is it not inescapable that in a city whose population comprises 80 per cent poor people and whose structural legacy cannot be got rid of in the foreseeable future, a sizable portion of the poor should be living in the outlying areas? Would it make any sense to provide services at sites which are needed for roads, bridges, and community facilities or constitute road berms or embankments of drains and railway tracks?

Clearance was part of an overall development effort – an effort that had suffered badly due to pressure of vested interest. Even when funds were provided, schools were not built for years, roads and bridges were not constructed. Costs of development projects mounted. River fronts were uglified, natural landscape and ridges were damaged; and areas surrounding historical places were turned into filthy slums. All this happened merely because of the presence of a few squatters who, probably, themselves would have shifted to alternative sites but were prevented to do so by those elements in society who had invariably found it convenient to coin the argument of human consideration to hide their vested interest in politics and properties.

The extent of the imbalanced approach would be evident from one example. An old property was acquired in 1965 for constructing a school building for children. Compensation was paid to the claimant. But the vacant possession was not secured merely because of the presence of 39 squatter families who were supported by a pressure group. Even after the provision of funds, the school building could not be constructed for eleven years. All this happened in the name of human consideration. No one cared to assess the suffering to which thousands of poor innocent children were subjected. They had to run the risk of crossing the busy highways. They had to face the cold biting winds of Delhi winter. In the summer season, an incredibly hot tent was their only protection from the scorching sun. During the monsoons, a wet sticking site was often the base of their class rooms. All this had happened for eleven long years. How many children fell sick, or even died? Who cared to assess? What matters was the political considerations, the voting-disposition of the squatters. This was the true face of 'practicing humanism'- pseudo, superficial, shallow and in fact, inhumanism in the name of humanism. It did not bother if education of thousands of little children was adversely affected, or their health and intellectual capacity was irreparably lacerated. To the human eye of vested interests all this was invisible.

I would cite another case to show how on account of continued squatting our poor country had incurred heavy costs, beside suffering environmental degradation.

Construction of Under-bridge, "M" Avenue, Chanakyapuri, was considered absolutely necessary to meet the increasing demand of traffic between South Delhi colonies and New Delhi areas. The work was held up for five years. By the time the squatters were cleared in 1976 and resettled in the resettlement colony of Dakshinpuri, the cost of the project had increased three-fold. And it was not only the cost but also the additional burden on the rolling stock, additional consumption of petrol

> and diesel, additional time and energy in commuting longer distances that mattered. Could a poor country afford wastage of resources in this matter? After the bridge has been constructed and squatters cleared and resettled at proper sites, not only uncertainly of the squatters had ended but also a vital traffic link established, providing convenience to thousands of commuters and saving their time and energy in reaching their destinations.

No one contested any of the sworn facts, or denied the existence of any document or data cited, or the numerous benefits, including in terms of money saved and environment improved, that accrued to the city in general and slum dwellers and squatters in particular. Nor could any witness be produced to rebut that the policies and procedure had a number of precedent in the pre-Emergency period and had the approval of the Union government and Parliament.

But who was interested in truth or justice or fair discussion on the facts presented? The Shah Commission and the politico-bureaucrat caucus of the Home Ministry had been working at tandem to design a frame-up, to hide material evidence, line up false and tutored witnesses and create an intimidating atmosphere in which no one would dare to loosen any nut or bolt of the frame-up. In support of this assertion of mine, it may be best to let the relevant paras of the aforesaid affidavit speak for themselves.

The bewildering predicament in which conscientious officers found themselves was personified by Ranbir Singh, an executive officer of the DDA, who, when unjustly harassed by Justice J.C. Shah, reacted on April 1978, in sheer disgust, on the lines the gist of which was as follows:

> I was a revenue officer from Haryana on deputation to the DDA. Due to hostile attitude of Bansi Lal, the then Chief Minister of Haryana, I was forced to resign. For the purpose of pension, I lost 19 years of service. Now, I am being victimized merely because I carried out the approved policy of the government and the DDA in the same manner as was being done before the emergency.

The Fact Finding Committee was totally prejudiced. It intentionally suppressed material facts. Why did it pick up either the Vice-Chairman or the executive officers? What about several intermediary officers? Why did the Committee ignore the written records, such as the registers of surveys, allotment slips, the minutes of various meetings, past precedents, demolition duty-rosters, police *roznamcha* reports, etc.?

How can I defend myself against the state apparatus? I had made a request for legal assistance. But the same was refused. On the other hand, both the government and Commission are assisted by highly paid counsels (P. N. Lekhi is getting about Rs.900 per day and Karl Khandawals Rs.1600 per day, besides other remunerations for advice, discussions, etc.). In these circumstances, can there be a fair and just exposition of the entire case? I do not think there is any precedent anywhere where a public servant who has discharged his duties in accordance with the old policies and practices had been put in the dock and subjected to all type of questioning without getting any support from the government or from any other source.

Against the tutored witnesses, who made earlier depositions without caring to show any sanctioned building plan or any written documents in support of their legal ownership, I can hardly do anything. The Commission may send its own officials to see that the structures, which were not vacated voluntarily, are still standing. Only those who were willing to shift by securing alternative allotment actually moved; otherwise how could so many structures be still standing in those very localities. You doubt our version about the voluntarily movement. We know the truth – we who daily meet the people. In those days, conditions were different. Now, if you ask anyone to stand in queue at the bus stand, he will slap you. In those days if you suggested to the unauthorized builder or encroacher to remove his shack or structure by simultaneously offering him an alternative site or structure, he would thank you profusely and avail of facility of free transport for himself and his family.

Ranbir Singh, an officer with a golden heart and full of compassion for the poor and down trodden, said all this with a lump in his throat. The statement was a true expression of a tortured mind. I had myself often wondered whether there was really any other way of tearing the wall of hostility except by striking my head against it.

How intense was Shri J.C. Shah's bias and how intimidating was his fulmination against those officers whose statements or documents did not fit into his pre-conceived notion would be clear from a few typical happenings which I briefly give below.

On 16 December, 1977, Ranbir Singh, Executive Officer, DDA tendered evidence before the Commission in respect of the alleged demolition in Kappashera. When Ranbir Singh tried to defend himself and repeated his assertions, even when such threatening words as "do not try to temporize with what you are saying" were earlier used by Shri J.C. Shah, the latter got exasperated and gave an open hint to Ranbir Singh. He used the following words:

> "I can understand your taking a position that Mr. Jagmohan told you to go and you, as an officer, thought that you have got to carry out the order. That one can understand".

Ranbir Singh had submitted to the Shah Commission that, in village Kappashera, action had been taken by the Municipal Corporation under its building bye-laws, and he had gone to the site to arrange for allotment of alternative plots, as per usual practice. He further submitted all the 'demolition slips' had been signed by the Corporation Staff, Shri J.C. Shah countered by observing that one of the slips had been signed by Ranbir Singh. Shockingly, Shri J.C. Shah did not refer to as significant words as these: "As per orders of the Zonal Assistant Commissioner, Rural, Municipal Corporation". What could be more clear than the following note dated September 18, 1975 of Shri P.N. Vinayak, Zonal Assistant Engineer, Municipal Corporation, on demolition duty roster:

> "As per orders of the Zonal Assistant Engineer (Rural), demolition action of about 34 small shops and factories etc. were taken along with the DDA staff (E.O.(d)) at Kappashera, Mor and Gurgaon road".

In view of this note recorded on September 18, 1975, could there be any doubt under whose orders work was carried out? Yet, Shri J.C. Shah tried to find an escape route for the Corporation officials and to shift the blame to the DDA officers who, unlike Corporation officials, were not toeing the Commission's line and helping it to weave a pre-conceived pattern.

I learnt in the last week of November, 1977 or thereabout, Shri J.C. Shah himself visited village Kappashera and Samalka, and obtained complaints from the villagers. Soon thereafter, the CBI officials attached to the Shah Commission went to the village complex of Samalka-Kappashera and brought the complainant-cum-witnesses to the office of the Shah Commission, and recorded their tutored or manipulated statements on the same day, viz. 9 December, 1977.

On 16 December, 1977, Sat Prakash, another Executive Officer, DDA, was also examined. When he stated that no 'stay order' was shown to him at all and thus defended the position of the DDA, Shri J.C. Shah threatened him in the following words:

> "Well, if it is found that this is true, it is a serious contempt of court for which the penalty may be serious for you."

Again, when Sat Prakash stated that no other officers of the DDA were present, J.C. Shah again threatened him in the following words:

> "I take a very serious view of things like this and if it is found that it is true, people who have been responsible for this sort of behavior would come to grief".

At another place, Shri J.C. Shah again remarked:

> "It (court) must take serious notice of action of this nature by the officers of the DDA who ought to know how they are to behave."

On 16.12.1977, Mrs. Agya Rajinder Kaur was suddenly called to the Commission, when a tutored witness, S.P. Gupta, alleged that on 23$^{rd}$ September, 1975, Kaur had threatened him in the Delhi High Court with the arrest under MISA if he (S.P. Gupta) did not withdraw the stay order. Actually, there was no stay order and this was evident from the copy of the High Court order sheet. Nor was Mrs. Agya Rajinder Kaur concerned with the alleged demolition. When she appeared before the Commission, she denied the allegations. As she started saying that she could not be in the High Court on the alleged date, being on leave, Shri J.C. Shah was furious and threatened her.

On April 7, 1978, Shri Mahabir Singh Gola came to give evidence to support Singh's contention that certain groups of individuals had agreed to shift from their haphazardly and insubstantially built unauthorized structures in low lying area to the nearby newly developed colony of Jehangirpuri. Gola wanted to produce a register which contained a resolution of the area Panchayat in favour of shifting *en bloc*. The moment Shri J.C. Shah noticed the register, he realized that such pieces of evidence of the persons, alleged to have been 'bulldozed', would not at all fit into his pre-determined conclusions. Hardly had Gola uttered a word in support of Ranbir Singh's version **that** Shri J.C. Shah interrupted him. He first held veiled threats, then open ones. He virtually had the register snatched from witness's hand. When the witness tried to stick to his stand in his own rustic and simple language, Shri J.C. Shah threatened him with prosecution. By that time, the witness had lost his balance, and had become somewhat incoherent. Shri J.C. Shah did not stop at that. He shouted for Ranbir Singh from the audience. He asked Gola to vacate the witness chair and threatened Ranbir Singh with prosecution for 'arranging' such witnesses. The few conscientious people were aghast, but the arranged audience laughed and jeered. Why could not Shri J.C. Shah, instead of shouting at the innocent witnesses and repeatedly intimidating them with prosecution and 'serious consequences', ask any local engineer of the Municipal Corporation' or the Delhi Administration to report about the level from where the squatter and slum dwellers were keen to shift and get relocated in the newly developed resettlement colony of Jehangirpuri?

In connection with the general matters pertaining to 'demolition'/ 'clearance', it was brought to the notice of Shri J.C. Shah, both in writing and orally, that there were instructions of the Lt. Governor as well as of the Central Government to the effect that the Central Demolition Squad, attached to the DDA, could be availed of by other agencies, and there was no need to duplicate arrangements in this regard. When, in connection with the Kappashera case, it was pointed out that the Delhi Municipal Corporation officers had obtained the services of the DDA Demolition Squad and a letter to this effect had been written by one O.P. Gupta of the Municipal Corporation, Shri Shah wanted to see the file. On the following day when the file was brought and an attempt was made to show him the letter in the presence of the public, Shri J.C. Shah made disparaging remarks, and without even going into detail, threatened and harassed the person who had brought the file. It was evident from the records that the letter was genuine and had all the entries for receipt and dispatched existed. Yet so inclined was Shri Shah to harass and brow-beat those who wanted to state the truth, supported by contemporaneous records, that he went on passing all types of disparaging remarks and defaming and demoralizing them.

One of the mechanisms that the scheming mind of the politico-bureaucrat caucus of the Home Ministry had devised was to set up a committee of two hand-picked officers. It was, ironically named as 'Fact Finding Committee', though its sinister but hidden agenda was to subvert facts and bypass written records by obtaining tailor-made oral statements from officers by building an intimidatory atmosphere around them. What was still more diabolical, the two-member committee was to be headed by R.C. Jain whose animus against me had a long backdrop, especially after his nefarious and manipulative role in the VIP Land Grab Scandal got exposed in the Supreme Court and also in Parliament.

As indicated in the opening part* of this chapter, R.C. Jain who was known to Lt. Governor Baleshwar Prasad, took over as Special Assistant in early 1972. Both of them had developed weakness for residential plots. They did not show respect for the superior claims

*Paras 6 and 7 and footnote may be seen.

of others, in accordance with the fair and settled principles of allotment. When I tried to explain the correct position, Jain poisoned the mind of Baleshwar Prasad. He was given the impression that I was a stumbling block. Since I could not be got rid of, my appointment being in the hands of the Cabinet Committee, Jain thought of a device to cut me off. He got appointed his close friend and batch-mate. V. Shankaran, as Commissioner in the Delhi Development Authority, and started dealing with him directly eliminating me in the process.

My relationship with Jain was further embittered by the aforesaid VIP Land Grab Scandal which came before the Supreme Court in Writ Petition No. 340, 1972 (original jurisdiction). The crux of this Scandal was that, in an unholy collaboration with certain members of the nominated Managing Committee of the New Friends Cooperative Housing Society, Lieutenant Governor Baleshwar Prasad and his Special Assistant, R.C. Jain, removed some old members/ allottees of the plots from membership of the society and got themselves enrolled through their close relations as members and allottees in the vacancies. The allottees included Baleshwar Prasad's nephew, S.V. Purushottam, whose address was given care of K.K. Shrivastava, Chief Secretary, Delhi Administration, and R.C. Jain's wife, Mrs. Mohini Jain, whose address was not given care of her husband but as Benaras Art House. There was an obvious attempt to hide their own identity.

Everything was done in what the Supreme Court described, in its order of April 4, 1975, as "undue haste". The Chief Justice observed: "Undue haste in rushing through the allotment procedure and the list of new allottees speak for themselves." A letter was obtained from the President of the nominated Managing Committee of the Society on 26 January 1974 (Republic Day) and replied on the same day by the Lieutenant Governor, giving approval to the deletion of the old members and enrolment of the new ones (VIP), including his nephew and Mrs. R.C. Jain.

Jain knew that I would never be a party to such an act. So he maneuvered to keep me out. Apparently, he persuaded the

Lieutenant Governor not to show the case or file to me. He also knew that it would be difficult for the Lieutenant Governor to overrule me on the file.

To look into the manipulation and deletion of old members and enrolment of new ones, the Supreme Court appointed Justice Debabrata Mukerjee, a retired judge of the Calcutta High Court, as Chairman. Mukerjee held that the deletion of the old members and enrolment of new ones was illegal. The findings of Mukerjee were confirmed[17] by the Supreme Court.

Parliamentary proceedings for the period April-May 1974 were also revealing. Chandra Shekhar, A.B. Vajpayee and other senior members of Parliament vehemently criticised the enrolment of the VIP members. Jyotirmoy Basu, M.P., disclosed that R.C. Jain had met senior officers and VIPs and obtained their signatures on the application forms for membership of the society and allotment of land. H.N. Mukerjee described R.C. Jain and his unholy coterie as 'miserable criminals' and their act as ' black guardedly' operation.

The manner in which R.C. Jain conducted the affairs of the 'Fact Finding Committee'[18] was in line with his record of manipulation in the VIP Land Grab scandal. An impression was created in a subtle way that the officers of the Central Bureau of Investigation had been put on the track of DDA officials. The attempt was to overawe the junior officers, create a fear psychosis and obtain incriminating statement against me. They were made to believe that slums and squatters clearance was some sort of a criminal action from which they could escape by blaming me for decisions as well as for implementation.

It was on the basis of cooked-up oral evidence and suppression of practically all material documents that the 'case-summaries' were

---

[17] S.C. Judgement in three Writ Petitions No.340 of 1972; 1526 of 1972; and 286 of 1974.

[18] On 25th May 1977, the Union Home Ministry issued a notification appointing a 'Fact Finding Committee' to collect facts about "the programmes for slum clearance , removal of encroachments, demolition, beautification, etc." It comprised two members – R.C. Jain and D.K. Aggarwal. The appointment of R.C. Jain, who was to act as the senior member of the Committee, was another malafides act of the Home Ministry caucus.

prepared by R.C. Jain's Committee and lapped up by the Shah Commission whose overflowing bias has already been brought home by giving several specific examples. Here, in a different context, I give, as examples, brief particulars of the cases which show how scheming could R.C. Jain be in creating false evidence and how some other sordid acts of the drama were being played in Shah Commission's office.

After the statement of R.M. Vats, the then Commissioner, DDA, had been formally recorded by the Fact Finding Committee, he was lured to make an off-the-cuff remark over a cup of tea. He is supposed to have said that at my instance, he went to the Prime Minister's house during the period of my visit to Vancouver (Canada) to attend the United Nations Conference on HABITAT in May 1976. Words were put in his mouth to say that he saw me, Tamta, Bhinder, Ailawadi and others visiting the Prime Minister's house regularly, and that I had instructed him to take the files and papers to discuss the cases in the Prime Minister's house. Casual remarks, supposedly made, were reduced to writing subsequently by Jain and sent to Vats in the form of a letter for confirmation. Vats was in a fix. If he denied, he would incur the displeasure of Jain and his links or associates in the power structure; if he did not, he would feel the prick of conscience and would also have to explain which files and records he had taken to the Prime Minister's house. He chose the middle path. He denied the material portion but remained silent over my suggestion to visit the Prime Minister's house, in my absence, to attend to the visitors who came there practically every morning in connection with representations and grievances concerning various departments, including the DDA. The incident is significant not for what Vats said or did not say, but for the manner in which incriminating statements were sought to be obtained and witnesses later on confronted with such statements before the Commission.

S.C. Dixit, Deputy Commissioner, had experience similar to Vats'. My successor advised Dixit to coordinate the correspondence of various branches of the DDA with the Fact Finding Committee. Dixit had nothing to do with the clearance of Turkman Gate area or any other clearance. One day, he was asked by Jain to discuss the progress of the correspondence. After discussion, Jain vaguely spoke about the Turkman Gate incident. Being not conversant with the background and facts of the case, Dixit gave a casual reply. To his great surprise, Dixit, after a day or so, received a letter from Jain, stating that during our discussions you informed the Committee that force was used in demolishing houses and that this information was being placed on record. A bewildered Dixit had no other option but to reply that he was not concerned with the Turkman Gate case and was, therefore, not in a position to say whether force was used or not. What happened subsequently need not be discussed here. My purpose is only to indicate how certain statements were sought to be extracted and placed on record.

R.C. Jain returned the notes and letters, sent by some branches of the DDA, which explained the correct position. Instead, he confined himself to the oral statements, extracted from junior officers in a closed room. It did not matter to him if such oral statements were at variance with the written records or minutes of the meeting. For instance, a junior officer was made to say that there were elements of surprise in the organisation of clearance operations, though the written records would show that survey of squatters was generally conducted before-hand and the squatters' families given clearance/ allotment slips in advance. Hardly anyone complained about the element of surprise. Moreover, after June 1976, all decisions in respect of clearance were taken by a Coordination Committee comprising senior officers of various departments and organizations, specially set up for the purpose. How could there be any element of surprise when clearance operations were being carried out practically every day, and the operation in a particular area was usually spread over a number of days.

Jain also conveniently forgot that the procedures followed in regard to the clearance and resettlement of squatters were the same as in vogue during the period Jain himself had been working as Special Assistant to the Lieutenant Governor. If there was anything legally or administratively wrong in the procedure, why did he not get it corrected? It is ironical that those officers, who had themselves been party to certain procedures and practices, are today, without any compunction of conscience, denouncing them as something illegal and irregular, deserving punishment.

The atmosphere in the Commission's office was anything but solemn. Nor was it conducive to dispassionate search for truth and justice. Some story-weavers, such as Inder Mohan and Siraj, were invariably there with their tutored witnesses. They were also accompanied by a few other chips of the same block. Their pre-arranged task was to sneer, jeer and overawe me. What pained me most was that this sordid act was being staged with the connivance of the Home Ministry's politico-bureaucrat caucus which was hardly distinguishable from officers managing the Commission's office. Much as I wished to believe to the contrary, Justice Shah seemed to have totally surrendered his judicial acumen and experience to the whipped up hysteria of the time, which was rendered all the more intense by the personality-oriented biases.

"He lies like an eye witness", says a Russian proverb. Mrs. Anaro, a false witness, started blurting out her tutored version, forgot to say something about which she had been told. Someone shouted from the audience – Jagmohan's story! Then, the needle went on the "tutored groove of the gramophone" and she spoke in one breath. She said, "while our houses were being pulled down, Sanjay and Jagmohan were drinking at the site." No one asked her where and when this happened, and what time and date was it. No one questioned her about my identification, particularly when she repeatedly spoke about my non-existent office in Jhandewallan and her supposed meeting with me in that office. Thousands of my friends and acquaintances and a large section of Delhi population know that I have not touched any intoxicant all my life. Yet, the bizarre, totally concocted story of Mrs. Anaro, was broadcast with all salt and spice, from the national hook-up of the All India Radio. What does this show? Regard for truth and justice? Or respect for judicial norms and values? Or resort to villainous trapping of innocence? Or heartless butchery of rectitude?

What happened on 23 December 1977 at about 4 P.M., when Kayam-u-din tendered his evidence, was equally revealing. After Kayam-u-din said something which P.N. Lekhi, government counsel, 'assisting' the Commission, did not expect him to say, the latter gesticulated nervously to the operator of the tape-recorder and the loudspeaker and the tone of the instruments was lowered (if not switched off temporarily). Thereafter, Lekhi went to the dais of the witness and whispered something to Kayam-u-din who replied rather loudly: "I am not one of those whom you tutor, 'rehearse' and bring as witness." Then, it was the turn of "social worker", Siraj Piracha to go to the chair immediately behind the dais of the witness and suggest to Kayam-u-din to send his written statement afterwards. Kayam-u-din shouted back, "I would not give any written statement. All this happened within the hearing and sight of Justice Shah. Any Judge who was not over-possessed by his bias would have immediately hauled up all those who were involved in such clumsy frame ups. But Justice Shah did nothing. His attitude looks all the more astonishing when it is contrasted with fury and fulmination which he displayed against Ranbir Singh, Satya Parkash and Agya Rajinder Kaur who dared to tender record-based evidence which did not fit into his pre-drawn conclusions.

In his over-anxiety to justify his pre-determined findings, Shri J.C. Shah resorted to suppression of material facts on an unimaginable scale and adopted patently illegal procedures which would have embarrassed even the judges of the Court of the Star Chamber of medieval times. Without passing any written order, he would make one insulting observation or the other, whenever his attention was drawn to certain irrefutable facts. I give below particulars of the statements/events/cases which show that, with regard to Squatters' and Slum Clearance and Resettlement Work, all concerned institutions, all relevant agencies were fully in the picture, and nothing was done at the 'whims and fancies' of any individual.

i) While intervening in the debate on the motion of the President for his address, Prime-Minister Indira Gandhi made a statement in the Rajya Sabha on January 8, 1976, underscoring once again that the programme of clearance of slums and squatters was one of resettlement and not of demolition.

ii) Later on, as reported in the *Hindustan Times* of July 19, 1976, Prime Minister herself made a surprise visit to resettlement colonies of Khichripuri, Mangalpuri and Trilokpuri and made personal inquiries about their new conditions of living. She planted few trees in the green areas, earmarked for parks in Trilokpuri Resettlement Colony.

iii) At a party forum, Mrs. Indira Gandhi did some plain speaking to her senior colleagues. Addressing the All India Congress Committee on May 30, 1976, she bluntly told them that they had in the past not cooperated with the authorities and obstructed the government projects of slums and squatters clearance etc. on one pretext or the other such as 'election time, monsoon, hot or cold weather'. She berated their attitude as anti-national.

iv) On August 28, 1976 the Parliamentary Consultative Committee for the Ministry of Works and Housing took up for discussion the programme and pattern of clearance and resettlement of squatters and slum dwellers in Delhi. As reported by the *Times of India*, the Minister of State, H.K.L. Bhagat, providing the Committee all relevant data, had said: "About 1,25,000 squatters' families have been allotted plots, and so far 400 km of roads constructed and facilities of water supply, drainage and street lighting etc. made available." Again, at the time of laying foundation stones for 30 posts offices in the resettlement colonies, H.K.L Bhagat lauded the entire work as outstanding. According to the report of the *Hindustan Times* of November 25, 1976, he had underscored that resettlement of seven lakh squatters and slum dwellers, in a few months was a great feat and could spur other metropolitan authorities to accelerate planning and implementation of their projects.

v) On May 14, 1976, the Chief Executive Councilor of Delhi Administration, at the time of presenting Budget of the Delhi

Development Authority for the year 1976-77, said that the DDA had emerged as the biggest resettlement and development Agency in Asia and that, in order to decongest the Walled City, it had resettled 1000 squatters in occupation of steps of Jama Masjid and also 460 junk dealers of Motia Khan, 700 motor parts dealers of Kashmere Gate, 320 wood merchants of Desh Bandhu Gupta Road, and 900 fruit and vegetable merchants of Subzimandi.

vi) The Planning Commission recognized the financial and environmental benefits of public lands, being cleared and squatters being resettled at one go. After having discussions with Chief Executive Councilor, both P.N. Haksar, Deputy Chairman of the Planning Commission, and I.K. Gujral, Minister of State for Planning, agreed to make available, through the Ministry of Works and Housing, larger funds for the overall scheme of clearance cum resettlement cum redevelopment.

vii) Quite a few sites were taken up for clearance and resettlements on the genuine and pressing demands of educational institutions and patrons of architectural and historical legacy of the country. This is what Dr. Mulk Raj Anand, art-critic and literary writer of international fame, wrote to me on September 12, 1975 about the Hauz Khas monument: "I feel ashamed to think that when other nations have built their cities, suburbs and villages, all in 25 years, we cannot, because of our democracy, clear even a small slum in one of the most beautiful spots of Delhi, where the DDA has spent so much money. I only hope that you may be able to do something before the end of the year. All our welfare work is waiting for the Community Centre to be free of pollution, mosquitoes, and germs."

viii) In similar desperation, Khurshid Alam, Member of Parliament, and son-in-law of the founder of Jamia Millia, and former President of India, reminded me about our joint inspection of the Jamia Millia complex and recalled: "You

> agreed that unauthorized construction of residential houses in the campus adjoining the main building of the institution was most undesirable and immediate steps were required to be taken to remove the unauthorized construction. I have been receiving repeated reminders from the Vice Chancellor, Jamia Millia, about this matter as they feel very strongly about it and naturally they are very apprehensive that slum conditions will prevail all over the campus if immediate steps are not taken to remove the unauthorized construction. I would, therefore, request you to please initiate immediate action in this regard."

When, as detailed above, Prime Minister Indira Gandhi had explained to Parliament the core object of the scheme, viz. resettlement; when she herself had made several visits to a number of resettlement colonies; when the Consultative Committee of Parliament had discussed the matter threadbare; when the Union Ministers held various functions at sites; when the Delhi Administration and Metropolitan Council warmly applauded the scheme; when the Planning Commission agreed to provide larger funds; and when eminent public men, such as Khurshid Alam Khan and Dr. Mulk Raj Anand, demanded immediate action to save the educational institutions and historical monuments from squatters; how could anyone with a modicum of regard for fairness go on propagating that everything, including matters pertaining to lands, housing, slums and squatters, was being done arbitrarily at the dictates of single individual who was not accountable to anyone.

In the capital, the Prime-Minister's residential office had always been active, especially during Indira Gandhi's regime. The local groups of farmers, traders, industrial labourers or their representatives had an easy access to what came to be known as, Indira Gandhi 'morning darbar' (PM's Public Hearing). Her instructions, if any, on their grievances or demands used to be conveyed to the local functionaries by her personal staff at the residence, such as R.K. Dhawan and Fotedar. After the declaration of Emergency, Sanjay Gandhi's role in PM residential office became far more pronounced than before. Prime Minister's messages, instructions or suggestions, indicated through Sanjay Gandhi, were no different from these communications through Dhawan. So far as my Department or Authority was concerned, nothing, as brought out in this and earlier chapters of this book, was conveyed or said by Sanjay Gandhi which had no precedent or approval of the pre-Emergency period. In any case, it was Prime Minister's prerogative to make whatever arrangements she considered most appropriate for dealing with public grievances. The pace of our work, undoubtedly, increased manifold. But in principles, procedures and parameters, they remained the same.

As a public-man and youth leader, Sanjay Gandhi made a praiseworthy contribution by ensuring that the political elements did not obstruct, as they used to do before, the process of implementation. And I said so publicly, while reiterating that I had continued to follow the same principles, policies and procedures of clearance, resettlement and redevelopment as were followed by me in the case of much appreciated first project of Nigambodh Ghat in 1967.

It was, in fact, the Shah Commission and the Home Ministry caucus which had crossed all limits of legal subversion. It insisted, despite protests, on splitting the Inquiry into two stages – a method which no other Inquiry Commission had adopted and which was subsequently declared illegal and unconstitutional by the Delhi High Court. At the first stage, the witness, even when he made a concocted and rehearsed statement, contrary to documents on the records, could not be cross-examined. His untested statement, with all its false, fabricated and defamatory contents, was given wide publicity in the national media. In this unworthy venture of image-smearing, the Home Ministry caucus played a major role.

To me, it was quite clear that Shri J.C. Shah was committing a grave illegality and virtually abetting the offence of defamation. But I had no means to fight the issue by challenging it in a writ-petition, I had no legal counsel. Nor had I the financial resources to engage one. In any case, I had never imagined that there could be one-man

Commission who would stubbornly close his eyes to plethora of documents, including records of Parliament. Hit by the hot and dusty winds from all sides, I made a valiant attempt to suffer through the crisis and leave it to the future historians to explore whether the near fatal infection emanating from the inner rot of the Indian society and the state had not made Shri J.C. Shah morally sick and hysterical, and also incapable of distinguishing city's ravagers from its protectors and planners. His undisguised glee in picking up the wrong end of the stick, his injudicious insistence in deviating from a legal and well-established procedure, and instead adopting a procedure and publicity campaign that had the effect of undermining my reputation were all morally untenable acts. They were also found to be wholly illegal and unconstitutional by the Delhi High Court in its Judgement of December 19, 1979[19], as would be enunciated hereinafter.

The development in this regard occurred on a separate plane, but the issue of Shri J.C. Shah's mental attitude was the same.

On November 21, 1977, Mrs. Indira Gandhi sent a written statement to the Commission in which she, *inter alia*, protested:

> The rehearsed statements before the Hon'ble Commission, reinforced by leading questions from the Hon'ble Commission and at times uninhibited expressions of conclusions, have been broadcast by the press, the radio and the television. Every person who has appeared before the Hon'ble Commission has been free to make reckless statements with impunity without fear of cross-examination by the concerned parties. There has been grueling and long drawn cross-examination by the Hob'ble Commission itself. Can there be any semblance of a judicial atmosphere when the proceedings are continuously punctuated with cheers or jeers, sarcastic remarks and thinly veiled insults to witnesses? That this should not only be permitted but also be

[19]Smt. Indira Gandhi and Another Vs J.C. Shah Commission of Inquiry: Cr. M (M) 539/78 & Cr.(M) 540/78. Absence of dispassionate objectivity on the part of one-man Commission has been analysed in detail in the subsequent portion of this chapter.

> given wide and repeated publicity clearly demonstrates the political motivation behind the appointment of the Hon'ble Commission. The entire proceedings, accompanied as they have been with loud blare of publicity, in disregard of the procedure contemplated by the Constitution and prescribed by law and in violation of the principles of natural justice, have caused irretrievable damage to me. They have turned the bar of the Hon'ble Commission into a legal platform for malicious political propaganda and have assumed the character of a trial by the press. At the same time, the relevant official records, which would have become public if the evidence of the Central Government had been recorded first, and would have helped present a balanced picture of the various events to the people, have not been disclosed.
>
> It was also strongly urged that the Commission was precluded from prescribing any procedure of its choice. The procedure prescribed under the Commission of Inquiry Act was the only procedure which was in consonance with the provisions of Article 21 of the Constitution, and it had been followed by all earlier commissions of great repute and standing, including the Das Commission, Khanna Commission, Takru Commission, Sarkaria Commission and Mathew Commission.

Similar was the lines on which Pranab Mukherjee, Minister of State in the Department of Revenue and Banking, articulated his grievance against the wholly untenable 'procedure of two-stage inquiry' and denial of right of cross-examination at the first stage. He said:

> I confess, I do not understand how it is possible in practice to segregate those two questions. By the very nature of things, the evidence which points to the commission of an excess will, also, tend to indicate 'who is responsible' for it. An offence and an offender must necessarily co-exist. One without the other is inconceivable. Thus, the so called two questions are inseparable.

Earlier, when I attempted to draw attention of the Commission to the Central government's decisions and Parliament's approval of the pre-Emergency days, and also of the procedures and practices then in vogue, Justice J.C. Shah showed his irritation in no uncertain words, remarking: "We have no time to hear Krishna Menon's type of speeches". I was shocked and bewildered. Justice J.C. Shah had all the time to hear the stories of Mrs. Anaro and the like, which had concoctions writ large on their faces. But he had no time to see any document or record which would conclusively prove that all plans, policies and procedures were the same during the Emergency period as they were during the pre-Emergency days.

Nothing but Justice J.C. Shah's deeply entrenched bias, and the influence which the Home Ministry's politico-bureaucrat caucus exercised over him, could explain his attitude. As observed by the Delhi High Court in the judgement, cited above, even while Emergency was on, Justice Shah had denounced it in a printed article and also at a public meeting presided over by him. The High Court had also noted that the Chairman of Inquiry Commission did not refute the allegations of Mrs. Indira Gandhi that he held parleys with the Union Home Minister and had become a virtual adjunct of the Home Ministry which was following a scheme of calculated political denigration and character assassination under the guise of a judicial inquiry.

The historic importance of the Judgement of the Delhi High Court, referred above, lies not only in quashing the proceedings against Mrs. Indira Gandhi but also in thoroughly exposing the absence of bonafides on the part of the Shah Commission. It was delivered by Justice T.P.S. Chawla* on December 19, 1979. The judgement is replete with observations and conclusions which show that the Shah Commission is not entitled to credence even with regard to key issues of both facts and law, having been virtually swept of its feet by his inner biases and outer glare of publicity and power. Here are some of the instances.

---

*Justice T.P.S. Chawla was well-known for his legal acumen and scholarship. He retired as Chief Justice of Delhi High Court.

In regard to the transcripts of the tapes, the High Court has pointed out: The transcripts have, of course, been signed by the Chairman, Shri J.C. Shah; but their accuracy leaves much to be desired (p.582). Who could have injected inaccuracy in these transcripts? The answer may be found in between the lines of the following observations of Justice T.P.S. Chawla:*

> I made many requests to counsel for the Union to have the accuracy of the transcripts checked with the tapes. At one stage, I was told that steps were being taken in that direction. But, ultimately, I was informed that, for some reason or other, it was not possible for the officers of the Union to correct the transcript or certify its accuracy(p.582).

About the participation of the Government counsel, P.N. Lekhi, the High Court has said: "The statement of the Chairman that he has 'not allowed counsel for themselves to participate in the proceedings' does not concord with his description of what has been happening." (p.596). Referring to the arguments given by Shri J.C. Shah in support of his first stage of Inquiry, the High Court has underlined: "It causes the statements of the Chairman, in his various earlier orders, that he was unable to discern 'who is responsible for the commission of the excess', to become incredible." In respect of Article 352, the High Court has remarked: "The Shah Commission is aware of the amendment of article 352 but slurs over it".

"History of liberty is the history of procedural safeguards". And this is what Justice T.P.S. Chawla has said about the procedure followed by the Shah Commission: "It is implicit in the reason given by the Chairman (Shri J.C. Shah) that he knew the procedure adopted by him was irregular. The construction of the rule and the section he himself propounds makes the conclusion inevitable". "The procedure laid down contains internal contradictions, and the Shah Commission also went against regulations which the Commission

---

*The observations, quoted here, from the Delhi High Court Judgement of Justice T.P.S. Chawla, delivered on 20.12.1979, are as reported in the Indian Law Reports (Delhi). In Cr M(M)539/78 Cr M(540)/78.

had itself framed". Every time the Chairman (Shri J.C. Shah) expounds the two stage theory, it breaks down in the process of the statement. The confusion is more than I can unravel".

Deprecating the Shah Commission's procedure of deploying the investigating agencies in 'ferreting out' the subject of inquiry, Justice T.P.S. Chawla has underscored: "In all common law jurisdiction, the law is firmly set against roving inquiries. The Supreme Court has refused to countenance them, and so have the High Courts. Our law does not tolerate them because they are unfair to the individual and capable of working immense injustice."

After discussing the procedure followed by the Commissions of Inquiry, set up in the past, Justice T.P.S. Chawla has pointed out that the Shah Commission is the only Commission which deviated from the legal and established procedure:

> Invariably, the Central Government and the Memorialists have been required to produce their evidence first, whether orally or by affidavit. The respondents, have been called upon to produce their evidence only thereafter. That was the procedure followed by the Das Commission; and, also, by the Khanna Commission. The Takru Commission did the same. Likewise, the Sarkaria Commission. In the Parnell Commission, appointed in 1888, the very first in England, that was the procedure which was followed (p.822).

The judgement has also pointed out that there was a close liaison between the Shah Commission and the Union Government:

> "The Commission relied upon the opinion of the Law Ministry, which it obtained in anticipation of the objection. It adopted the opinion of the Ministry, with all its errors and fallacies. The opinion of the Law Ministry was outrageously wrong. Its superficiality is stunning. The learned men in the Law Ministry looked only at the Official Secrets Act and the Indian Evidence Act. Their eyes never lifted towards the Constitution at all. To them the fundamental principle of collective responsibility, so vital for the existence of the Cabinet system, was unknown.

> Thus, by one indifferent stroke the Law Ministry would have felled the entire Constitutional structure in this country".

Justice T.P.S. Chawla has also noted: "The Chairman, Shri J.C. Shah, does not refute the allegation that he has held 'parleys' with the Home Minister and the Home Secretary and discussed matters relating to the scope of the inquiry" (p.621).

In view of all this and what he terms as 'statutory rules of natural justice', Justice T.P.S. Chawla has firmly ruled: "I have come to the conclusion that the procedure devised by the Shah Commission was contrary to the Commission of Inquiry Act" (p.835). The Chairman J.C. Shah "acted in violation of the Constitution or, at the very least, intimated that he intended so to act. If a person announces that he intends to follow an unconstitutional procedure, it seems to me that his jurisdiction is forfeited. He is no longer acting 'in discharge of the duties imposed or in exercise of the powers conferred; upon him by law. Nor is he exercising 'legal powers'."

Apart from declaring the proceedings of the Shah Commission as null and void, the Delhi High Court's ruling had shown how the Commission and its 'manipulative adjuncts' in the Home Ministry had driven themselves to a blind alley of confusion, contradiction and inconsistencies. Hardly anyone had realized that, enroute, their reckless driving had hit and injured an earnest wanderer in search for an ideal city of Ninth Delhi. His physical injuries would, perhaps, be healed soon and turned into scars. But scars are, after all, scars. They would not vanish so easily from the surface, given the unhealthy state of our democracy at present. The solace, however, was that, with hot and dusty winds losing their fury and with truth, by virtue of its having no tactics, remaining straight and steadfast, the scars, had started withering away faster than even the most optimist observer of the scene could think of, especially in the context of the virtually inexhaustable arsenal of lies built around the slum-clearance-cum-resettlement scheme of Turkman Gate area. To this arsenal, I would take the reader in the next Chapter.

CHAPTER VI

# CLEARANCE OF TURKMAN GATE SLUMS: FACING AN INEXHAUSTIBLE ARSENAL OF LIES

*Politics bereft of principles are the death traps;*
*They kill the soul of a nation.*

— Mahatma Gandhi

*A calculated set of calumnies is like a cluster of oil spots on a clean table which, even when washed, leave ugly traces; the cleaner the table, the more messy and irksome look these traces.*

— Author*

Turkman Gate derives its name from Shah Turkman, a famous saint, who died on February 19, 1240 A.D. His real name was Shames-ul-Arifin. He was also called Hazrat Biyabani, a saint of forests and wilderness, a recluse. His tomb, a white marble grave, is located within a graveyard of Turkman Gate in which there are a number of brick-built graves, presumed to be those of his followers.

The site, where Turkman Gate now stands, was on the bank of River Yamuna in the thirteenth century. This is borne out of the fact that the grave of Queen Razia Sultana (1236-1239), who was buried on the bank of the river, is located near Turkman Gate. In the vicinity, a city was founded by Mubarak Shah, in 1344, in the area lying between the present Ajmere Gate and Turkman Gate. But he died before any construction could be carried out.

In 1638, the Mughal Emperor, Shahjahan, decided to shift his headquarters from Agra and build a new Capital on the banks of the Yamuna. Here, a massive Red Fort, with its mighty walls, gates, towers and battlements, was constructed in about eight years. The

* The quote is from author's newspaper article, published under the title: *Media and Governance.*

Fort was a self-contained imperial township, accommodating about 5,000 persons. In course of time, a city grew around the Red Fort with a protective wall completed during Aurangzeb's time. It had a number of gates. Turkman Gate was one of them.

In the vicinity of Turkman Gate, a riotous mob was fired upon by the police, on April 19, 1976, under the orders of Additional District Magistrate. Six rioters, unfortunately, lost their lives. But none of them was affected by the clearance cum resettlement cum redevelopment work, which had been carried out by the DDA, from April 13 to 27, 1976, in accordance with the scheme sanctioned in the pre-Emergency period, by the then Delhi Improvement Trust, Delhi Municipal Corporation and Central Government. Almost all the rioters came from outside the pocket cleared. Soon after the termination of Emergency, an extremely ugly game was played by a variety of interests around this event to 'fix' the former Prime Minister, Indira Gandhi and her son, Sanjay Gandhi, and also exploit the issue in communal terms.

The event is of pivotal importance for understanding the origin of the tragedies that have been visiting Ninth Delhi from time to time. It shows in ample measure how dirty and diseased are the mental slums of Indian polity, how vicious is the grip of falsehood on the nerve centres of our social system, how a terrible deluge of disinformation and distortion could be brought about by a vengeful caucus and a section of media who specialise in relying more on hearsay and concoctions than on documents and concrete evidence.

## Chequered Backdrop

The case has such a long, chequered and intricate background and so many Goebbels-like lies have been packed into it that, without a documented and detailed narration and analysis, neither truth can be effectively brought home nor its implication for the future well-being of Ninth Delhi understood.

The seven-acre pocket, near Turkman Gate, constituted the worst slum of the Delhi-Ajmere Gate area. An improvement scheme was formulated for it, as early as 1938, vide Delhi Improvement Trust's Resolution No.200 of February 28, 1938 which, *inter alia*, observed:

> The necessity to alleviate slum conditions behind city- wall between the Delhi Gate and Ajmere Gate has burdened the official and public conscience for at least 12 years, but so far without result...The effect of unhealthy conditions of life is demonstrated by the statistics of tuberculosis, infantile mortality and enteric fever...The Trust ought to frame an improvement scheme, in view of the fact that a number of buildings used as dwelling places are unfit for human habitations.

On the basis of this Resolution, an improvement scheme and Land Acquisition Notification were issued and published in the Government of India *Gazette* on March 19, March 26 and April 2, 1938. The sanction of the entire improvement scheme was accorded by the Competent Authority (Chief Commissioner), and published in the government's *Gazette* of May 4, 1946. The pocket of seven acres of land, in question, was thus covered by the Improvement Trust's Resolution, the improvement scheme/Land Acquisition Notification, and the Chief Commissioner's sanction. Subsequently, after coming into force of the Slum Areas (Improvement and Clearance) Act 1956, a notification, dated April 24, 1957, was issued, declaring the entire area of Delhi Ajmere Gate Scheme as slum area. The notification described the areas as "unfit for human habitation and detrimental to safety, healthy, etc."

The private properties were acquired and a number of awards were drawn up in 1948, 1949, 1950, 1951 and 1952. The possession was taken in mid-fifties. The "Nazul"/ government land as well as the lands belonging to erstwhile Delhi Municipal Committee were either purchased by the Delhi Improvement Trust or got transferred for the purpose of execution of the scheme. Some properties in the area, which belonged to the custodian, were obtained by transfer from the Ministry of Rehabilitation in early sixties, on payment of compensation calculated in terms of the provision of the Slum Areas (Improvement and Clearance) Act, 1956.

**Mismanagement by the DIT/DMC and Transfer of Slums-work to the DDA**

In 1960, the slum clearance work was entrusted by the central government to the Delhi Municipal Corporation. From 1960 to February 1974, this work remained with the Corporation. In these fourteen years, the performance of the Corporation was found to be dismal. The Central government noted that a number of schemes had remained unimplemented and hundreds of tenements built with the funds made available for the purpose were either lying vacant or had been unauthorisedly occupied. In April 1976, about 1500 tenements, built with the slum clearance funds, made available by the Central government, were lying vacant, and another 600 had been unauthorisedly occupied, mostly by new squatters. The gross mismanagement of the scheme by the Municipal Corporation was adversely commented upon by the Public Accounts Committee. The wastage of central government funds and aggravation of the problem, consequent to the unauthorized occupation of hundred of tenements by ineligible persons, were also severely criticised by other public authorities.

Following these and similar other critical comments and recommendations made by the Lieutenant Governor, the entire work pertaining to slum clearance was transferred to the Delhi Development Authority in February 1974. Clearly, the objective was to prevent further wastage of public funds and secure speedy implementation of long pending schemes, such as the Turkman Gate Scheme.

About five years before the aforesaid transfer, the Delhi Municipal Corporation revised the scheme and also divided the occupants of the premises in two categories – unauthorised and authorised. The Corporation stipulated, vide its Resolution No.559/C&C, dated July 21, 1969 that unauthorised occupants were not entitled to any alternative accommodation, while the authorised occupants should be allotted flats elsewhere and brought back to the site after redevelopment and reconstruction.

While carrying out the scheme, the above decisions of the Corporation were broadly followed by us. In fact, a comparatively more liberal approach was adopted and alternative plots – both residential and commercial – were allotted even to the unauthorised occupants,[1] including the recent ones, without even charging any damages for the period of unauthorised occupation.

We had no doubt that voluntary and willing shifting would be secured if the following incentives and inducements were given:

(i) Those who continued to occupy the premises even after acquisition or those who had been paying rent or "damages" would be given tenements in Ranjit Nagar near Patel Nagar.

(ii) Those who were rank squatters and were not entitled to any alternative accommodation, according to the resolution of Delhi Municipal Corporation, would be given plots in the trans-Yamuna resettlement colonies of Trilokpuri and Nand Nagri.[2] For the surplus population, such as squatters and unauthorised occupants, an official seminar held in February 1975, on the suggestions contained in my book, *Rebuilding Shahjahanabad: The Walled City of Delhi,* had recommended resettlement in the trans-Yamuna area. These recommendations had been accepted by the Central government.

(iii) Those who wished to take flats built by the DDA under the Low or Middle-Income Group Housing Schemes would be allotted those flats by relaxing the normal conditions of registration and participation in the draw of lots.

---

[1] These concessions were given on compassionate grounds. They were also to serve as inducements to ineligible families for moving to the new areas and thus facilitate total clearance of the slum.

[2] The resettlement colonies of Nand Nagari and Trilokpuri had been developed, across the river, like many other such colonies. They had well-organised lay-outs and basic civic services. New development works, in the trans-Yamuna area offered vast employment opportunities. Distance wise, too, only a bridge had to be crossed from the new residence to the old place of work.

## Clearance After Liberalization of Resettlement Pattern

The clearance work, which commenced on April 13, 1976, proceeded smoothly and peacefully. On April 19, 1976, however, there was a riot in the vicinity, due entirely to the family planning camp in Daujana House locality and incitement by the extra-conservative elements opposed to sterilization on religious grounds.

The District Authorities, under the orders of Magistracy/Police, resorted to firing to control the rioting mob. There were some casualties, the number and other particulars with regard to which have been discussed in a subsequent section of this chapter.[3] We had carried out hundreds of clearance-cum-resettlement operations, both before and during the Emergency, and there was no disturbances anywhere.

The work was carried out slowly and smoothly. It was spread over a long span of time – from April 13, 1976 to April 27, 1976, though the number of premises to be handled was not large.[4] The deployment of the police force was in accordance with the instructions of the Lieutenant Governor, issued in 1967. Similar deployment had been done in practically all clearance works undertaken *before* the Emergency, and even *after* it was lifted.

Bulldozers were used as a labour-saving technique and for clearing the debris speedily and pulling down the vacated buildings from which window and door frames and other salvageable building material had already been taken by the previous squatters and slum-dwellers. This practice, too, had been followed for the last eight years. Free transport was provided to the families effected for carrying their belongings as well as building material.

The work of clearance in Turkman Gate was, moreover, not taken up suddenly. Before this case, six built up pockets, *katras,* involving 642 families, had been subjected to similar treatment, of clearance and resettlement. The detailed particulars of the localities have been given in **Appendix CVI-(i)**.

---

[3]From these particulars, it may be noted by the reader that none of the casualty was affected by the slum clearance work; the rioters had come from outside.

[4] The number of premises involved was 120.

In essence, Turkman Gate was a simple slum clearance and resettlement project. The conditions from which the slum dwellers and squatters were relieved were sub-human and their premises were described as "squalid, overcrowded, ill-ventilated and ill-serviced and those that bred deadly diseases of 'tuberculosis and enteric fever'. This description was given by the Delhi Improvement Trust Resolution No.200, passed as far back as February 1938. One could well imagine the horrible conditions that obtained in 1976, when the clearance was done. The reactions of Jawaharlal Nehru and Marshal Clinnard, during their separate visits to this area in mid-1950, have already been mentioned in earlier chapters. It was the inexcusable inefficiency and callousness of the two main organizations, the Delhi Improvement Trust and the Delhi Municipal Corporation, which were dealing with the Scheme from 1938 to 1974, coupled with the narrow and nihilist politics of slums, that had added to the problems and made our task of implementation extremely difficult.

As briefly indicated earlier, all categories of squatters and slum-dwellers received alternative allotments and were most liberally treated. Those who had any semblance of legitimacy, that is, the occupants whose 'premises' had been acquired by the Improvement Trust, after paying due compensation, but who had continued to stay, were given tenements in Ranjit Nagar, near Patel Nagar. In terms of land values, conditions of living, healthy environment, employment opportunities and potential for brighter future, nothing could be more beneficial than these allotments. Close to Ranjit Nagar, new residential, industrial and trading complexes, such as Naraina, Mayapuri and Iron Merchants-Kabari markets, had been developed by the DDA. About 1000 units had started functioning, and more were coming up at a fast pace. A number of avenues were open for securing gainful employment and also for learning modern manufacturing and trading skills. The monthly rent, or installment for acquiring ownership, was low, only Rs.22. Thus, this resettlement was a great boon to the erstwhile slum-dwellers, a highly rewarding journey to a new life of progress and prosperity.

Even rank squatters who, according to the resolution/decision of the Delhi Municipal Corporation, quoted earlier, had to be summarily evicted, were given alternative[5] plots in the Resettlement Colonies, across river Yamuna, which were fast growing in popularity and where about 18000 families, covering a population of about one lakh, had already been settled. In addition to residential plots, small commercial plots were allotted to these squatters who were earlier running petty shops within their living spaces or by encroaching upon the pathways. All damages for the period of unauthorised occupation were also waived. Never before had so many concessions been offered to ineligible category of squatters. It was natural for all of them to accept the offer and move to the resettlement colony of their choice.

In view of the better living conditions that all categories of slum-dwellers of the 'cleared' pocket, secured under our programme of clearance cum resettlement, a number of occupants of other such pockets petitioned[6] to the Central government and DDA, *even after the Emergency was over,* to shift them. This is what, for example, residents of Katra Daulat Ram in Turkman Gate complex wrote on August 1, 1977 to the authorities concerned:

> Presently, we are living in a deplorable and scornful position due to unhealthy atmosphere. There is suffocation and congestion due to large population. It is a tiny hell on the earth. There is foul smell in the atmosphere. Mosquitoes breed their eggs on the heaps of the dirt which spread malaria fever and other chronic diseases. Many persons have been suffering from T.B., asthma and other diseases.
>
> Houses have been constructed in disorderly manner, with *kacha* sand and weak materials. There is no ventilator, windows and exhaust for throwing bad smell out of the house. No human

[5] This allotment pattern was designed to serve as additional incentive to secure early implementation of the long pending Slum Clearance project.

[6] While reproducing such petitions/applications, I have retained their language, in original, even when these were somewhat deficient in grammar or choice of words.

> being can live in these houses. The life of these houses is over and may collapse at any time. Most of the houses are in dangerous condition and we fear that they may collapse during the rainy season.
>
> In view of the above noted circumstances, we hope that our DDA and our ruling Government in the hands of Janta Party may consider our grievances on priority basis and arrange immediately to shift us from this hell and get rid of us from the ensuing calamities of the nature.

### *Cause and Context of April 19 Riot*

Coming to the factors and forces that caused the incident of rioting on April 19, 1976, it was quite clear from day one that the Daujana House family planning camp was the sole cause. In this connection, it may be underscored, even at the cost of repetition, that on account of the liberal treatment accorded to the slum dwellers and squatters of all classes and categories, and the confidence generated in them by the speed of development work at the new sites, there was no violence anywhere, either before or after the Turkman Gate incident, though about seven lakh people were resettled.

There is a plethora of contemporaneous documents and other hard evidence which support the above contention of mine. In all the reports of the CID (Special Branch) from 13-14 April to 19-20 April 1976, there was not even the remotest suggestion about any resentment against the demolition/clearance work of the DDA in the Turkman Gate area. On the other hand, the reports, during the said period, were full of warnings about the tension that was being built up due to the sterilisation drive and rumours spread by its opponents.

In the report of April 13-14, 1976, under the heading "Indian Union Muslim League" the following extract had appeared:

> Iqbal Ahmed, Secretary, Delhi Unit of the Muslim League, Shahiruddin Ashrafi and Abdul Khan are reported to have met in the Delhi Muslim League office on 13-4-1976 and decided to instruct selected League workers to spread rumours in areas

of Muslim population, alleging death of certain persons due to sterilisation.

In report No.81/76, dated 14-15 April 1976, under the heading "Jamat-e-Islami" the following paragraph had been recorded:

> Awil Ul Jafar, Mohd. Amin, Mohd. Rafiq, Faras-at Huss Mohd. Ahasan, Mohd. Shafi Monis, Amir Halqa UP and Dr. Nizatullah Siddique (Aligarh) Member Majlis-e-Shoura of JEI met Mohd. Yousuf, Amir JEI, on April 14 in Tis Hazari Courts. During the course of talks, Mohd. Shafi Monis informed the Amir that he had met the Ibrahim Sulaiman Sait, President IUML a week ago, and had requested him to use his good offices for exemption of Muslims from forced sterilisation, as ML was the only party which could take up the Muslims' cause at the present juncture....

In report No. 82/76, dated April 15-16 1976, the following lines had been highlighted:

> Syed Abdullah Bukhari, Imam Jama Masjid, while addressing a Friday congregation (about 3,000) today (April 16) said that the people would soon be asked to keep their mouths absolutely shut. He also alleged that the beggars, physically handicapped persons and pavement vendors, were being subjected to forcible sterilisation.

Again, from report No.83/76, dated April 16-17 1976, the following information had been culled out:

> Ibrahim Sulaiman Sait, President, IUML, visited the Party office Urdu Bazar Jama Masjid on 16-4-76 evening when he was apprised by Iqbal Ahmed, Abdul Ahmed, Suleman Saliq and Shahir-ud-Din Ashrafi of Imam Abdullah Bukhari's Friday speech particularly on the issue of sterilisation of Muslims.

Another extract from the same report under "Indian Union Muslim League" was as follows:

> It has been reliably learnt that Shah-u-Din Ashrafi, an active ML worker, met Ibrahim Sulaiman Sait on April 17, and reportedly suggested that ML workers should court arrests against the Government's campaign for alleged forcible sterilisation.
>
> There was some commotion in Matia Mahal, near Daujana House Family Planning Camp, on April 18, 1976 when some hot words were exchanged between one Idris and his supporters on one side and the protagonist of family planning on the other. Tension mounted in the area when some stones were reportedly thrown on a family planning van.

In report No.85/76, dated April 19-20 1976, the following paragraph appeared under the heading "Muslim Organisations – Muslims Personal Law Board":

> Majlis-e-Amla of Muslim Personal Law Board met at Delhi on April 18, 1976. During discussions, Ibrahim Sulaiman Sait and Yousuf Patel criticised the Government for allegedly resorting to forcible sterilization and said that such action amounted to interference in the religious affairs of Muslims. The MPL Board passed a resolution criticizing "forcible" sterilization as inhuman....

The above reports of the Special Branch of the CID were made in the normal course of work and there was no reason as to why they should be favourable or unfavourable to either of the two organisations of the government – the DDA or the family planning department of the Delhi Administration. The reports made before the incident must be taken as fair, objective and reliable for assessing the cause of riot. Reporting subsequent to the incident of April 19, 1976 could be biased and attempts could be made to deflect the responsibility of those senior functionaries of the Delhi Administration, under whose orders the Daujana House family planning camp was being run, in a particular way, and to shift the blame to the DDA.

The riot first started at the Daujana House camp on the morning of April 19, 1976. This would be clear from the police wireless messages. Hartal was organised, and religious emotions were aroused on the issue of compulsory sterilisation. The daily summary report of the CID for April 19, 1976 had also held that the disturbances on April 19, 1976 were caused by persons from other areas.[7]

Six persons died in the incident and their particulars are as follows:

1. Salaudin s/o Mohd. Din, r/o 1942, Kucha Chelan Delhi.
2. Mohd. Shahid s/o Mohd. Yazin r/o 1674, Suiwalan, Delhi.
3. Mohd. Arif s/o Mohd. Bashir r/o 2393, Kucha Mir Hashim, Delhi.
4. Sagir Ahmed Amir s/o Majid Ahmed r/o 3989, Gali Khane Khan, Jama Masjid, Delhi.
5. Om Parkash Omi s/o Meeru r/o 3870, Khirke Tafazal Hussain, Jama Masjid, Delhi.
6. Abdul Malik s/o Abdul Haq r/o 2406, Turkman Gate, Delhi.

It should be clear that, except for one person who came from Turkman Gate area but whose premises had not been affected by clearance work, all other were outsiders and had come from Suiwalan and Jama Masjid area.

The report of Additional District Magistrate, Ashok Pradhan, made in the evening of April 19, 1976, had also underlined that the family planning drive and incitement by the Imam of Jama Masjid were the main reasons for the riot:

> Earlier, in the morning, Imam Jama Masjid rang up ADM Central Ashok Pradhan and S.H. Naqvi, A.D.M.(s) and alleged that in the family planning camp, being run at Daujana House, forcible sterilisations were being carried out, and that there was

[7]Despite a number of crude efforts made by the Shah Commission's office and the Home Ministry politico-bureaucrat caucus, whose bias against Mrs. Indira Gandhi and a few others of her perceived supporters, had by then become history, could not inflate the figure of casualties or include any person whose premises had been affected by the clearance work.

> a lot of resentment amongst the Muslims of the area against the use of coercive methods. He also threatened to personally lead a group of men and women and offer arrests against the alleged high-handedness in the family planning campaign. The Imam made a speech at about 9.30 A.M. against the family planning in the Jama Masjid area from the P.A. system, installed at the mosque. Shortly thereafter, at about 9.50 A.M., a car carrying a doctor to the family planning camp at Daujana House was stopped in Bazar Matia by some miscreants, the driver was beaten up and the doctor assaulted. The atmosphere became tense and the Bazar was closed down. A number of women, assembled there, made a vain bid to mob the organisers of the camp, shouting slogans. The Imam himself came to the family planning camp at Daujana House at about 10.45 A.M. and tried to incite the crowd, mainly consisting of women.

In his deposition at the "assistant stage"[8] Ashok Pradhan also disclosed the following facts:

> ....the first incident was at Daujana House...Actually, if Imam Sahib had not come to the spot (Daujana House) that day and he had not gone to the Turkman Gate area, the things would not have gone beyond control as it happened later...I told Imam Sahib that I was appealing to him as a man and not as ADM and would request that he should leave the spot (Daujana House) otherwise there will be bloodshed....
>
> But by the time, I could handle the situation at Daujana House itself Imam Sahib had left for Turkman Gate. Imam Sahib was opposed to the (family planning) and in the morning

[8] Since the enactment of the Commission of Inquiry Act in 1952, the Shah Commission was the only one which followed, despite protests, a procedure of splitting the inquiry into two stages. At the first stage, there was no right to cross-examine. As analysed in the later part of this Chapter, it was seen as the most glaring manifestation of Shah Commission bias. The Delhi High Court declared this procedure as illegal. The malafides were seen in the attempt to identify those who would justify their action and tailor oral evidence to concentrate attack on them and defame and denigrade them.

> he had rung me up on the telephone and told me that if they did not stop he would himself lead women folk and court arrest in protest thereof...

This disclosure lent further support to the conclusion that the riot had occurred due to strong resistance to the family planning programme and incitement of Imam Sahib, and not due to the clearance cum resettlement work of the DDA. It was also confirmed by R.K. Ohri, Superintendent of Police, who stated, in his deposition before the Commission, that Saxena, SDPO, had told him that there was resentment against family planning, and not against 'demolition'. K.S. Bajwa, former SP (CID), also stated that there was no intelligence report with him before April 19, 1976, indicating any resentment due to the clearance work in the Turkman Gate area.

So far as the DDA was concerned, the work was going on smoothly and steadily, without any indication of resentment. The strength of the police deployed was not significant. There were only three Sub-Inspectors on April 13, 1976, one Inspector and two Sub-Inspectors on April 14, 1976, one Sub-Inspector and one Inspector on April 15, 1976, one Inspector and one Sub-Inspector on April 16, 1976, one Inspector and two Sub-Inspectors on April 17, 1976. This was obviously not the strength which suggested any likelihood of violence or trouble. The operation, in fact, was so smooth that the necessity of keeping a full contingent of DSP (Demolition Squad) was not felt by the clearance party from April 13 to 19, 1976.

On April 18, 1976, being Sunday, the clearance party of the DDA did not come to the site, but a very small bulldozer continued to work, clearing the debris by the roadside. If the persons affected with the clearance operation had been really angry with the DDA, they could have certainly attacked the unprotected bulldozer which was functioning with a lone driver without the assistance of any member of the clearance party.

On the morning of April 19, 1976, the DDA staff at the site suspended the work after noticing certain developments emanating from Daujana House and Jama Masjid area and of aggressive movement of Imam Sahib around family-planning camp. The aggrieved persons, if any, would have satisfied, had the cause of tension been clearance. But the real cause was different – the emotional reaction to the Daujana House, Family Planning Camp and the speeches made by the leaders of the community to the effect that Islam did not permit sterilisation. Earlier, Lieutenant-Governor Kishan Chand had issued public statements, warning that those who opposed the family planning campaign would be severely dealt with.

It should be quite clear that the Deputy Commissioner, other district officers of the police and magistracy, the Inspector General of Police and the Lieutenant-Governor had full information about the strong resentment that was being built against the family planning drive. And yet no steps were taken to relieve the tension. On the contrary, public warnings were given by the Lieutenant-Governor to the opponents of the family planning on April 10, 1976 and April 15, 1976. While inaugurating the family planning camp at Daujana House on April 15, 1976, Lieutenant Governor warned that the Delhi Administration would not tolerate any opposition to the family planning.

If DDA's action was evoking resistance or there was any resentment because of it, why could not a simple letter or note be sent to me by the Inspector General of Police or any of his staff, the District Magistrate or the Additional District Magistrate, the Chief Secretary or the Home Secretary, Lieutenant Governor or his staff, etc. If anyone had written to the DDA, advising suspension or stoppage of clearance operations, and if the DDA had not acted on the advice or started arguments about it, the blame could be passed on to it. In the long history of its clearance-cum-resettlement drive, not in a single case I had taken action against the advice of the police or magistracy. All sorts of oral statements, unsupported by written communications, even in cases where such communications must be sent, have been made before the so called Fact Finding Committee and Shah Commission, with their explicit or implicit encouragement, to escape responsibilities and unfairly blame others.

After the incident of April 19, 1976, it was the family planning camp at Daujana House that was ordered to be closed by the

Lieutenant Governor and no suspension or termination of clearance work was ordered. Had he thought that the riot was due to slum-clearance work, he would have got it stopped. The authorities were aware of the real cause. Kishan Chand and Mohsin, Deputy Minister (Home), visited the site after April 19 and neither of them ordered or advised stoppage of clearance work.

The clearance work in the pocket of Turkman Gate could not have led to resentment because an unprecedented liberal treatment was accorded by the DDA in matter of allotment of alternative flats and plots. The extent of liberal treatment can be seen from the fact that 28 plots were allotted against premises No. 1920/IX; 22 plots against 3299/VIII; 19 plots against 3271/VIII; 14 plots against 3333/VIII; and 22 against 3375/VIII. The two mosques in the area, which had been badly damaged due to the unauthorised constructions on the walls, by the squatters, were renovated by the DDA. This act was especially appreciated by the Muslim community. It also found a mention in the report of the Special Branch (CID) as an indication of tension-free atmosphere obtaining at the site. Subsequently, an additional piece of land was also leased to one of the mosques for its use.

In so far as the issue of deployment of police is concerned, there were standing instructions of the Delhi Administration/ Lieutenant Governor on the subject. These were issued about *eight years* before the Emergency, vide No.50(6)/67-L&B, dated July 27, 1967. A copy of this order has been given in Appendix CVI-(ii). The position with regard to the communications sent to various authorities has also been elaborated in this Appendix. Clearly, the practice followed in this connection was in vogue in the pre-Emergency days. And it was followed even in the post-Emergency days.

While dealing with the clearance-cum-resettlement-cum-redevelopment projects of Nigambodh Ghat, Purana Quila, Hazrat Nizam-ud-din etc, I have already explained, that the bulldozers were used in such cases as a labour saving device and for speeding up clearance and development work. No new method was adopted in the case of Turkman Gate's pocket. In fact, even after the Emergency, the practice had not changed. In this connection, I quote from the note of the Executive Officer (Demolition), dated May 14, 1977, which he wrote in connection with the clearance operation in Jafrabad area during the Janta Party regime:

> Clearance operation in Jafrabad, where 3,000 to 4,000 *sirkies* had come up recently, was undertaken. Yesterday, two companies of the armed police were also requisitioned. We had arranged about 125 beldars and labourers. Since they refused to cooperate, they were detained by the local police. Most of these *sirkies* were removed by the unauthorised encroachers themselves. In the meantime, about 200-300 women collected around the jail van. The force was collected and brought to the location where 2 companies of the DAP were kept standby by the local police. The unauthorised encroachers indulged in setting fire to their sirkies at about 15-20 locations. This fire was witnessed by ADM(E), DIG(R), SP(E) and all other officers.

There are a number of other cases in which similar procedure has been adopted after April 1977. These cases include demolitions in Motia Khan, Subzimandi and Geeta Colony etc. In the last mentioned colony, a number of persons were also arrested. Shri J.C. Shah and its virtual adjunct, the politico-bureaucrat caucus of the Home Ministry, never paused to think that the excesses, in true sense of the expression, were being committed by the Janta government itself. They were too biased, too supercilious, to note the stark contradictions in their public postures.

Equally stunning was the superficiality of a section of 'eminent' journalists. Their savage disregard for the elementary norms of verifications of even easily ascertainable facts, and slaughter of individual officer's reputation, built over years of hard and honest work, were deplorable acts in themselves. But the manner in which the concocted stories of the self-styled social workers and other vested interests were lapped up and published, with impunity, in their books, made their venture all the more painful. It left a long trail of sciatic behind.

As underscored by me in the earlier chapters, I, being an executive head of a city planning and development body, had no concern whatsoever with any issue which had led to the declaration of Emergency or unwarranted arrests during its period. With regard to the contents of these books, which pertain to the justification or otherwise of the declaration, or its fair or unfair use for overcoming what was seen by the Prime Minister as a grave national crisis, I am in no position to say anything with authority.

But, in so far as the contents relate to "the demolitions of poor men's houses", "rendering thousands of families homeless", I can firmly assert that they are immeasurably false and, in fact, betray an ignorance even of the elementary provisions of Delhi Master Plan, and also of the policies and procedures, which had been sanctioned by the Union Cabinet and Parliament, and which had been in force for over a decade, before the declaration of Emergency. The projects executed were not of demolitions but of clearance cum resettlement cum redevelopment. Not a single family was rendered homeless. All aspects of the matter, including its background, precedents of the pre-Emergency days and numerous social, economic and environmental benefits that accrued to the individuals, the families and the city as a whole, have been brought out in detail, in earlier chapters, citing supporting data, documents and other contemporaneous records. An in-depth study of these chapters would show how unfair could the Indian set-up be to those who are committed to the performance on the ground rather than keeping the plans in the folded files and talk incessantly about them.

**Loose Journalism**

In the circumstances and the manner in which Emergency was declared and operated, one would have expected that the leadership in the intellectual arena would have put in all out efforts to make a new beginning and devote special attention to the problems of loose journalism. About a century ago, the Father of the Nation, had said:

> The sole aim of journalism should be service. The newspaper press is a great power; but just as an unchained torrent of water

submerges the whole country-side and devastates crops, even so an uncontrolled pen serves but to destroy. If the control is from without, it proves more poisonous than want of control. It can be profitable only when exercised from within.

Unfortunately, a sizeable segment of Indian journalist, has remained oblivious of the need to control from within. It has treated its freedom as an end in itself. It has not seen it as a means to the end of creating an organised, peaceful, prosperous and value-based society. By ignoring such an end, journalism in India has not played its much needed part in preventing the country from moving from one crisis to another.

In India which has undergone desertification for hundreds of years and where post-independence leadership has remained indifferent to the need of removing the after-effects of this desertification, the danger of chaos and collapse is real. Here, the house is made of combustible material and can catch fire easily. It was, therefore, all the more incumbent upon the journalist in the post-Emergency period to exercise some control from within and act with care, caution and balance. But exactly the opposite happened. On the very heels of the decision to withdraw Emergency and hold Lok Sabha Elections, a number of them brought out books in which truth about the development of Ninth Delhi was heartlessly butchered, not only by throwing all crucial records to the winds but also by virtually 'outsourcing' their work to exploiters of combustible material.

Without citing any document or giving identifiable particulars, Kuldip Nayyar, in his book, *Judgement*, had asserted that in Turkman Gate incident: "Roughly, 1000 properties were demolished and about 150 people killed". Mark these assertions and set them against the data, documents and other records, particularised under sections (i) *Chequered Backdrop;* (ii) *Transfer of Slum work from Municipal Corporation to the DDA;* and (iii) *Clearance After Liberalisation of Resettlement Pattern of this chapter.* The merciless slaughter of the truth would be self-evident.

And how did Kuldip Nayyar discharge the obligations that his journalist ethics demanded? By not visiting the area, even after the Emergency, where '1000 properties' were brought down and '150 occupants' killed. Had he taken the trouble of travelling a few kilometers from his office / residence, he would have found that all the premises (land and structures) were owned by the DDA and not a single person affected by the clearance had been killed.

The lapses which Uma Vasudev committed in her book, *Two* Faces of *Indira Gandhi*, were of the same class as those of Kuldip Nayyar. She did not make any independent inquiry. She solely relied upon her source, Inder Mohan, who turned out to be a master story weaver and whom, later on, a Delhi Metropolitan Magistrate Court pronounced as unreliable, with a marked disposition not to care about a number of material contradictions his various versions contained. The stories which he told her and which she merely put within inverted comas read like a fictional script of a Hindi movie.

The extent to which the fanciful accounts could be given by Inder Mohan, and used by Uma Vasudev, could be gauged from her reference to Inder Mohan's meeting with me on "September 19, 1975 in my spacious office on the eighteenth floor of Vikas Minar". She did not know that DDA's office shifted to Vikas Minar in July 1976, that is, about nine months after Inder Mohan's alleged meeting with me. Even after shifting to Vikas Minar, my office was on the fifth floor. Clearly, even Inder Mohan's fertile imagination and his expertise in coining allegations could not cross all the barriers of truth.

He also appeared to have misled Uma Vasudev about my Padma Award. She wrote: "Jagmohan's controversial role during the emergency finds an ironical twist in the fact that he was awarded the Padma Shri for his 'significant contribution in the formulation and implementation of the Delhi Master Plan, for playing a pioneering role in the planning and implementation of their development projects, and for breaking new grounds in the matter of slum clearance'." This award was given to me, not in emergency, but on January 26, 1971. In **Appendix CVI-(iii)**, I have given a note which shows how vast and vicious was Inder Mohan's network of lies not only with regard to my actions in securing implementation of Delhi Master Plan but also in respect of my stand to safeguard the country's integrity when I was sent as Governor of Jammu and Kashmir to frustrate the diabolical plan of the ISI of Pakistan to grab the Valley through acts of terror and subversion.

Besides the concocted story of Ranjit Hotel, for which the writer was, later on, convicted by a Delhi Metropolitan Magistrate for defaming me and the details in respect of which have been given in a subsequent portion of this chapter, D.R. Mankekar's book, *The Decline and Fall of Indira Gandhi* contained the same fanciful account of Inder Mohan, which Uma Vasudev had put within inverted comas. The only difference was that Mankekar, by and large, gave the impression that it was his own account. He, too, had not taken the trouble of visiting the site or perusing any documents or contacting me on phone. On the other hand, he resorted to reckless statements in other arenas of city's development as well, exposing both his prejudiced mind and his utter lack of knowledge on the subject. For example, with regard to the acquisition of Munirka land, he had alleged,: "They (the land-owners) were paid compensation at the rate of Re.1 or Rs.1.50 per square yard. The Delhi Development Authority later charged Rs.l00 to Rs.150 for the same land." The facts are that the undeveloped land was acquired on the basis of two notifications, issued on November 13, 1959 and 24 May, 1961, that is, decades before the Emergency. The compensation was determined by the courts on the basis of market value prevailing at the time of notification. The two bed-room flats, with a separate living and drawing room, kitchen, bath, lounge and a verandah were allotted to the individuals in the middle-income group at price ranging from Rs.40,000 to Rs.45,000. This included the cost of development of land, provision of municipal services, and community facilities like parks and school sites, and construction of the flat itself. In fact, the boot was on the other leg. Whereas the allottees of the DDA flats were paying about Rs.400 per month as hire-purchase installment at that time, the prevailing rent in the locality was

Rs. 600 to Rs. 700 per month. In other words, the allottees were virtually earning a premium of Rs. 200 to Rs. 300 per month without undergoing any trouble that a private house builder had to face in Delhi. This is a typical illustration of the fact that, in our set-up, those who try to solve some basic social problem get brickbats, while those who sit back and do nothing either get away with their indolence and lack of initiative or at the most get a mild, casual, reprimand of a general nature.

*Delhi Under Emergency* was another book of the same genre. Its authors, John Dayal and Ajoy Bose, had claimed that they had given blow by blow account of the excesses committed. But every blow they described was nothing but a massive punch of superficiality. They spoke through persons specially "selected" to say what the authors had already decided to write. For example, they presented a very dark picture of Mangolpuri Resettlement Colony, through one Dwarka Prasad. Yet this was the colony which elected the Congress candidate in the Municipal Corporation election of June 1977 with overwhelming majority, when most other constituencies voted against the Congress. I am not concerned with the Congress victory or defeat. All that I wish to demonstrate is that the account of John Dayal and Ajoy Bose about the conditions of living in the resettlement colony of Mangolpuri was false. Had the conditions been so horrible as the authors had indicated and the resettlers so bitter as they wanted us to believe, would they have voted so enthusiastically for Sajjan Kumar, a Congress candidate, particularly when he had wholeheartedly supported the clearance-cum-resettlement drive? The truth is that the squatters, who were previously living in utter misery in scattered clusters with practically no civic amenities, were overwhelmed by the benefits of resettlement and development and expressed their gratitude in no uncertain terms.

Dayal and Bose had also made incorrect observations about DDA's functions in regard to implementation of the Master Plan. The task assigned to the DDA was not merely housing, as Dayal and Bose asserted, but to secure planned development of the capital. The residential, industrial, commercial, green and institutional components of the Plan had been earmarked under the statute, and the DDA had not developed any commercial slant. It had auctioned, as it had been auctioning since 1962, commercial sites with the approval of the Central government and Parliament. So far as residential land is concerned, no more than one per cent had been sold through auction restricted to those who had no other plot or house in Delhi. The remaining residential land had been disposed of, at fixed rate, worked out on a no-profit-no-loss basis.

Michael Henderson's book, *Experiment with Untruth,* was another untrue account based largely upon the version of story-teller, Inder Mohan, who, in fact, constituted the common source of most of the falsehood that was written in the above mentioned books about the so-called demolitions and making squatters and slum dwellers homeless. The clearance was done from the public land needed for public purposes and alternative sites were simultaneously made available with facilities for transport. Today, all of these allottees are secure in their possession, live in organised lay-outs in thriving colonies, with community facilities, and new opportunities to build a great future for themselves and their children.

Apart from indicating how attempts were made to mutilate the positive aspects of the history of Ninth Delhi's development, above brief narration and analysis speak volumes about the health of an influential section of the media in the years immediately following the end of Emergency. How was it that most of the 'eminent journalist-authors' saw practically everything through the coloured spectacles of Inder Mohan. Had they exerted themselves a little, seen even a fraction of records of pre-Emergency period, visited a few sites or picked up phone to contact those whose hard-earned public standing they were ruthlessly demolishing, they would have discovered the truth about our Clearance cum Resettlement cum Redevelopment projects and also about the Turkman Gate Slum Clearance Scheme. They would have had also to find answers to quite a few questions and propositions of fundamental significance, as set out below:

(i) In the wake of its intoxicating victory in the General Elections of March-April 1977, the Janta government dissolved the Delhi Metropolitan Council and the Delhi Municipal Corporation. In the fresh Elections, held in June 1977, the Congress party won only ten seats in the Metropolitan Council and twenty seats in the Municipal Corporation, and all of them were from the constituencies dominated by the voters of the resettlement colonies. How was it that the resettlers who were so 'brutally treated', as was made out by the journalist-authors in their books, voted for Mrs. Indira Gandhi's party, when practically every other constituency in the city of North India, be it in State Assembly or Lok Sabha, voted against her party?

(ii) What policy, programme and procedure were being followed from the day of Nigambodh Ghat / Yamuna Bazaar clearance on June 17, 1967 to the day of declaration of Emergency on June 25-26, 1975? How did they differ from what was done during the Emergency? Further, had not the political parties, which later on combined to form the Janta Party, consented to whole-heartedly support the said policy, programme and procedure in various official meetings held in 1967? How had all this been labelled inhuman, after about a decade, by the same leaders?

(iii) If the afore-said policy and practices were inhuman, what prevented the Central government and Union Parliament, when the Janta Party came to power in March, 1977, to annul the earlier decisions and issue fresh orders, prescribing new policy and procedures? Why were old policies and procedures of deploying additional police continued during the Janta regime as well?

(iv) How did Turkman Gate Slum Clearance Scheme, sanctioned decades earlier by the Delhi Improvement Trust and Delhi Municipal Corporation, suddenly become communal and linked to the concocted lines such as: We would not allow second Pakistan? Is it not that, exasperated by the gross mismanagement of its funds, the Central Government, in 1974, transferred the entire slum clearance scheme to the DDA for effective implementation?

(v) How was it that neither any eminent journalist nor any other votary of true information ever speaks of 1,000 alterative allotments made, including those of 200 newly built flats in Ranjit Nagar, near Patel Nagar, to the occupants of 120 slum premises of Turkman Gate? Why were Muslim Leaders, such as Sheikh Abdullah, not taken to Ranjit Nagar, but only to Trilokpuri where rank and recent squatters who were not eligible under the Turkman Gate Slum Clearance Scheme and/or Municipal Corporation Resolution Scheme were given plots on compassionate grounds?

(vi) Were not employment opportunities increased on a massive scale by simultaneously shifting, in the vicinity of Resettlement Colonies, huge whole-sale markets, such as Fruit and Vegetable, Truck and Tempo Terminals and Depots and Repair workshops, and also by establishing new residential, industrial and commercial estates in Naraina, Mayapuri, Okhla, etc.?

It is, indeed, unfortunate that the journalist-authors of the genre, discussed above, instead of serving as a source of knowledge, wisdom and light, at a critical time in nation's history, had chosen to act as no more than a malfunctioning lamp that could set on fire the entire fabric of Delhi planned development. It is immaterial whether they did so on account of bias, ignorance, carelessness, or misplaced trust on persons like Inder Mohan. What is worse, they never acknowledged their professional and ethical lapses even when the correct facts, became as clear as day light.

In vandalizing truth, no less unedifying was the role played by most senior Civil Servants of the Delhi Administration. The statements made by them in the public or before the Inquiry

Commission and Committees were truly amazing. They contradicted their own written records. They had persuaded themselves to believe that the easiest way to get over the problem which they were facing was to feign ignorance or to pass the blame to the others. Unwittingly, they were admitting what poor stuff they were made of.

Lieutenant-Governor Kishan Chand, told the Shah Commission that he was merely a mute spectator, while four or five officers, who had direct access to the Prime Minister, "ruled" the city. Nothing could be farther from truth than this statement. If any officer was responsible for the emergence of a new power structure in Delhi, it was Kishan Chand.

Kishan Chand hardly made any secret of the manner in which he proposed to function as Lieutenant-Governor of Delhi. Soon after assumption of office, he publicly declared that he was a humble solider of Indira Gandhi and had taken up the job to serve her. This declaration betrayed his mental attitude and his general inclination to flatter or please the persons in authority. A few days before the imposition of Emergency, he openly organised deployment of Delhi Transport Corporation buses for transporting people to the rally outside the Prime Minister's house. He tried to victimise me for not allowing officials of the DDA to join the rally. He was anxious to have a massive rally. When Kishan Chand learnt that I had told my Special Assistant to get the staff intending to go to the rally marked absent, he got very annoyed.

Immediately thereafter, Kishan Chand moved the Ministry of Works and Hosing for my transfer, though the Appointment Committee of the Cabinet comprising Prime Minister, Home Minister, and the Housing Minister, on the recommendations of all concerned, including the Cabinet Secretary, had approved of my continuance for another year. A month or so earlier, the ESCAP, UN organization for South East Asia Region, had enquired from the central government whether my services could be made available to them for a period of three months for preparing a report. On receipt of this query, A.N. Banerji, Secretary, Ministry of Works and Housing, asked Kishan Chand whether I could be released for a period of three months. He replied, "What to speak of three months, I cannot spare him for three days." Yet, such was Kishan Chand's regard for principles and administrative propriety that as soon as he came to know about my attitude towards the rally, he moved for my transfer and suggested for appointment the name of U.S. Sirivastava who had helped him in the deployment of Delhi Transport Corporation fleet. Since, however, I could not be transferred without the approval of the Appointment Committee of the Cabinet, the move fell through.

As indicated earlier in the book, the programme of Clearance cum Resettlement of squatters and shifting non-conforming trade and industry was highly beneficial to the city. But as it began to be subjected to motivated criticism with the coming into being of the Janta Party regime, Kishan Chand started feigning ignorance and circulating the story of being "a mute spectator". Actually, it was he who had presided over a number of public functions organised by the DDA in the resettlement colonies, where he warmly eulogised the work of clearance and resettlement. He had himself visited the Turkman Gate area twice. Soon after the Turkman Gate incident, he had approved the proposals relating to the clearance of slums of Sarai Khalil and Gali Khan-i-Khana. He had also obtained special notes from me on the subject for incorporating them in his speech for the Governors' Conference and his annual address to the Delhi Metropolitan Council.

Notwithstanding the existence of all the above facts and massive circumstantial evidence, Kishan Chand stated before the Commission, that he was merely a "spectator", and that the Raj Niwas was a deserted place "in which not even dogs barked." For this statement, hardly any precedent can be found in the history of Indian Administration. Kishan Chand wanted the public to believe that if he had passed written orders, he did so merely to fulfill the statutory obligation, and if he gave oral orders or approval, he had been ignored. What was the necessity of anyone ignoring him when he would have signed the file in any case? Kishan Chand, without any compunction of conscience or regard for elementary fairness, adopted the attitude: "heads I win, tails you lose".

With easy conscience embedded in their mental self, the other senior functionaries of the Central Government, the Delhi Administration and the Local Bodies, too, changed colours with the alacrity of a chameleon. A sudden realization seemed to have dawned upon the erstwhile Municipal Commissioner, B.R. Tamta, that 'demolition' of illegal encroachments and constructions was something of an evil to which he had been drawn under the threat of Maintenance of Internal Security Act. His statutory obligations and oath of office did not require him to do so. Likewise, F.H. Mohsin, Deputy Minister, Home, in Mrs. Indira Gandhi's Cabinet, discovered new flaws', while deposing before the Shah Commission, in the Turkman Gate Slum Clearance case.

Mohsin had gone to the Turkman Gate, when the work of clearance and resettlement was going on. He had also met H.K. Lal, Deputy Commissioner (Slums). He did not get the work stopped. Nor did he tell H.K. Lal what modifications, if any, were required. On return to his office, he did not take up any issue with the Home Minister or the Prime Minister. Clearly, at that time, F.H. Mohsin did not think that anything wrong was being done. As he was an 'obliging witness', the Commission did not ask him obvious questions that needed to be asked to find the truth.

The tragedy of senior functionaries, such as Kishan Chand, B.R. Tamta and F.H. Mohsin, was that they had no real attachment to the idea of creating a planned, balanced and disciplined city. With no intellectual base in their understanding of the new needs of an expanding metropolis of a developing country and with no commitment, they could easily drift from one position to another. But in my case, the issue was one of standing by my 'infant of mental self', Ninth Delhi, whom I had been protecting against all kinds of marauders and nursing it with my blood and sweat for the last decade. The small minds in the offices of the Shah Commission and in the Home-Ministry's politico bureaucrat caucus were incapable of understanding it. Being a prisoner of their frame-up plan, they were all-out to suppress written records and create false evidence by a sheer sleight of an intimidatory hand. Worse, the improprieties in their approach were accompanied by the attempts to make other speak lies.

Had I termed spectacular development as sinister demolitions, benign resettlement as brutal homelessness, and also described three-decades' old and sanctioned Turkman Gate Slum Clearance Scheme as an anti-Muslim project, specially and suddenly conceived by Sanjay Gandhi and I to 'prevent a second Pakistan from coming into being', I would have been spared all the bouts of harassment and hostility, all the vicious attacks of disinformation and defamation. But the network of falsehood, howsoever deftly woven, could not hold for long. It developed holes, and truth began to trickle down, drop by drop. In this regard, an episode is worth recalling:

> After the proceedings of the Shah Commission, on 7th April 1978, a group of young men, whom I had seen practically every day in the Commission's room, engaged me in a friendly conversation in the lawn outside. I had seen them prompting some people to jeer and sneer at me. But now their tone was conciliatory. I soon discovered that they had no ill-will against me, and were basically of amiable disposition.
>
> Jagmohanji, so the gist of their talk went, people of Delhi are generally appreciative of what you have done in regard to planning and development of city. You have been coming all alone to attend the commission's proceedings. We have ourselves been heckling you. But you have stuck to your stand gamely. We appreciate all this. We commend your courage and stoic calm. But one thing we do not understand. Why don't you name Sanjay Gandhi?
>
> My dear friends, I replied, You are mistaken. I am stating what in essence is the truth. I am not shielding anyone. By the very nature of my job, I could not have been concerned with the imposition of Emergency or arrests under MISA or censorship of media. I have never justified any of the decisions pertaining to these matters.
>
> So far as the so-called demolitions in Delhi were concerned, the policy and procedures had been settled by the Central

government, Parliament and statutory authorities long before the Emergency. From the Nigambodh Ghat and Hauz Khas years of mid-1960's, both Indira Gandhi and Sanjay Gandhi were aware of the salutary impact which the schemes of clearance cum resettlement cum redevelopment were having on Delhi's landscape. But the problem was the local leadership of their party. Sanjay Gandhi, in fact, did a commendable service to the city by ensuring that the politicians with narrow outlook, did not interfere, as they used to do in the pre-Emergency times. I have always acknowledged his positive and dynamic role in this arena. In any case, how does this render my action illegal or wrong in any way.

Let us face the truth. I got the schemes of clearance and resettlement executed because I believe in their intrinsic merit. I saw in them real humanism, real justice – justice not only to the individuals but also to the society. All those who are today pretending ignorance or saying that they acted under compulsion were earlier singing songs in praise of what was done. This is morally nauseating. It also shows that they did something in which they themselves did not believe. In other words, they were untrue to themselves. I ask you, if a person is not true to himself, would he be true to the society, true to the state?

Unfortunately, we are missing the central question and going to peripheral one. Unless we learn to insulate slums from politics and adopt a fair and firm approach to basic civic issues, our cities will remain ugly and disorganized. They will continue to provide abundant material for denigration of our culture and civilization to a Katherine Mayo, a Renold Segal, a Naipaul, a Louise Malle.

My reply was, perhaps, much longer than what was expected. I noticed that the atmosphere was getting a little tense. I quickly expressed regret for having "bored" them. They laughed, shook hands and parted company.

The atmosphere had definitely changed. But the heavy dust of disinformation, and distortion had already touched the highest level.

F.H. Mohsin had also told the Shah Commission that President Fakhruddin Ali Ahmad was unhappy, without indicating whether correct picture had been presented to him or not.

Towards the end of May 1976, H.K.L. Bhagat, Minister of State for Works and Housing, and I had met the President. He was in a relaxed mood. With grace and charm peculiarly his own, he talked informally. I explained to him what had been done in the Jama Masjid complex and what was proposed to be done further. I also showed to him a few photographs. The President was visibly happy over the clean environment that had been created around Jama Masjid. He himself spoke of the significant improvement that had also been effected by us around Central Idgah, Qasabapura – Motia Khan, where Mughal Emperor Aurangzeb said his prayers. The President, too, had been offering his Id prayers in this Idgah, and had been noticing, with admiration, the growing elegance of the large park being laid at the land around Idgah, which was earlier under unauthorized occupation of junk stores and in insanitary conditions, emitting offensive smell.

The President expressed the hope that, likewise, the visitors to Jama Masjid would not now see the slums on the staircases. He, however, had a few reservations with regard to the sites of relocation. Apparently, the powerful vested interests had been working on the mind of the President. He was given the impression that small shopkeepers had been sent miles away. The President was surprised when I informed him that all the shopkeepers working on the staircases had been accommodated in the 350 shops built in Urdu Bazaar in the Jama Masjid complex itself, and that only workshops, lathes, and petty repair and welding establishments, which had no real link with the Jama Masjid complex, either by way of cultural heritage or by way of conforming units, had been allotted alternative sites in the newly developed complex in Mayapuri, where hundred of industrial and warehousing units had already been shifted from Motia Khan / Idgah Iron Merchant and kabari Markets.

The President was further surprised when I told him that even those who had been carrying out business on the basis of 'teh-bazari'/

license, covering only about 3 to 4 sq.yds of space, had been allotted plots of hundred sq.yds. in Mayapuri, where the average price, at the time of allotment, was about Rs.1000 per sq.yd. In other words, each of the allottee had got a plot worth Rs.1 lakh. If the allottees took initiative and made use of the valuable allotments made to them, they could definitely carve out a bright future for themselves and their children. In Jama Masjid complex, they were condemned to perpetual misery with no scope for future improvement. They had only temporary license of 3 or 4 sq.yds. and were at the mercy of the local body.

In respect of the Turkman Gate area, too, I explained the entire background of the case which apparently had been kept away from the President. I told him how the scheme of slum clearance had been conceived as far back as 1938, how the premises had been acquired in 1948-52, how the dilapidated and dangerous buildings were collapsing, how the occupants were living under fear of death, how the Corporation Resolution had provided for allotment only to the old slum-dwellers, how we had liberalized these provisions and made allotments even to the squatters and fresh entrants, and how against 120 premises cleared, about 1,000 alternative allotments, including 200 flats in Ranjit Nagar (Patel Nagar) area, 400 residential plots and 200 commercial plots had been made. All this background and analyses came as 'revelations' to the President. He did not react in words. But the expression on his face seemed to be posing a question to his inner self: How is it that, out of dozens of deputations and individuals who had met him, no one had given him a complete picture and practically everyone had been talking only of being thrown miles away.

As if intending to divert the subject, the President said a few warm words about the manner in which the DDA had carried out the shifting in Sarai Khalil area. He also talked about the general scheme of redevelopment of Shahjahanabad, and desired to know as to what had happened to the recommendations made in my book[9] about

[9] The book the President was referring was: *Rebuilding Shahjahanabad: The Walled City of Delhi.* It was published in 1974.

reservation of land in Mata Sundri Road complex for being used for redevelopment of the Walled City. H.K. L. Bhagat informed the President that he was taking special steps to ensure that the land in question was made available for purpose.

The disinformation and distortion, launched through multiple agencies and individuals, and linking of my earnest efforts for ensuring planned and disciplined development of Delhi, with the 'Emergency issues, was oppressive in itself. But what was far more depressing was to see encouragement being given to nihilistic forces which were out to inject more contaminated blood in the veins of the city and render a substantial part of it perpetually paralysed.

The story, which crossed all limits of villainous concoction was the one that appeared on the front page of the *Indian Express* of April 19, 1977, under the title: *The Day of Bullets and Bulldozers* regarding an alleged event that was said to have occurred on the evening of April 18, 1976. It, *inter alia,* said:

> At around eight on the evening of April 18, Qyamuddin and three other residents of Turkman Gate went to Hotel Ranjit on hearing that Sanjay Gandhi and his group had come there.
>
> Conferring on a plush room of this hotel which overlooks Turkman Gate were Jagmohan, then Vice Chairman of the DDA, Ramesh Dutta, troop leader of the now defunct Nehru Brigade, two unidentified women and Sanjay Gandhi.
>
> After a wrangle with some hangers-on outside, Qyamuddin and his companions got into the room. Qyamuddin pleaded that demolition should be stopped till alternative accommodation could be provided. Sanjay said not a word. Jagmohan told them to get out and burst forth in rage; "We will do what we want. We won't allow a second Pakistan here". Qyamuddin and friends retreated hurriedly."
>
> Inder Mohan and Siraj Piracha, both social workers in the area, used to meet Jagmohan quite often. He had told them about his pet theory more than once. If Muslim communities, such as the one around Jama Masjid were not dispersed, there would be no national integration.

Every component of this story had been manufactured, with malafides intentions, to serve as an inexhaustible arsnel of lies to bombard my little fortress of tenacity till it was reduced to a few scattered stones and rubble. After the above publication in the Indian Express, it was reprinted in the Seminar (June 1977). It was also published by a few other magazines as if the writers had personal knowledge and were present at the time of the alleged confrontation. D.R. Mankekar in his book, *Decline and Fall of Indira Gandhi*, went a step further. He wrote with the authority of a researcher and an impartial eye-witness.

Soon after its publication, I wrote to the Indian Express: "Turkman Gate story, published in your paper, so far as it pertains to me, is a figment of imagination". My letter to the *Seminar* read:

> Your write-up, so far as it pertains to me, is wholly incorrect and highly defamatory… a sheer concoction…. I hope you will agree that for a sensitive person there is no greater torture than the mental torture of being subjected to false accusations. Nor can there be any greater injustice to history and public information than the publication of such inaccurate and motivated reports…

I sent similar letters to the editors of the magazines in which this story appeared. What did the 'apostles' of freedom of expression do? They did not even acknowledge my letters, what to speak of publishing them.

I was deeply dismayed. But what could I do? I had only my cynical mood to keep company. With the pall of gloom around me, the thought of giving up the unequal fight often sailed across my mind. With no less frequency, however, my true instinct would assert itself and remind me of an old adage: 'For evil to prosper, all that good men have to do is nothing.' And I would begin to argue with my dejected self: since the story in question was a product of a highly crafty and conspirational mind, to let it pass would not only mean my own moral capitulation but also result in swelling the ranks of wrong doers who could imperil the future of the Ninth Delhi in more than one way.

Eventually, my inner compass took me to the right course. I decided, whatever be the cost and whatever be risks of undergoing further harassment, to expose the sordid net-work of calumnies by filing a criminal defamation complaint[10] in the Metropolitan Court having jurisdiction in the matter.

The culprits and conspirators had imagined everything else except the probability of someone having the courage, in the vicious environment prevailing around him, to challenge their concoctions in the Court. But when the unlikely event happened, they found their castle of lies had been built with supercilious carelessness and had huge irreparable gaps. The visibility of the Turkman Gate site from Ranjit Hotel was not feasible. No room or floor number was specified. None of the persons who was stated to have barged into the 'room' was forthcoming. On the alleged day, Sanjay Gandhi was in Shimla[11] with his mother, Prime Minister Indira Gandhi. The writer of the story admitted that what he had penned was told to him by Inder Mohan and Siraj Pracha. Arun Shourie, who had subsequently taken over as Editor of the Indian Express intimated to me on May 23, 1990:

> You will recall that there has been a case in court in which you had complained about an item that had been published in the Indian Express in 1977 with regard to the Turkman Gate demolition. My colleagues and I have examined the news item in question and are satisfied that there was absolutely no basis other than hearsay for having included in the article the defamatory portion which is the subject of the complaint. I cannot tell you how all of us regret the embarrassment caused to you by the item and, may I say, to the paper itself by the

[10]Case number 168/2; dated 8/6/79; decided: 20.7.92 by Metropolitan Magistrate.

[11]The circulation/publication of the concocted story suddenly ceased, when an American journalist, after an interview with Sanjay Gandhi, noted that, as per written records of the Central and State governments, including those of the Indian Air Force, was with his mother, Prime-Minister Mrs. Indira Gandhi. Those Journalist/author who had earlier written the story, found that they had a common informer – Inder Mohan. But they all kept quiet, not having the moral courage to own the lapse.

> publication of such an item. If at any stage you feel that you would like me to acknowledge this fact publicly or if you would want me to inform some forum about this on behalf of the paper, I would gladly do so. You are, of course at liberty to use this letter in any forum or way you deem fit.

In view of the total exposure of their fabrication, the accused had really no defense. All that they could do was to cause delay by repeatedly raising flimsy issues and then going in for revision to the High Court if their plea was rejected by the trial court. My cross-examination covered about 50 pages. The intention was to tire and harass me. But I did not give up. After 13 years, the verdict was pronounced. The Metropolitan Court was so incensed by the outrageous concoction that it awarded four months' imprisonment to the reporter who first wrote the story. Inder Mohan's conspirational game of story weaving also stood exposed. In its order, the Court observed: "His (Inder Mohan's) evidence is self-contradictory, full of material contradictions. He is not a trustworthy witness and no reliance can be placed upon his evidence."

The verdict was, undoubtedly, a triumph for truth, a heart-warming victory for steadfastness and tenacity of purpose. And yet, in the end, I was left asking myself quite a few tentalising questions: How many lethal missiles fired from the seemingly inexhaustible arsenel of lies could I neutralize? How many death-traps dug by the unprincipled politics of the country could I outflank? How many unwholesome legacies, riddled with divisions and discords, could I do away with? Clearly, in absence of an effective answer to these questions, I could not entertain any hope of successfully attempting to lay a new path, through a new gate, to a new city. The basic issue, as I saw it, was not merely to undo the damage done to a tormented soul battered by calumny and injustice; it was to spin a new moral fabric for the capital city and realise the ideals of the Republic in deeds and on the ground.

CHAPTER VII

# NEED FOR CIVILIZATIONAL REGENERATION AND SECOND RENAISSANCE

*Political and civil liberty is and will always be the most sacred of all blessings, the worthiest object of all endeavour, and the nucleus of all culture: but the only firm foundation on which this glorious edifice can ever be erected is nobility of mind. We have to begin, therefore, by creating the citizens for a Constitution, before we can give a Constitution to the citizens.*

— Johann F. von Schiller

In the foregoing six chapters, I have made an earnest attempt to hold a mirror to the momentous events, having a bearing on the development of the capital of the Republic, which show how multiple infections have virtually made a semi-permanent abode in the body-politic of the city and the state. While proceeding with my narration and analysis, in the context of my personal experience and on the basis of unimpeachable data, documents and contemporaneous records, I have placed my finger on what I consider to be the lapses of historic proportion in various arenas of our public life. Every serious reader and well-wisher of the city, I hope, would reflect, whether the national aspiration, *Satyamev Jayate* (Truth Alone Triumphs), is not being pursued in the reverse and whether the exploitative forces, embedded in some of the diseased seeds of our democracy have not been extending their domain at an accelerated pace.

As elaborated in Chapter II, titled *Tragedy of A Self Destructive Democracy:Phenomenon of Unauthorized Colonies and Constructions,* the city has, of late, seen a massive onslaught of rapacious and ruthless elements. Wounds after wounds[1] have been inflicted upon the hapless cityscape. But the unkindest cut of all has been the approach of the leadership of practically every political party to condone, and even reward, illegal acts, howsoever blatant, to secure 'group votes' of the 'ravishers' at the time of municipal, state and Lok Sabha elections. No principle, no norms, no value, no past solemn declaration, and no court-verdict or its repeated denunciation have mattered. All that is sought is power — power not for doing long term good to the city or the state but for attaining short-term personal and political gains, forgetting all the time that ignoble and unjust means could give birth only to a deformed and disoriented city.

Why has all this happened? Is it not due to our poor understanding of the ideal of democracy and still poorer application of its core values at the ground level?

Abraham Lincoln's classic definition of democracy as 'a government of the people by the people for the people', has an inbuilt fascination. It casts its spell on most of us. But when it is operationalized on the ground, a number of practical questions, with their hidden complexities, stare us in the face: What is the character, calibre and capacity of those who constitute the people as well as of those who would come to rule them in their name? What historical and cultural legacies do they carry, and what are the ethical or unethical norms which have got woven, over the years, into their civilizational fabric?

[1]In Chapter I, titled: *City and its Leadership and its Civilizational Contours*, I have particularized a function where-in Ms. Sheila Dikshit and Ms. Sonia Gandhi distributed 'provisional regularization certificates' to 'all the 1639' unauthorized colonies, as if by being first permissive to the wholly illegal acts of land racketeers, and then 'rewarding' them was an 'achievement' which should be flaunted about, as the Delhi assembly elections (December 2008) and the Lok Sabha elections (May 2009) approached. The opposition leaders were no less vociferous in competitive negativity. No one in the top leadership bothered to even think over the manner in which 'we-the people' were conducting ourselves, displaying either our greed or our indifference.

A true and meaningful democracy requires, by and large, healthy voters, healthy leadership, healthy social and cultural environment and a healthy disposition to adapt to the changes that are fast occurring in the contemporary world. Those nations that remain unmindful of these requirements and profess adherence to the democratic structure by following its outward frame would create democracies that are superficial and shallow. Such democracies would generally represent the collective weaknesses and not the collective strength of the people. They would ensure dominance of regressive elements in the society and promote evils of deception, duplicity and demagoguery. They would be propelled by forces of greed and intrigue and produce manipulative politicians rather than principled statesmen. They would impose a tyranny of its own kind. They may free the hand that moves towards the ballot box but keep the mind that guides the hand enslaved.

Individuals and the society with a narrow, selfish, sectarian and parochial outlook, would happily elect a government with the same outlook. Such a government would certainly reflect the 'will' of the people. But what sort of 'will' would it be? Would it not be a lethal 'will', a poisoned sandwich on the plate of the nation? The peoples and their chosen rulers would merely reinforce each others' weaknesses and push the national maladies to a point of no return. For every issue, involving a choice between 'right' and 'wrong', between a short-term gain to a political party and a long-term goal of nation building, the selfish and vested interests would whip up mass hysteria and browbeat saner elements into submission. Clearly, what was needed in the post-1947 India was not merely a democracy in its structural form, but a democracy that had, at its roots, nobility-oriented individuals and society, and which drew its sustenance from the purified blood stream of a civilizationally regenerated nation.

With the inclusion of democracy and adult franchise as basic provisions of the Indian Constitution, special efforts were needed to upgrade the intellectual and moral capacities of the voters and build an environment conducive to reform and reawakening of the society.[2]

Though an ancient civilization, with a set of elevating values, rooted in contentment, compassion, a sense of balance and harmony, and an overall spirituality of outlook, India had, for centuries continuously suffered a steep decline and contracted a number of social evils that are inherent in subjugation, poverty, ignorance, general insularity and freezing of mind. These evils, these infected and rotten eggs in the historical baggage of post-independence India, had to be done away with.

The Indian leaders, who came to the helm of affairs at the time of independence, were talented and well-versed with the affairs of the modern world. They gave an excellent constitution to the country and created sound and solid institutions to meet the constitutional goals. But they bypassed the central issue. The nation required not only constitutional provisions but also constitutional morality, not only institutions,but also men and women of character and calibre to run them. They did not adequately realize that if the right kind of voters, right kind of voters' representatives and right kind of cultural and civilization ethos were not brought into being, the constitutional goals would develop distortions, and democracy would get deformed.

The items of triumph and tragedy, which I have recounted, and subjected to virtual x-ray in the six chapters, should impel us to raise

---

[2] Dr. H.N. Kunzru had cautioned against universal adult franchise. He feared that this would provide wide scope for demagoguery. He wanted that beginning should be made with about 40 per cent adult franchise and universality should be about in fifteen years or so during which the remaining electorate could be educated. Earlier, C. Rajagopalachari, too, had warned: "We all ought to know that Swaraj will not be a better government or greater happiness for the people. Elections and their corruption, injustice, and the power and tyranny of wealth, and inefficiency of administration, will make a hell of life... Hope lies only in universal education by which right conduct will be developed. It is only if we succeed in this that Swaraj will mean happiness, otherwise, it will mean grinding injustice and tyranny of wealth."

At the time of adoption of the Constitution, in his concluding speech, Dr. Ambedkar had also struck a note of sceptism: "Who can say how the people of India and their parties will behave?".

a number of crucial questions about Indian democracy, as it is practised at the ground level of the republic's capital.Is it fulfilling the objectives for which it was chosen as a mode of governance? Is it leading to order or disorder, coherence or confusion, cleanliness or corruption, justice or injustice, good or bad administration? Is it resulting in improvement or deterioration of ethical standards of the society? Is it facilitating or obstructing regeneration of those forces that once made the Indian mind powerful and profound on the one hand and gentle and non-acquisitive on the other? And how is it impacting the evolution of India's vision for the future?

To a discerning eye and dispassionate observer, the answers to the above and allied questions would be clear:there are far too many straws in the wind, which should serve as strong warning signals at various governance fronts. They point to the urgent need for enlarging and deepening of national capacities at these fronts, and also for weaving the enlarged and deepened capacities into a pattern of regenerated civilization and system of governance. All along my core formulation in this regard has been: unless the Indian mind is retrieved from its debasement, and the people remain what they are, no administrative, economic or constitutional reforms can save the country from the ever deepening quagmire of inefficiency, corruption and malpractices.

I should underline that, according to the way I look at governance, its span extends across the entire canvas of the life of a nation. It involves not only administrative or managerial capacities but also the social, political, intellectual, cultural and moral capacities of a system in its entirety. And the best governance set-up is the one that harnesses all these capacities and directs their focused beam on the resolution of the problems that confront the nation. If, for example, intellectuals provide no fresh or creative ideas, or if the culture of a nation is not generative of values of honesty, dedication, compassion and the like, the quality of governance will suffer, no matter how well-conceived constitutionally its institutional arrangements are, and how updated and progressive its economic policies and programmes.

During my long[3] journey in public life, I had a close look at contemporary Indian society, to peep into its soul and to probe its inner layers. I came in contact with a wide spectrum of people, from the *jhuggi* dwellers to Prime Ministers, from small vendors to top businessmen, from the simple and dedicated civil servants to power-drunk bureaucrats. I passed through several cold deserts as well as green pastures. I viewed different scenes from different pedestals and from different angles.

One common factor has stood out in all my experiences and in the perceptions I gathered. There has been a grave national ommission in attending to our fundamentals. The consequence of this omission has not only been a colossal casualness and corruption in public life, but also an ever-increasing incapacity of the country to cope with manifold challenges that have arisen during the past 68 years and many more that are bound to arise, in a still more complex form, in the coming years. For the crisis is not merely structural; it is rooted in the recesses in our souls. It is a crisis not only of governance but also of the governed; it is a crisis of character, of commitment and of conscience; a crisis that is in-built in the spiritual and inspirational vacuum that we have created and the poor moral and social order that we have brought about.

When, in the early 1990s, songs in praise of the new economic reforms were being sung at their loudest and an impression was being created that the solutions to all the problems of the Indian economy and administration had been found, I had, in the fifth edition of my book, *My Frozen Turbulence in Kashmir*, which was being written at that time, commented on the superficiality of the entire approach:

---

[3]I had the opportunity to serve the country on several occasions in different arenas of public life in different capacities. I have held several assignments in the civil service, from the junior rungs to the top. I have worked as Lieutenant Governor/Governor for about 10 years. I have functioned as a member of Parliament for about 14 years and assessed the proceedings of the Lok Sabha and Rajya Sabha, both from the opposition and treasury Benches. For about five-and-a half years I had the privilege of being a Union Cabinet Minister, holding a variety of portfolios—communication, urban development, poverty alleviation, culture and tourism.

It is being argued that new propositions would pull the country out of crisis. This argument ignores the nature of the crisis and its roots which lie embedded in the social ethos and cultural forces that govern the life of the country—the forces that have seeped into its bloodstream and made deep inroads into its polity, its business, its industry, its administration and other institutions. To proceed with 'economic reforms', without reorienting these fundamental forces and without infusing new spirit in the institutions, would only amount to pursuing a mirage.

Today, the country is abandoning its adherence to the concept of welfare state by transposing its own faults—faults of its ethos—to these concepts. After a few years, the country would once again transfer its own infirmities—infirmities of its current culture—to the concepts of free market, liberalization and globalization,and denounce them. A new person with a new portfolio, a new 'package', a new 'action-programme', accompanied by a new set of drumbeaters, would arrive. All the while, the country will go on sinking deeper and deeper into trouble. The malady is in the heart; attending to the periphery would not do.

For instance, it is being claimed that, with the deregulation of the economy and dismantling of the public sector, an era of progress would dawn and corruption would decline. Soon, the hollowness of the claim would be discovered because nothing is being done to change the ethos, the cultural and social traits, which breed corruption. In the absence of internal cleanliness, malpractices would merely get transferred from one sphere to another.

Whether type A or type B of the economic system or approach is more suitable is not the issue. My basic contention is that the recent measures, apart from being faulty and risky in many respects, would not yield any worthwhile results. Under the new dispensation,the plot of the story may undergo a change, the stage may have a different setting, the actors may speak in different languages and adopt different styles of acting, but the drama would end essentially on the same unsavoury note.

Would anyone who is willing to look dispassionately at the post-reform period of 25 years[4] seriously dispute the truth of this contention? If he does, let him answer a few basic questions. Have the institutions of governance started functioning more efficiently and effectively? Has the incidence of corruption in our public life declined and have we, the people, become more alive to our civic and national obligations, and do we now maintain a narrower gap between what we say and what we do?

The answer to all these questions is, clearly, in the negative.This is so because the approach adopted was hollow, superficial and devoid of deep thinking and sustained motivation. That is why, while we have been talking of reforms and using beautiful and borrowed jargon like good governance, the fatal flaws of our polity and administration have been deepening.

Few of us realize that, besides the much adumbrated economic reforms of 1991, there have been scores of reform commissions and committees since independence. They were setup by the Central and State governments to bring about positive changes in the machinery of governance. A number of measures were also taken to strengthen the law and augment the institutions. A Central Vigilance Commission was appointed in 1964 and a vigilance officer was attached to each ministry. The anti-corruption laws were amended. The definition of public servants was enlarged. The possession of assets disproportionate to the known sources of income of the public servant was also brought within the ambit of criminal misconduct. The burden of proving innocence was shifted to the accused. Substantial modifications were also made in the income tax, excise

[4] It needs to be clearly understand that here I am not expressing preference for any ideology or model of economic development. I am merely underlining the primacy of civilizational regeneration. Unless a fundamental upgradation of social and cultural milieu is simultaneously brought about, no change in economic ideology or political regime would yield the desired results.

and custom laws and in various financial regulations to curb black money and *hawala* transactions.

But what has been the outcome of all these commissions and committees, all these modifications in law, and all these expansions in the institutional framework?

Beginning with the jeep scandal of 1949, there has been a virtual flood of cases of 'scams', 'scandals' and 'swindlings'. Of late, this flood has changed into a torrent. The 2G Spectrum case has broken all records of malfeasance, involving a loss of about Rs. 1,70,000 crore to the government. The Commonwealth Games, the main objective of which was to enhance the country's standing in the comity of nations, has caused a huge dent in its reputation and that too, after consuming about Rs.18,000 crore of the national exchequer.The Bellary Mines cases, besides causing irreparable damage to the environment, have resulted in swindling of public revenues on a massive scale. Global Financial Integrity's Report puts the estimates of Indian wealth stashed abroad at US$ 1.4 trillion. The volume of black money, which was believed by noted economist Nicholas Koldar to be 4.5 per cent of the country's gross domestic product in1955, has now, according to a study by Arun Kumar of Jawaharlal Nehru University, risen to about 50 per cent of the gross domestic product. The 2010 findings of Transparency International have underscored the fact that India has more black money than the rest of the world combined. Even the statutory organizations, the supposed citadels of fairness, such as Public Service Commissions, have fallen prey to corrupt practices. Two Chairmen of the Commission, one of Punjab and other of Maharashtra, were prosecuted. The army too has not remained unscathed. A senior Major-General was recently court-martialled and imprisoned on charges of criminal misconduct in supplying poor quality food to the troops stationed at Siachen Glacier in Ladakh. Not to be left behind, the media, the so-called custodian of clean public life, has often resorted to the unethical practice of giving extensive publicity to vested interests by way of 'paid-news'.

What is of particular significance is that these cases involve almost all the important segments of society: ministers, members of

Parliament, senior civil servants, chief-executives of corporate houses, army officers, men and women of the media. It makes no difference what their political affiliations are, what economic ideologies they profess, what profession they follow, and whether they belong to autonomous organizations or independent regulatory authorities.

It is, indeed, a tragedy of monumental proportions that all this should be happening in a country about which world renowned American historian, Will Durant, in his 10-volume *Story of Civilization,* written a few years before Indian independence, had said:"Perhaps, in return for conquest, arrogance, and spoliation, India will teach us the tolerance and gentleness of mature mind, the quiet content of the unacquisitive soul, the calm of the understanding spirit, and a unifying, pacifying love for all living beings."

Do attributes, such as "the quiet content of the unacquisitive soul" and "gentleness of the mature mind", have any meaning in presentday India?In any case, the pertinent questions that arise from this are:how is it that practically every element of the social structure and every component of governance machinery is afflicted with the same malady? What is the common base from which this malady springs? And why is it worsening, despite various economic, political and legal medicines administered from time to time?

To my mind, the answer to all these questions is one. The common virus that has afflicted all of them floats on top of the social and cultural environment of the country and no one can escape from it. The air around is thick with pollution and the Indian mind and soul stand chronically contaminated.

The experience of the last 68 years of independence supports my formulation. It has shown that it is not possible to build a clean and honest system of governance on a diseased mindscape, a disabled soul, and in the degraded social and cultural environment which such a mindscape and such a soul give rise to. Strong laws are necessary. Well-structured and effective institutions are a must. The personnel to implement the laws and run the institutions have to be knowledgeable and trained. The overall mechanism of deterrence has to be potent. But all these are of no avail if the fundamental issues pertaining to the mind and soul of India remain neglected, and if the negative values are allowed to surround us.

History tells us in no uncertain terms that every turning point in the march of civilization has been preceded by a fundamental change in the minds of the people. From the mid-15th century, Europe commenced its long journey from the medieval to the modern age, when the Renaissance started unleashing forces that stimulated the public mind and made it intellectually vigorous, culturally sensitive and socially humane. From the awakened mind sprang the scientific temper, the spirit of inquiry, the ideas of progress and disposition to shake off the unjust impositions of the Church and the State.

Likewise, before the ideas of equality, liberty and fraternity created the French Revolution and made their impact on the social, economic and political structures of the European nations, the writings of Thomas Paine, Rousseau and Voltaire had transformed the intellectual and cultural environment and weakened the 'sacredness' of the Royal and Episcopal authority. With the fall of the barriers in the mindset of the people, the fall of the Bastille and other citadels of illiberal regimes was only a matter of time. An era of inner changes was bound to give birth to a new order.

It was the inner change that was most needed in post-1947 India, and it was this very pivotal need that was neglected. The leadership in all spheres of public life—political, social, intellectual and cultural—should have taken measures to create a climate from which a nobility-oriented society and State could emerge. A modern constitution and five-year plans for economic development alone were not enough. The leadership should have been instrumental in the formulation and implementation of a national regeneration programme by way of which the country would have been relieved of all the garbage that had collected in her courtyard during the long period of decay and degeneration of her civilization, and at the same time dug out the buried treasures of her life-elevating ideals towards which the great reformers of the first renaissance, such as Raja Ram Mohun Roy and Sri Aurobindo, had repeatedly pointed to. The leadership should have realized that without inner energy, the institutions created by the Constitution could not develop the animation that was needed to keep them clean, creative and constructive.

We seem to have forgotten that it was the renaissance of the later 19th and early 20th centuries that had caused an extensive inner change and shaken the 'sleeping giant', as Vivekananda called India, out of its stupor. He himself was the personification of the 'awakened giant'. Like a hurricane, he appeared on the scene, blowing out the desert sand and bringing to the surface the treasures of Indian thought. He forcefully reminded the diffident Indians of his times that they were heirs to a profound philosophy of life, the core doctrine of which was: 'Every individual is potentially divine and his "self" is a part of the Great Self and his soul a speck of the Oversoul'. Vivekananda's exhortations to the masses were: "Lift up your head. For each one of you carries God within.... You are infinite, deathless, birthless.... You yourself are the proof of God!'Thou are That'.[5]

Such clarion calls made by Vivekananda during his extensivetours across the country generated a wave of self-confidence in thepeople and also a will to stand up and be counted. An intellectual and spiritual environment conducive to the growth of cultural assertion and freedom was created. It influenced a wide spectrum of leadership, from the apostle of non-violence, Mahatma Gandhi, to the towering militant, Subhas Chandra Bose.

It was because of a substantial regeneration of the Indian mind and an awakening of the Indian soul that Gandhi was later able to build a 'nobility-oriented' mass movement that brought India her

---

[5]Vivekananda synthesized all the healthy strands, schools and systems of Indian thought, from the Vedic times to his own, and presented the outcome in the form of a clean and comprehensive doctrine which he termed Practical Vedanta. This doctrine rests firmly on the shoulders of the basic philosophy of the *Upanishads*. But he emphasized that man's higher purpose of approximating to the Supreme Self could best be achieved by positive action, by serving the divinity in the human being, all over the human race.

The profundity of Upanishadic thought has been widely acknowledged. As great a thinker as Arthur Schopenhauer has observed: 'In the whole world, there is no study— so beneficial and so elevating as that as *Upanishads*....It is destined, sooner or later, to become the faith of all the people.'

freedom in a unique way. The country acquired a dignified pride in the pattern of thought which its ancient civilization had evolved.

A sizeable section of the society was fired with new inspiration and experienced a new awakening. A number of reform movements in the political, social and cultural arenas ensued, paving the way for India's freedom. These movements also brought to the forefront clean and conscientious leaders whose rectitude rested on the 'nobility of temper' that the high ideals of Indian philosophy had generated.

As a result of the total neglect by the post-1947 leadership, the renaissance, which in any case was not so strong as to blow away all the dirt and dross of over 1,000 years of decay in India's civilizational ethos,began rapidly losing its reformative impulses. It soon became extinct and the result is the deterioration in the standard of public life and the virtual subversion of all the constitutional objectives that we intended to achieve. For example, the constitutional goal of socio and economic justice has been 'attained' by creating the largest disparities of income in the world. The ever increasing migrants to the major India cities are finding shelter in the hell-hole of slums. About 38 million are afflicted with serious water-borne diseases. Over half the world's most polluted cities are in India. All this—alongside an increasing number of luxury houses, posh malls and sprawling golf courses.

Legal provisions and national pledges notwithstanding, Forty per cent of child marriages in the world occur in India. A recent report of the Naad Foundation, which was released by the Prime Minister on 11 January 2012, shows that 59 per cent of Indian children between 0–5 years of age have stunted growth.

The position with regard to crimes against women is extremely disconcerting. In 2011, there were as many as 24,206 registered cases of rape, as against 2,487 such cases in 1972, showing an increase of 791 per cent. The outrageous gang rape of the 23-year-old student on the night of 16 December 2012 in a moving bus in Delhi, and her death a few days later, showed to what level of depravity a section of Indian citizens have descended; their beastly instinct does not even spare a five-year-old girl.

Here, it may be relevant to draw attention to the parallel developments that have taken place on the international stage. After the Second World War, the United Nations Educational, Scientific and Cultural Organization was set up in 1945. Its Constitution declared: 'Since wars begin in the minds of men, it is in the minds of men that defences of peace must be constructed'. The objective was to provide the international community with a new mindset. But no concrete or meaningful action followed. Consequently, the character of the economic, social and cultural forces, emanating from an aggressive and dominating mind, continued. So did violence and brutality. And the 20th century turned out to be the bloodiest; more people died in this period than during the entire march of human civilization preceding it. Today, terrorism, a savage product of a savage mind, is spilling innocent blood on an unprecedented scale.

I have no doubt that, if the fundamental aberrations of the Indian State and society have to be corrected and if the arteries of the system, clogged as they are at present, have to be restored to health, India would have to experience another renaissance, a renaissance which is far more potent and pervasive than the first one. It must penetrate every nook and corner of Indian life and help in creating a new set of values which would elevate the minds of the people and underpin, albeit imperceptibly, all societal and State actions.

The key question is how to go about this great task. Arising out of this question are a number of subsidiary questions of vast dimensions and depth. These are: What are the measures and movements that need initiation? How should the social order be purged of selfishness, shallowness and hypocrisy? In what manner can the vicious cycles of backwardness and poor leadership that have come to operate at various levels of the present-day 'democratic structure' of the country be ripped apart? How should intellectuals be mobilized and persuaded to undertake a mission of humanizing society and injecting in it values of honesty, compassion and commitment? What should be done to sensitize the youth to its responsibilities for building a dynamic and disciplined India? How should the business and bureaucratic elites be weaned away from their current mania for money-making? What, in brief, should new national aspirations, a new kind of lifestyle and a new kind of society and civilization be?

The basic inspiration, if it has to catch the imagination of the great mass of people and stir them, has to come from the unique set of philosophic values evolved during the heyday of ancient Indian civilization. These values have been warmly eulogized by eminent scholars and historians of civilizations. For example, British historian Arnold J. Toynbee, after making a painstaking study of various civilizations, came to this conclusion: 'The only way for salvation of mankind is the Indian way. Here we have the attitude and the spirit that flows from a true vision of spiritual reality.'

Since the ambit of this book relates primarily to the development of Ninth Delhi and there are obvious constraints to go into the entire set of values here, I would restrict myself to the exposition of two basic values to serve as illustrations for my formulation. One pertains to the ideal of *Karmayogi*, and the other to belief in the divinity of life, unity of existence, and the organic nature of the cosmic web of the universe.

The ideal of *Karmayogi* constitutes the corner-stone of Indian philosophy and ethics. In essence, it enjoins one to perform one's duty dispassionately and without entertaining any weakness for reward. I do not think a more lofty, a more elevating, a more solid and sound concept of work than this has been evolved in any other system of thought anywhere in the world. Resting as it does on detachment, dedication and complete selflessness, it cannot but ennoble the holder of power. A work undertaken by a State functionary necessarily involves exercise of power. If this exercise is actuated neither by weakness for reward nor by any other subjective consideration, it cannot lead the functionary astray, and no corruption, malpractice or injustice would ensue. The work gets performed honestly, objectively and effectively.

The Indian concept of unity of life, of belief in the indivisible and interpenetrative relationship amongst all elements of existence, and of recognition of the phenomenon of 'One in All and All in One', is so solid and sound in its fundamentals that it holds the key to the development of selfless behaviour and emergence of a balanced ,just, honest and harmonious social order. It orients the mind of the individual towards the realization that he or she is a part of the greater Self and should not do anything that has the effect of injuring a part of one's own self.

In the principle, 'One in All and All in One', notions of equality, liberty and fraternity are implicit. It virtually constitutes metaphysical democracy. If the same divinity is embodied in different individuals, they cannot but be equal. Liberty and fraternity would also be ensured as it would be unthinkable for divinity in one person to starve the same divinity in another person or do injustice to it in any other matter.

The promotion of these two values, coupled with similar promotion of other values of the system to which I have made a reference, would go a long way in creating a society with character, conscience, compassion and commitment.

I should underline that the system of values, out of which I have cited two as examples of their inherent nobility as well as of their utility, is not at variance with what goes under the rubric of secular humanism. The only difference is that within the system which I am advocating burns the fire of the civilizational and cultural pride which would convert concepts into convictions, and convictions into commitments, and commitments into solid and sustained actions that would give rise to a healthy and congenial environment.

The next question to be considered is, who will take the initiative and bring about the necessary change. Would it be political leadership or intellectual class or social and cultural organizations or upcoming younger generations with a fresh mind and an innovative outlook? Obviously, it would have to be a combination of all.Each one of them has to acquire a new motivation, a new sense of direction, and act with renewed zest and zeal not only in its own but also in allied fields.

Currently, a sense of unease[6] about the prevailing conditions is discernible in a substantial section of enlightened citizenry who are increasingly pressing for basic reforms. But these urges are scattered.They cross the minds of individuals and sail into nothingness. It is possible that one such individual who is more determined and focused will not allow this to happen. He or she would absorb them, become their symbol, and assume leadership of all those who feel the same but find no organized outlet for their expression. The leadership of such a person would result in enlargement and intensification of the urge for reform which in turn would strengthen his leadership.[7] Thus, the reformative urges and the leadership would reinforce each other mutually; one would strengthen the other. And a movement would be born.

This mutuality is absolutely necessary to usher in a second renaissance. A truly great leader is one who commences his mission by tapping the healthy forces that are already a part of the psyche of a section of the people, organizes them into a cohesive force, and propels them to a higher horizon to build a grand vision for reform and regeneration.

When I refer to a leader, I do not mean a single leader. It could be a group of leaders with similar aims and they may be working in

---

[6]The way *'this sense of unease'* sometimes finds a telling expression has been particularized by me in Chapter I and its Appendices: (CI-(i), CI-(ii), CI-(iii) and CI-(iv)). The contents of the 'edit-page' articles of celebrated journalists, such as Shekhar Gupta, Harish Khare and Ravinder Kumar, and the views of eminent public men and associations (Appendix C-I-(iv) speak for themselves.

[7]An easily intelligible example of this phenomenon is the reform of the management of the Shrine of Mata Vaishno Devi. I have added a brief note, as Appendix CVII-(i), to show how the urges of a motivated leadership and the urges of those individuals/pilgrims, who had been experiencing 'a strong sense of unease', got enlarged and intensified, and resulted in 'root and branch' transformation of the entire Katra-Vaishno Devi' Complex, yielding manifold benefits to the state and society.

(I have not included the particulars of this case in the main text to not only avoid interruption in the flow of readers' thoughts in respect of the main propositions enunciated here but also to make the background of Shrine reforms more clear.)

different arenas of public life. An intellectual, for example, may be working in the literary arena. Like Charles Dickens, he maybe writing novels and stoking social sensibilities of the nation by portraying, in his own artistic way, the current injustices and inhumanities of our systems. When sensitivity and compassion are deepened in the people, a mental climate conducive to reforms would come into being.

Instances are not lacking of great leaders emerging on the scene and bringing about a decisive turn in the nation's destiny.The inspiring leadership of Swami Vivekananda, Rabindranath Tagore and Mahatma Gandhi, in their respective fields, shows how a fundamental change in the nation's ethos, attitude and outlook could be brought about.

What India needs today is a great leader who would put himself or herself at the vanguard of a second renaissance which, by virtue of its own dynamics, would give rise to a band of 'renaissance heroes' in education, culture, politics and other walks of life, and fertilize and regenerate the mindscape of India. Such 'heroes' would bring the youth into their fold. They would ensure, in their own way, that the rich become less greedy and money-minded, and the poor refuse to lend themselves to exploitation by falling prey to 'vote banks' and caste-ridden politics.

For the emergence of 'renaissance heroes', the role of our educational system is particularly significant. If this system is so designed that, besides normal studies and cultivating a scientific temper, it engenders respect for the nobility of ancient India and a revulsion for the products of its degenerated past, then a strong foundational plank for the second renaissance would be created.

Our current educational system is in a poor shape. It neither provides quality education nor nurses positive values. Almost all the universities and deemed universities which are expected to function autonomously and serve as a power-house of healthy values and creative and constructive ideas, are facing a crisis. Self-serving politicians with little vision or motivation for nation-building are manipulating them.

Reconstruction of the educational edifice, both in structure and in spirit, would, therefore, have to proceed along with the reformative impulses that are necessary for generating a second renaissance. As a part of this reconstruction, the entire educational set-up would have to be placed under the charge of an independent regulator who would take particular care to ensure that the contents of teaching, *inter alia*, are oriented towards creating a new awakening in the country and absorption by the teachers and the students of those values and ideals of the philosophic system that I have outlined.

The youth emerging from a reformed and rejuvenated educational system would not only be inspired individuals with lofty ideals, but also become flag-bearers of the second renaissance. The teachers would play their own role in enlarging and deepening the renaissance forces and in rebuilding the national edifice on cleaner, purer and stronger foundations.

In the end, I reiterate that in the noble heritage of India lies embedded a powerful and profound mind and a pure and punctilious soul. The impulses generated by the combined impact of the measures and movements that I have outlined would rekindle that power and reawaken that soul. With this would commence the process of injecting fresh blood into the dying institutions of the State and society and making them vital and vigorous. New capacities—intellectual, moral and social—would be created inthe system, and India would move from strength to strength, from imbalance to balance, from callousness to compassion, from casualness to commitment, and from corruption to cleanliness.

# APPENDICES

## APPENDIX CI-(i)

There has to be something frightfully wrong with our capital city if its most prominent losers continue to so dominate our front pages. How else can you justify Madan Lal Khurana, Vijay Kumar Malhotra and Sahib Singh Verma, occupying so much real estate on our newsprint when they are only sulking all of the time?

They sulked, first, because two of them were done out of their chief ministerships. Then, they were denied cabinet berths when the Vajpayee cabinet was first sworn in. Now, they have been ignored even for a minor sinecure. They still sulk, but for once, they also celebrate. They have got the head of Urban Affairs Minister Jagmohan who is widely acknowledged, even by Congressmen, as the one BJP minister who was making a difference. He was generating such a positive buzz with his clean-up of Delhi that even the Congress was beginning to see him as a threat. Unfortunately, so did his own partymen and got him in the jugular.

The real story is not that the Delhi's BJP party leaders should hold the view that Jagmohan's kind of assault on the illegal builder mafia's unauthorised construction, polluting industries and encroachments was going to lose the BJP votes. The more alarming truth is that Vajpayee and his advisors bought that argument. If they still believe that our capital is a city run by the mafias, for the mafias and other special interest thugs who care a damn for the quality of the air we breathe, the congestion on our roads, power failures, water shortage, mess in the hospitals and so on, as long as property prices can boom, they live in very old times indeed.

Over the past three years, you have seen these three lead the campaigns against almost anything done to clean Delhi. First of all, in a breathtaking display of dadagiri they blocked the new Rent Act even after it had been cleared by the two Houses of Parliament and the President. The Supreme Court stated just yesterday (in the

Jayalalitha case) that the will of the people could not override the tenets of the Constitution. Here, mere muscle power of minor thugs has blocked both. Then, they opposed the removal of polluting industries – what else could they do when it was well known that a large number of the polluters were also power-thiefs, financiers and friends of the politicians and patrons of the ruling party? Then they sat on dharnas against the demolition of encroachments and, finally, led the private bus operators' and autorickshaw owners' protest against the Supreme Court's insistence on the switchover to clean fuels, particularly CNG (compressed natural gas).

It is, actually, OK for politicians so outdated and so illiterate to be ignorant of issues concerning modern urban governance. For you and I this city is a place where our children live and grow. For these types it is a piece of land to harvest votes from. They treat us not as living, demanding, concerned beings, privileged to be living in the nation's capital and therefore more aware and conscious than fellow Indians elsewhere. They only count us as votes.

The Prime Minister removed Jagmohan because he was convinced that his kind of activism was going to lose the BJP votes. How you wish he had paused to think why he should buy that logic from people, two of whom were directly responsible for losing his party a sweeping mandate that was always its own in Delhi. It would have required extraordinary talent to make the BJP lose its hold over Delhi and these three obviously have it.

The wide-spread support to Jagmohan…When was the last time when you saw such dismay at the departure of a Cabinet Minister anywhere? The only reason this happened is that we Dilliwalas have now begun to appreciate quality-of-life issues better than we traditionally do elsewhere in India. Recent years have convinced us that even in a city as chaotic as ours, it is possible to clean the air, remove the squatters – the rich with the clout of connections and equally the poor with the power of votes.

This winter, after two decades, you could see the con-trails of jets in the capital's skies, the smog that blocked them in the past having been swept away by Supreme Court's activism. If you too suffer from bronchial asthma, you can tell the change in air quality in each breath.

You see so many more stars in a night sky. Who is going to vote for foul air now? People won't vote for or against CNG. But they would also not vote to return to days of coughing, wheezing and smog when even a test match could not start before lunch at Ferozeshah Kotla for lack of visibility.

Much as we fret that it has become a jungle, Delhi is not rural Bihar and thank God for that because as India urbanises at a fast pace, it is the capital that must set the agenda. It is not only the centre of power because it is the seat of government but also because the nation's elites live here and even their children must survive in this city at least until they are old enough to go overseas for education. It is, therefore, that when an Uphaar fire tragedy happens in Delhi, it creates a very new culture of concerned civic activism. How many of us, on the other hand, even remember the Dabwali (in Haryana) fire in which over 400 children died? But post-Uphaar activism has now defined new safety standards in places of entertainment all over. Even judicial activism against pollution had to begin only in Delhi. Now it will set standards for all of India.

You have to shake up Delhi to move India today. If the 1984 massacres of the Sikhs had been confined to Kanpur or Patna, the follow-up would not have been a fraction of what we have seen in Delhi. After all, just a year earlier, more than 3,000 Muslims had been massacred in one day at Nelie in Assam. Who remembers that story? How many people have been prosecuted for that? Even on urban governance, it is Delhi that has moved ahead when even Mumbai has declined. It is such a pity that so many polluting vehicles that Delhi is discarding are now ending up not only in small towns around the country but also in middle-metropolises like Ahmedabad, Bangaore and Pune. But it is a matter of time before awareness travels there as well and when it does, it would translate into more votes for better air, water, transport, education and health care. Not for land-grabbing, polluting, thieving old mafias as the BJP's trio of losers in Delhi seems to believe. The Prime Minister's, let us hope meanwhile, was a momentary error of judgement which he would rectify simply by ensuring that his new urban affairs minister is not persuaded to change his predecessor's script by the same things.

APPENDIX CI-(ii)

# JUNKING JAGMOHAN

That Jagmohan has been persuaded or pressured to overcome his resistance to accepting another portfolio in no way dilutes the negative side of the clear signal sent out by his removal from the Urban Affairs Ministry. Over the next few days the line likely to be put out is that the spirit behind entrusting tourism to Jagmohan was to inject dynamism into a department that has floundered despite all the attractions of this land. It simply will not wash. Even those who do not accept Jagmohan as a genius in the management of urban affairs will concede that he has always displayed total commitment to his job – whether during his assignment with the Delhi Development Authority, as Lieutenant Governor, or finally as Cabinet Minister whose task centres around critical aspects of the Capital. Not for nothing did Indira Gandhi recall him to boost the flagging construction projects for 1982 Asian Games. Not for nothing did VP Singh dispatch him to Srinagar to fire the first shots against the gunmen who had come close to taking control of the Kashmir Valley.

It is true that almost all through his career he has run foul of politicians whose racketeering he disrupted, as well as that section of the bureaucracy that believes with a religious faith not unmixed with self-interest that it is duty-bound never to rock the boat. Yet when he did enter electoral politics he was a three-time winner from what is deemed the most intelligent electorate in the coup.

The politicians' equivalent of thieves-honour is what has united them against Jagmohan for it was under their patronage that the master plan was rendered meaningless and encroachments flourished. And when the apex court found no local agency seriously following its instructions it was Jagmohan who filled the breach.

There may be some truth in the charge that he was demolishing vote banks, in the process he was also cutting off the funding-line that runs between the various disreputable lobbies and their politician associates. The grapevine has it that adding to the tirade against him were a host of media persons who claim protracted occupation of government accommodation as a birthright.

All that added up to the kind of pressure that the Prime Minister chose not to resist – even at the cost of his promise of good governance losing all credibility. The talk of the town suggested that shifting Jagmohan was utterly questionable but perhaps a sound political decision. This newspaper refuses to accept that interpretation of "politically correct."

APPENDIX CI-(iii)

# THE HINDU RATE OF GOVERNANCE

The Prime Minister, Mr. Atal Behari Vajpayee, has just effected a kind of reshuffle in his Cabinet. The exercise is supposed to have re-established his authority over his own Government. If this turns out to be so – and, it will be a big "if" – it would merely signal a return to a semblance of constitutional normality. After all, the Prime Ministerial supremacy is the *sine qua non* of effective governance at the Centre.

The question, however, is whether this one-time show of Prime Ministerial assertion, if at all, would be sufficient to help the Vajpayee regime break out of the Hindu rate of governance, which after three years of the first genuine non-Congress Government in New Delhi appears to have become our defining arrangement. Many years ago, Professor Raj Krishna had popularised the concept of "Hindu rate of growth", which tried to explain the pattern of minimalist rate of growth in the Indian economy. Prof. Raj Krishna had posited a certain kind of immobility of institutional arrangements, cultural preferences and intellectual predilections that did not allow the Indian economy to achieve a rate of growth higher than a paltry 3.5 per cent. The economy finally managed to break out of this stranglehold in 1991; but, as our current economic difficulties so painfully remind us, unless the process and substance of Government is liberated from the Hindu rate of governance, the gains on the economic front may well be jeopardized and there will be no satisfactory solutions to the challenges before the Indian state.

If an assertion of Prime Ministerial authority over his own Government is not sufficient enough a condition, then what would it take to break out of the Hindu rate of governance? It would not do, for example to be content with the limits of a coalition arrangement; coalitions at the Centre are fast becoming a recipe – and, an excuse – for minimalist performance by leaders who are expected to provide leadership and by administrators who are supposed to implement policies and programmes. Almost all the Chief Ministers are convinced that performance on the administrative front does not matter – and, does not yield the commensurate electoral dividends – as much as their capacity to perform competently a few familiar political managerial chores. Inversely, an incompetent Giridhari Gamang would find himself replaced by an indifferent and insensitive Naveen Patnaik; the ritual democratic accountability had been performed without any relief to the citizens.

Nothing drives homes the invincibility of this Hindu rate of governance more than the near-starvation deaths in Orissa and other parts of the country. What is more, it took a proactive Supreme Court to shake the governing process out its institutional slumber. Neither the Prime Minister nor the ruling party at the Centre nor in Orissa displayed the minimum of moral conscience in the matter; the belated response, again, is bureaucratic.

For the last three years, the NDA Government has taken great comfort in measuring its success by the past failure of others. After three years the joke is now on the NDA crowd. The joke is particularly cruel because the NDA crowd continues to take a partisan pleasure in the pronounced inadequacies of the Sonia Gandhi Congress. The toll this rite of partisanship is taking on the entire process of governance was touched upon, if only just partially, by Mr. Arun Shourie, a few days ago in the Rajya Sabha during the debate of disinvestment: "You are just now saying that it is all the failure at this Government or that Government. I am telling you that it has become a pervasive characteristic of Indian governance. That is the real problem".

The extent to which the BJP leadership has happily house-trained itself in the Hindu rate of governance can be judged from the ejection of Mr. Jagmohan from the Ministry of Urban Development. Here was one administrator who was willing to follow the classic textbook approach: spell out the larger vision of a city two or three decades down the line, conceptualise a plan of action in tune with that vision, prioritise the tasks in the plan of action, summon the supervisory energy, attend to the nuts and bolts of details, stay unwavering in achieving the task at hand, despite the opposition from the vested interests.

There has been not a single rumour, leave alone a allegation, that in his drive to clean the capital out Mr. Jagmohan was susceptible to the familiar charm of the slumlords and the builders lobby. He obviously had the mandate of his Prime Minister and his Government. It was the backing of his Prime Minister that enabled Mr. Jagmohan to stand up to a whole array of opposition voices, from within and outside his own party. And just when he was on the verge of proving the point that it was possible for a good man, with the requisite dedication, integrity and competence, to move an agenda, he finds himself thrown out.

The presumed political costs of Mr. Jagmohan's anti-encroachment drive have apparently been cited to the Prime Minister, and the local party bosses have been allowed to have their way. The half-hearted explanation that Mr. Jagmohan's successor in the Ministry of Urban Development would not tinker with his priorities does not wash. The Hindu rate of governance would not let a Jagmohan break out of the stranglehold. The Jagmohans of this world would always displease some sections; after all the society is forever engaged in an intense struggle over collective resources. The idea of good governance is to ensure that the choices this struggle produces are in the larger interest (as collectively defined at any particular time) as well as are morally defensible.

The question, then, becomes that if Mr. Jagmohan had to be defrocked as the Minister for Urban Development because he was generating too much political costs, what is the guarantee that a painstakingly hard-working Minister like Mr. Shanta Kumar would be allowed to finish the task of streamlining the public distribution system.

Sooner or later, Mr. Shanta Kumar's efforts would start hurting some vested interests. Or, for that matter, how long would Mr. Arun

Shourie be shown the prime ministerial indulgence. Already Mr. Shourie has earned the displeasure of the corporate crooks and their political stand-ins; he has invited the charge of breach of privilege for daring to call a political operator's bluff.

Even more pertinent a question presents itself: can individual Ministers – however competent, however dedicated, and however sincere – break out of the Hindu rate of governance without the Prime Minister of the day providing a hands-on leadership. Even if they could create little islands of ministerial efficiency, they would hardly change the fundamentals without a new collective approach.

Without a Prime Ministerial commitment, courage and clarity about our national vision, about what is right for India in the long term, what are the costs and who would pay these costs and who need to defer gratifications, there would be no breaking out of the Hindu rate of governance.

The imperative of the day and the age is an inspired and inspiring Prime Minister who would use the vast authority of his office to reorder the institutional arrangement and administrative energies of the Indian state in a manner that would excite and mobilise this disparate, multi-cultural society. The historic onus is on Mr. Vajpayee. He must begin by coming to terms with the inadequacies of the RSS world view. He is welcome to perform the *guru dakshina* once a year but he must mentally exorcise himself of the antediluvian demons that abound in the RSS mythology. Only then would it be possible for him to demand and get cooperation from political foes and friends in breaking out of the Hindu rate of governance.

## APPENDIX CI-(iv)

A few typical comments of public spirited individuals and organsiations on the drive launched by me to bring about a pattern of governance which is just, principled and result oriented:

(i) Air Marshal M.S. Bawa (Retd.), President, Citizen Alliance for Promotion of Responsive Governance, in his letter of April 28, 2000, wrote:

It has been heartening to follow up the actions you have been taking and particularly when we read in the Hindustan Times of 28th April, 2000 it really assured us that there are still people in this great country of ours who would stake their all for a righteous task. We assure you Sir that you will not find out movement wanting and we shall be right behind you and that also not very far… We commend you for your courage and steadfastness in the face of tremendous odds and the up-hill task that you are engaged in. One thing you must take pride in is, that there are a small handful of people who will stake their all with the hope to pull the country out of the quagmire that it has been landed in. History shall only remember those who put their everything on the chopper block for the country and not those who plundered it. May God give you courage to hold your own and not succumb to any pressure.

(ii) The Efforts Group of Delhi Citizens Action Group for Promotion of Responsive Governance spoke in the same strain in its letter of May 23, 2000:

We admire, appreciate and congratulate you on your bold step to take head on the builder mafia. Your honest efforts to restore Delhi is laudable. We assure you all the support in your endeavours.

(iii) The noted Non-Governmental Organisation, Common Cause, in its communication of April 15, 2000, said:

A very welcome news has been highlighted in today's Hindustan Times, that you have taken the steps of initiating strong action against depredations which builders and plot-holders have been causing in construction of high-rising and multiple flat buildings in Delhi. It is very unfortunate indeed that this has been allowed to be perpetrated by the concerned authorities of Delhi, ostensibly on the strength of approval by certain elements among politicians.

(iv) Referring to the 'expose' of the misdeeds which came to light during my weekly public hearing, Ashwani Kumar Aggarwal of the Traffic Advisory Committee, wrote on June 5, 2000:

It (public hearing) is very much commendable. Everybody is happy and contented that there is somebody who can hear his woes patiently and illegal action are undone promptly. You have the guts to take action against the people who have links with the land mafia.

(v) The letter of September 10, 2000, from Shri S.P. Sharma of Ashok Vihar was of its own kind. He observed:

Now Hon'ble Minister Shri Jagmohan Ji wants to do right things and the pressure on him is mounting each day to incapacitate him... Yada Yada Dharmamsya............ I pray to Lord Krishna to bless our Hon'ble Minister to be able to deliver justice to the suffering masses then he will not have to take the trouble to descend on our Holy Earth to do the same job.

(vi) Anil Agarwal's letter of June 6, 2000, took my stand to a very high pedestal:

I have heard/read a lot about you... In our country, you fall among exceptional people like Mahatma Gandhi ji, Chandra Shekhar Azad ji, Subhash Chandra Bose ji, Lal Bahadur Shastri ji etc... These people have contributed and repaid to this country last end of their heart... Sir, you are going on the same line and your bold approach /feelings are similar to them.

APPENDIX CII-(i)

# Jagmohan's is only sane voice, says SC

**EXPRESS NEWS SERVICE**
NEW DELHI, SEPTEMBER 13

THE Supreme Court has lauded the stand taken by the Union Urban Development Minister Jagmohan on the shifting of non-conforming industries out of Delhi, saying he seems to be "echoing our words" and was the "only sane voice" in the usual humdrum.

In contrast, the three-judge bench headed by Justice B.N. Kirpal observed yesterday that the Delhi government, the MCD and the DDA seem to be adopting a stand which would make the apex court totally helpless as various orders passed by it had gone totally unimplemented.

While hearing the PIL filed by environment activist M.C. Mehta on the shifting of polluting and non-conforming industries out of Delhi, the court directed that a nodel cell be set up under the Ministry of Urban Development.

The nodal cell should be headed by Jagmohan and should have members selected by him who will work under the direct supervision and guidance of the Ministry, the court said. Any laxity on their part would be sternly dealt with by the court, it added.

The SC said this seemed to be the only answer in view of the fact that the government had neither shifted the industries by December 1999—the court's deadline —nor had it made any provisions to justify their continued existence in violation of the Master Plan.

In response to the Delhi government's proposal to regularise these industries by carrying out changes in the Master Plan, the Urban Development Ministry had, in its affidavit to the court, said: "No amendment in the Master Plan of Delhi may be done to cover inaction or failure on the part of local government or local agency to enforce their by-laws."

Any changes in the Master Plan or its norms to accommodate illegal activities, the Ministry said, would not only put premium on lawless activity but would also cause injustice to the law abiding citizens. The court agreed with the Ministry's viewpoint and strongly pulled up the Delhi government, saying it wanted to "encourage legalisation of illegal activities which resulted in the prevailing 'jungle raj' in the Capital as far as violation of law was concerned".

The court also said that the

**CONTINUED ON PAGE 3**

# 'Jagmohan's is only sane voice'

FROM PAGE 1

nodal cell will examine the issues connected with the problems of pollution due to the presence of non-conforming industries in residential areas. It would have all powers under sections 3(3) and 15 of Environment Protection Act for closure of illegal units. The SC directed local government agencies and industries to render aid to it to implement the court orders. Appearing for the Ministry, Additional Solicitor General Kirit Rawal expressed surprise over the "brazen" way the government had acted by not implementing court orders and had, instead sought changes in the Master Plan.

## APPENDIX CII-(ii)

**Summary of the serious lapses, brought out in the discussion paper, circulated at the Town Planner Symposium, to consider Khanna Committee Report.**

(1) While the Khanna Committee submitted its report on May 13, 2006, the Lok Sabha passed the Delhi Laws (Special Provisions) Bill on May 11, 2006 and Rajya Sabha on May 15, 2006; thereby providing another proof that the exercise undertaken through the Committee was not *bonafide* and was designed to obtain recommendations to justify the pre-determined decisions.

(2) The Committee's observation that the planning processes are flawed is based upon hearsay and not on any scientifically conducted field survey.

(3) Another argument made by the Committee to build the argument of flawed planning process is that lower order plans such as zonal development plans and implementation or layout plans have not been prepared in time by the concerned authorities. As far as preparation of zonal development plans is concerned, all the eight zonal development plans for urban Delhi, where most of the problem of violations exists, have been prepared by the DDA.

(4) The Committee contend that there is no proper institutional "mechanism in place at present to allow interested parties to formally approach the authorities for seeking modifications/ relaxations vis-à-vis existing building codes and land use regulations, from time to time on justifiable grounds. It is not understood why there should be additional relaxation after law, rules and regulations have been framed.

(5) Rule of Law is established to govern the civil society, based on certain shared values, including those of probity, accountability, liberty, transparency, equity, etc. It is not lawful to establish committees and pass laws in order to protect violators of another law, be it urban and regional planning or any other aspect of the civil society.

(6) Both experts are the Fellow Members of the Institute of Town Planners, India, a professional body of town planners regulating their professional conduct in the public interest. Following are some of the chief objectives of the ITPI as noted in its Memorandum of Association.

   (a) To advance the study of town planning, civic design and kindred subjects and of the sciences and arts as applied to those subjects;]

   (b) To promote planned economic, scientific and artistic development of towns, cities and rural areas.

Whether the members of ITPI have served any of the above objectives of the Institute by signing up the Khanna Committee report, which has condoned all forms of violations of the planning law and Master Plan for Delhi of which at least one member was the custodian at one point in time.

Clearly, the Khanna Committee report has faltered on all the principles of planning and good governance. It proposes to regularize all violations. It will spell disaster in the form of more unplanned development for the citizens of Delhi in the years to come. Expect another regularization committee being set up by the Government of India in 2020 if not earlier. Good societies cannot be built on the basis of violations of the rule of law.

APPENDIX CIII-(i)

# MINISTER OF TOURISM AND CULTURE
## Excerpts From Tour Notes of Maharashtra: Pandharpur, Dehu, Alandi, Pune – April 13 – 14, 2003

In continuation of my previous tours of Maharashtra, I undertook a visit to the above cited cities / towns. The main objective was to create a clean, convenient and soul-lifting cultural-tourism-circuit on the traditional Palkhi route which is taken by lakhs of 'Warkari'-processionists every year. This tradition is embedded deep in the mind of the millions of followers of Sant Gyaneshwar of Alandi, Sant Eknath of Paithan and Sant Tukaram of Dehu. Those who accompanied me on this route included Shri Amitabh Kant, Joint Secretary (Tourism), Government of India, Shri Ashish Kumar Singh, Managing Director, Maharashtra State Tourism Development Corporation, Shri S.K. Mitra, Superintending Archaeologists (Aurangabad Circle), Shri Gopal Reddy, Collector, Sholapur and others. Shri Balasaheb Vikhe Patil, Union Minister of Industry, and Shri Ramdas Athavale, Member of Parliament, accompanied me to Pandharpur.

### PANDHARPUR

I was shocked to see that this nerve centre of "the great Maharashtarian pilgrimage" was practically without any civic amenity. Public conveniences were conspicuous by their absence. The River Front was stinking because of the open defecation around. At one corner, a little away from the habitation, there was only one small shed, open from all sides. This was the only shelter from the scorching sun or the rain. For 'darshan' of the deity, hundreds of pilgrims were seen waiting in a narrow lane, amidst insanitary conditions. The incipient callousness of the governance machinery – central, state or local lay bare before my eyes.

It was agonizing to note that, even after 55 years of Independence, millions of pilgrims were being treated as herds of cattle who had to fend for themselves and put up with conditions that were clearly sub-human. The tolerance-level of the pilgrims and their passivity were simply amazing.

The following measures need to be taken up immediately:

(i) In view of the attitude of the State Government and the local bodies, as exhibited in the past, initiative should be taken by the Central Government in the Ministry of Tourism and Culture.

(ii) A new tourism circuit, along the Palkhi route, should be sanctioned, covering all important cities and towns that are traversed by the pilgrims.

(iii) A set of shelter sheds, dormitories and rest houses as well as a set of modern public conveniences should be built on the land that is available with the State Government/local body / Trust.

(iv) The River Front should be developed, staired all along the slope and elegantly landscaped.

(v) The encroachments that have come-up on the river side of the road should be removed and alternative site provided, wherever merited.

(vi) The Yatra should be so regulated that there is no congestion in the narrow street which should be effectively paved and suitably covered to provide shelter from rain and sun.

(vii) Sanitation of the town should be improved, more sewage treatment plants installed and regular fogging and spray of gamaxine done.

(viii) After the set of building referred to at (ii) above have been constructed, no open defecation should be tolerated and necessary watch and ward staff appointed to ensure healthy and clean maintenance.

(ix) A team of highly motivated local non-officials and officials need to be set up to help in the execution of the entire project.

## DEHU

Here, the conditions are comparatively better; but the water-front has a lot of scope for improvement. A few shops would also require relocation. A blue-print for both internal and external redevelopment should be prepared. While the internal work should be left to the Temple authorities, the outer work could be handled / financed by us.

## ALANDI

As in the case of Dehu, the temple and surrounding area need effective redevelopment. These are old properties which should be got cleared from the squatters and reconstructed with a lot of open space.

**(Jagmohan)**
14.04.2003

All concerned

APPENDIX CIII-(ii)

# PART I

A brief account of what was done with regard to a few representative cases of each distinct category, at the National Level, to set up Great Green National Cultural Hubs under the New Initiative Programme.

## AJANTA

In the spiritually elevating environment caused by the rising tide of Buddhist thought and in the wild solitude of dense and green forests and gentle and graceful streams, the Ajanta Caves were cut out of rocks and magnificent murals created on their inner walls by guilds of great artists and artisans from the 2nd century BC to the 6th century AD. Patronised by princes, these artists produced works of rare beauty which had both 'a sense of sublime' and a 'sense of design'. The inspiration was invariably spiritual. The figures were intensely human and mirrored the society and culture of the times.

Unfortunately, notwithstanding the superb quality of these 'monuments in mountains' and the world-wide reputation which Ajanta paintings had earned as being "the greatest artistic wonder of Asia", a slum cluster had come up at the very foot of the caves.

Under the New Initiative Programme, a determined effort was made to create a new environment. A civic-cum-tourist-cum-cultural complex was constructed about 3km from the caves. Here, amidst an elegantly landscaped space, a shopping centre with 72 units, including five restaurants, was set up. A large car and bus parking area, with scientifically designed pattern for circulation, was also brought into being. An information-cum-documentation-cum-interpretation centre was also set up. Another innovation was a green buffer that was created between the new centre and the cave complex.

The area vacated, after the clearance of the slums was landscaped, afforested and merged into the cave complex in accordance with an overall blueprint of creating the same environment in which the caves were hewed and murals painted.

The objective was to ensure that amidst the lovely greens of mountains and meadows of the Sahyadri range and the slow rustle of the Wagora river, the visitor to this massive complex of 29 caves could hear the 'voices of silence' which the Ajanta paintings transmit. Making use of latest technology, cool fibre optics light has been installed. This enables the visitor to see the paintings in all their artistic glory and absorb their message.

The ante-chambers of heaven, as the Ajanta Caves were once described, have been recreated. The soft music has been reinjected in the slow rustle of Wagora rivulets and the cosmic dance of the swinging trees on the Sahyadri hills made more meaningful and refreshing. Now, every item around the complex lifts the visitor upward and puts him or her in a frame of mind through which could be seen "the ordered pattern of the spiritual realities of the universe" and the true purpose of life in this world and beyond.

## ELLORA

Ellora rock-cut Temple Complex is another incredible masterpiece of cave art and architecture of India. Regenerative action has been taken to restore it to its true glory and greatness. Now the awe-inspiring spectacular panorama of Ajanta and Ellora serves a magnificent window to the great arts of India and also lifts the visitor to higher horizon of thought which has always been a noble and distinctive feature of Indian heritage.

## MAHABALIPURAM

The Mahabalipuram Complex, built in the seventh century, under the Pallava regime, covers some of the most remarkable Rock cut shrines of South India- Arjuna's Penance, a bas relief with life size images; Pancha Pandava Rathas, a set of five mini shrines carved out of one rock in the form of chariots; Mandapams, sculptural relief depicting stories from Hindu epics; and Shore Temple, cut out of a hard blackish leptinite, with a square lower storey and a pyramidal superstructure.

The masterly art exhibited here has been acknowledged by its inclusion in the list of World Heritage Sites by UNESCO. "This art is Indian with such purity of line, such nobility, such perfection that these works are indicative not of primitive society, but rather the zenith of a civilization."

Under our restoration, conservation and improvement Master Plan, a sparkling look has been imparted to this great heritage of India and its various temple sites integrated through elegantly laid green walkways and refreshing parks. The majesty of the sea adds its own charm to the delightful environment.

## KUMBALGARH

Kumbalgarh Fort is a telling example of how some of the *finest jewels of Indian heritage* have remained wrapped in obscurity for a long time. Till recently, few knew about the existence of this unbelievably imposing Fort which has been the *Eye of Mewar* and which has been described as the work of giants rather than of men and whose walls, in width, are second only to the world-famous *Wall of China* and can accommodate at a time 7 horses trodding abreast.

The antiquity of Kumbalgarh goes back to the time of Samprati, grandson of Ashoka. Located on the pinnacle of the world's most ancient rock, its great potential for defensive warfare was recognized by Mewar Ruler, Rana Kumbha, in the 15$^{th}$ century, who started building the Fort in its present form. In course of time, it became 'a lethal weapon against the assaults of the rulers of Delhi, Malwa and Gujarat.'

With its 35 kilometres long wall, 700 bunkers , 8 massive gates fitted with spikes and 'tier above tier' of battlement, rising to the summit, today it stands as a glorious symbol of Rajputs' indomitable courage and inflexible will. Its historic importance is enhanced by being the birthplace of Indian legendary hero, Maharana Pratap, and also by the location of scores of beautiful temples in its complex, such as Neelkanth, Namdeo, Ganesha and Yaga Vedi.

As a part of the New Initiative Programme, this massive Fort has undergone restoration under a plan conceived in the underground of its hoary past. Today, it stands with all its majesty and magnificence, inviting visitors to hear its countless tales of triumph and tragedy, defiance and defection, chivalry and chicanery, valour and treachery.

## PART II

A brief account of an example which shows how irreparable damage was prevented to national heritage by taking a principled and firm stand against the politics of populism and profiteering.

### TAJ MAHAL

The Taj corridor project envisaged reclamation of about 30 hectares of land from the Yamuna bed in the area lying between Taj Mahal and Agra Fort, and construction of a food and shopping plaza, amusement park, Appu Ghar and other buildings there. It was given out by the U.P. government that this project, which attracted wide public attention in June-September, 2003, was a part of a scheme which had the approval of the Union Ministry of Environment and Planning Commission and for which 50 per cent of the cost (Rs. 600 crore) would be met from the Central funds.

The project of interfering with the natural flow of the Yamuna and construction of buildings behind the Taj was inherently unsound and environmentally untenable. But the Uttar Pradesh government's response to the queries raised in this regard was vague. The reply of the Ministry of Environment, too, was not of much help; it would not go beyond saying it had not sanctioned any such project.

What I saw at the site was shocking beyond belief. There were scores of bulldozers, trucks and other machines inside the bed and a huge quantity of stones, clay and bricks had been stored nearby. Strong disapproval of what was going on was conveyed to the local officials who accompanied me to the site. They could not give any satisfactory reply to the question as to how a massive development-cum-construction work could be undertaken in the area falling within the prohibited zone of two "protected" monuments, the Taj and Agra Fort, without obtaining specific approval of the Agra Development Authority, the Archaeological Survey of India and other agencies concerned. All that they could say was that the entire matter was being handled at the State Government's level. The State Government and the Environment Ministry were told to get the work stopped.

After holding out a promise to look into the alleged wrong-doing in sanctioning the project, releasing the first installment of Rs. 17 crore and getting the work commenced without even calling competitive tenders, Ms. Mayawati suddenly called a Press conference and announced that she had demanded from the Prime Minister and the Deputy Prime Minister that I should be removed from the Union Cabinet forthwith. The issue assumed the form of a serious national controversy, particularly because the BJP and Ms. Mayawati's party, the Bahujan Samaj Party, were coalition partners in the state government. I stuck to my stand. The controversy ultimately led to the fall of the Mayawati government and the abandonment of the project.

Thus the Taj, India's most famous monument, whom Rabindra Nath Tagore described as "a tear-drop on the face of eternity", was saved from being ravished. Ms. Mayawati, however, saw it that in the parliamentary elections held shortly afterwards the followers of her party worked and voted against me. The intelligentsia, which had warmly applauded my stand during the period of the controversy, remained passive and did nothing to support me electorally, providing once again that in our country right-thinking persons do not assert themselves at the hustings and forget that the "the only thing necessary for the triumph of evil is for good men to do nothing.'"

APPENDIX CVI-(i)

# LIST OF BUILT-UP POCKETS CLEARED BEFORE THE CLEARANCE OF TURKMAN POCKET.

| S.No. | Name of the Property | Time of Clearance | No. of families Involved | Localities where Shifted |
|---|---|---|---|---|
| 1 | 4090-4094/XII Meena Bagh | June-July 74 | 140 | Sarai Rohilla, Moti Bagh, Ranjit Nagar |
| 2 | 7523/XV Katra Kareem Khan, Paharganj | July-August 74 | 150 | Ranjit Nagar |
| 3 | 416/XIV Sarai Rohilla | September 74 | 25 | Moti Nagar |
| 4 | Other small properties numbering about 12 | July-August | 100 | Moti Nagar, Ranjit Nagar, Sarai Rohilla |
| 4 | Katra Sheesh Mahal 630 | April 1975 | 170 | Mata Sundri Road |
| 5 | Kalan Mahal, Directorate of Education, Delhi Administration, Delhi | April 1976 | 50 | The occupants (19) who had some semblance of authority were given tenements in Mata Sundri Road while the Rank squatters (62) were given plots in resettlement colony of Seelampur |

## APPENDIX CVI-(ii)

**The contents of the standing instructions of the Delhi Administration/Lieutenant Governor, issued vide its orders No.F50(6)/67-L&B dated July 27, 1967 and the procedures followed both in pre- and post-Emergency days, of sending communication to the Police and other authorities.**

*Contents of the Order*

In the recent past a few major demolition-cum-clearance operations have been undertaken and many more have to be carried out in the near future. The problems connected with the operations are very complicated. A political slant is now sought to be given to every operation and strong resistance is being put up by vested interests. It is, therefore, absolutely necessary to strengthen the demotion-cum-clearance machinery and to make available its assistance to all the departments concerned.

All the Heads of Departments of Delhi Administration are directed to give the fullest cooperation and assistance to the (Demolition) Cell and attend to the requirements of the (Demolition) Cell on a high priority basis. Whenever any manor operation has to be undertaken at least the S.D.M., D.S.P. of the local area would remain with the demolition party throughout the operation.

It was in accordance with these instructions and the usual practice that communication No.P.A./V/76/Dem., dated April 7, 1976, asking for deployment of police, was sent by me to the DIG, with a copy to the District Magistrate and other concerned. This letter was written after discussions with the Lieutenant Governor on April 5, 1976 and taking his approval to the line of action contemplated. In this connection, it is relevant to compare the communication sent by me to the DIG with a copy of Deputy Commissioner, on April 7,

1976 with the following three communications sent to the Deputy Commissioner with a copy to the DIG in connection with three clearance operations undertaken before the emergency:

1. F.50(1)/67-L&B, dated March 6/7, 1968.
2. F.50(50)/68-L&B, dated November 7, 1968.
3. F.3(66)/73-CRC/DDA, dated February 12, d 1974.

From the above three communications and similar other communication sent from time to time to district and police authorities, with copies to civic authorities and Special Assistant to the Lieutenant Governor, it would be quite clear that the practice of deployment of police in the manner it was done in Turkman Gate was as usual and as before.

## APPENDIX CVI-(iii)

**A brief note regarding net work of lies spread by Inder Mohan to undermine my efforts to frustrate the design of subversionist, in Kashmir Valley in 1990. Inder Mohan manipulate a report in the name of a Committee of PUCL by 'acting' through a local member.**

The unclean hands of Inder Mohan, are seen in his letter published in *The Hindustan Times* of May 16, 1990. This letter was in response to a report which appeared in *The Hindustan Times* of April 30 under the caption 'PUCL Report Flayed'. After questioning the validity of the observations made in the report about the encouraging results achieved by the Governor and after claiming that the PUCL report was based on 'first-hand direct knowledge acquired by the team members', Inder Mohan wrote in the aforesaid letter:

> 'Why was Jagmohan so keen to oblige his Home Minister by releasing five hardliners in exchange for his daughter?'

Inder Mohan knew perfectly well from his first-hand knowledge that I was not the Governor of the State at the time of Rubaiya Sayeed's kidnapping (December 8, 1989) and her release (December 13), and that one of the reasons for my being sent to the State for the second time on January 19, 1990, was the total collapse of the Kashmir Administration and its virtual take-over by the subversives. But Inder Mohan's expertise in the art of disinformation impelled him to make the accusation, believing that a large segment of the Indian populace would not be remembering, in mid-May 1990, the true position of the case. His game plan, obviously, was to level false allegations after spicing them with seemingly acceptable slants of "first-hand knowledge" and hope that a sizeable section of the people would take it.

With regard to the flight of the Kashmiri Pandits, Inder Mohan's twisted report wanted the public to believe that it was not the fearsome environment, it was not the brutalized landscape, it was not the ruthless Kalashnikov of the marauders, it was not the bomb explosions and fires, it was not the threatening telephonic calls, it was not the hysterical exhortations for 'Jihad' from hundreds of loudspeakers fitted on the mosques, it was not the 'Tirana-e-Kashmir' of having Quran in one hand and a rifle in the other, it was not the fall-outs of grave human tragedies of Ganjus, Tikkus and Premis, it was not the sinister design of 'killing one and frightening 1,000', but the inducements of the trucks (without providing any particulars of the vehicles, their movement, or financial sanction) that had made the Kashmiri Pandits to abandon their homes and hearths in the cool and crisp Valley and to move to the hot and inhospitable camps of Jammu.

## APPENDIX CVII-(i)

**An example which shows how urges of an inspired leader and urges of those individuals who had been experiencing 'a strong sense of unease' got enlarged and intensified to cause 'root and branch' transformation of The Katra-Vaishno Devi Shrine Complex, rendering the exploitative politics of the vested interests ineffective.**

When I was functioning as Governor of Jammu and Kashmir in mid 1980's, I was persuaded by a friend of mine from Delhi to accompany him on his visit to the Mata Vaishno Devi Shrine at Katra. After this impromptu visit, I recorded a note which, *interalia*, said "If one were to see the moral and material degeneration of the present day India, all that one has to do is walk from Katra to the Mata Vaishno Devi Bhawan."

The entire route was virtually tree-less and unbearably hot, full of pointed and curving stones and pebbles, punctuated frequently with treacherous pot-holes over which one could, without extra caution, stumble and hurt oneself badly. Stray dogs and cows suddenly appeared as if from nowhere, exposing the 'Yatris' to further risk of injury. The breathlessness caused by the ascent and the stuffy atmosphere was relieved by wafts of air only to bring in a nauseating stench of urine and excreta of both humans and cattle. All along the route, there was not a single public urinal or toilet, forcing men as well as women to use the limited space available in the corners. The pestering beggars, which included a large number of children, evoked both anger and pity. Most of the owners of ponies looked as sick and famished as the ponies themselves. The cruelties inflicted upon the animals were heart-rending.

At the main Shrine complex itself the conditions were equally appalling. Malpractices were galore, insanitation insufferable, and eating places dirty and surrounded by junk and garbage. The natural beauty around the Cave had been marred by hideous buildings put up without any design or sensitivity. The entire offerings and donations were taken without any accounts by those who claimed themselves to be the custodians of the Shrine.

Pilgrimage, in its true Hindu tradition, is undertaken to meet 'gods', have face to face communion with them, attain a deeper state of spirituality and experience a higher vision of truth. In the ancient times, the pilgrim invariably encountered an elevating environment. A sublime environment evoked a sublime vision. And a feeling of being 'upward and divine' swelled from within.

But what happened during my journey from Katra to the Mata Vaishno Devi Shrine was an encounter not with an exhilarating air but a foul stench. Worse, it was being face to face, not with the spirits of the great souls and the seekers of truth but with the machinations of manipulators and corroded minds. Allegations and counter-allegations were galore. Accountability was conspicuous by its absence. Everyone passed on the buck to the other. I was deeply agonized, particularly when I learnt that the sub-human conditions had been persisting for over four decades, despite repeated denunciation by the press, pilgrims and top functionaries of the state and the central governments.[1]

If I got an opportunity, I resolved within myself, I would show how a spiritual wasteland could be regenerated and how the journey to the Shrine could act as a tonic, both to the body and the soul. And the opportunity came in the form of Governor's rule, when I enacted a law to establish the Mata Vaishno Devi Shrine Board with Governor as its Chairman.

Consequent to the reforms, under the Shrine Board Act, which withstood the constitutional test of the Supreme Court's scrutiny, all round improvements have come about. Culturally, the ancient philosophy of Shakti has been given a proper context and those who

[1]In the post-1947 India, the political and administrative establishments, by and large, have shown a marked disposition to leave the hard crust of the basic problems untouched.

are knowledgeable now see it as a science of the soul. Environmentally, the entire area in and around the Shrine has been upgraded and made congenial to the realization of spiritual powers. Economically, huge resources have been mustered and ploughed into the region for its development. Administratively, a new model for creative, constructive, and effective governance has been evolved and presented to the nation. And, above all, tradition and modernity have been synthesized in a manner which underlines the significance of both of them in building a new India.

There are hundreds of spirituality significant cities, sites and shrines, spread all over the country. If all, or most, of them are subjected to the same creative thought and constructive action, as was brought to bear in the case of Vaishno Devi Shrine, not only India's sacred geography but also its economic and social architecture would improve radically.

# APPENDIX SPECIAL

*Background of the India Gate Canopy controversy which was the genesis of my proposal for extending Rajpath to the River Front by way of Green Walkway and Corridors, and its subsequent amplification to develop a Great Green Vista to prop up Regeneration of Delhi City Mindscape.*

A fierce public controversy arose out of the proposal to install Gandhiji's statue under the India Gate Canopy, where the statue of King George once stood. The controversy, hot as it always was, came to a boiling point in July 1997. At that time, I unfolded in my speech in the Lok Sabha an altogether different proposal which was, later on, also published in the form of newspaper article in the Indian Express as well the Hindustan Times. This proposal was warmly applauded. The controversy about the statue died down. A vague sort of hope was entertained that one day my proposal would be executed on the ground.

To put the whole matter in perspective and explain the salient feature of the proposal, I can do no better than reproduce the aforesaid newspaper article which appeared under the title: *From Rajpath to the River Front Nothing But Green* and which read as follows:

> During the last few days, former Prime Minister Chandra Shekhar raised the issue twice in the Lok Sabha at Zero Hour. He expressed the view – rather strongly – that the chhatri should be demolished and Gandhi's statue set up at the site.
>
> Chandra Shekhar's view is opposed, equally strongly, by a number of eminent architect, town-planners and art-critics. This opposition, I may make it clear, is not due to any lack of reverence for Gandhiji but due to the incompatibility of the site and its surroundings with Gandhiji's ideas and philosophy.

I have an alternative proposal which, I think, will not only meet the approval of Parliament but also be accepted with enthusiasm by professionals and the nation as a whole. The proposal I have in view has the following main components:

- Extend Rajpath to the Yamuna river front. The only structure that comes in the way is the over 50-year-old National Stadium which could be reconstructed in or around the Nehru Stadium Complex. A vast green vista, stretching from Rashtrapati Bhavan to the river front, would come into being. It would be a visual delight in itself, besides creating an environment of peace, tranquility and dignity in the heart of the city.
- To add to the serenity of the complex, two underpasses would be constructed to take care of the north-south traffic.
- The new vista, though in line with Rajpath, would have an elevation towards the river front. Gandhi's statue would be erected on a green mound at a level higher than Rashtrapati Bhavan, at a point a little east of the present location of the National Stadium. The higher level of Gandhiji's statue would symbolize India's cultural value of according pre-eminence to the spiritual power in comparison with the temporal power.
- The green mound on which Gandhiji's statue would stand would be approached by a series of ascending concentric mounds, signifying Gandhiji's belief in always trying to move from the 'lower level of truth' to 'higher level of truth'.
- The proposed vista would meet the river front almost at a right angle, skirting the side of Purana Quila. At the meeting point, the charkha-shape landscape would be developed and a medium-sized dam constructed.
- The river front would extend, on its western side, up to Gandhiji's Samadhi in the north and to Kalindi Colony / National Bypass in the south. In the vast green river front, expression could be given to various ideas of Gandhiji in the fields of religion, culture, economy and social reform.

- In the proposed green belt, suitable spaces would also be earmarked for other great social and cultural reformers such as Raja Ram Mohan Roy, Justice Ranade, Swami Vivekananda and Sri Aurobindo.

Let us show some vision, some glimpses of the power of the Indian mind which was once our greatest treasure.

*With shacks, stores and sheds gone from the Yamuna River Front, an opportunity to implement the above blueprint has opened up.*

# INDEX

## By the Same Author

i) *Rebuilding Shahjahanabad: The Walled City of Delhi*
ii) *Island of Truth*
iii) *The Challenge of Our Cities*
iv) *My Frozen Turbulence in Kashmir*
v) *Soul and Structure of Governance in India*
vi) *Shaping India's New Destiny*
vii) *Crisis of Environment and Climate Change*
viii) *Reforming Vaishno Devi and a Case for Reformed, Reawakened and Enlightened Hinduism*

A few glimpses of the contents of some of these books and the propositions they put forward may be provided here for the interested readers.

### I. Soul and Structure of Governance in India

The book deals with larger and deeper issues of governance and offers concrete suggestions to tackle these issues. It also underlines that there is a melody of life which lives only in our mind and soul, and without this melody a stirring and elevating music of governance cannot be composed.

The book has fourteen chapters. Chapter-I outlines the current crisis of governance. Chapter II analyses the Soul and Structure of Governance in Ancient and Medieval India and comes to the conclusion: if there is nobility in the soul and the motivation is pure and the idealism high, the structure, even if it be not perfect, can lead to a life of honour, peace and prosperity.

Chapter III looks at the remarkable strength of the steel frame which the British constructed but also points out (Chapter IV) that the last years of the British governance in India were tragically inglorious. These were the years in which the steel frame assumed the form of a moth-eaten bamboo structure whose poisonous insects spread venom all along the line and left behind a trail of blood, riots and the biggest migration known to history.

Chapter V delineates Sardar Patel's finest hour. Chapter VI assess the performance of the Pre-Reform period (1947-1991) and Chapter VII of the Post-Reform. It brings out how the health of the governance machinery started deteriorating sharply from the mid-sixties when populism made a deep intrusion in Indian politics. For winning elections, reliance began to be placed, not on principles but on personalities, not on long-term perspective of nation building but on short-term personal and party gains.

Chapter VIII highlights the mind boggling challenges which the machinery of urban governance faces, and chapter IX deals with the external factor and forces which influence our governance capacity. Chapter X discusses New Public Management Movement.

The next four Chapters XI – XIV, present an exhaustive blue-print of Governance-reforms, with all its ground level nuts and bolts in place.

As India stands today, three courses for the future are open to her. She could put herself in a deeper trap of divisive forces and expose herself to a more serious risk of getting disintegrated. Or she may continue to live, like other Third World countries, with her contrasts and contradictions and with illusions of progress that shallow materialism often causes. The third course – the only right one – open to her is to follow the above blueprint of reforms. If she does so, she could effectuate one of the most humane, enlightened and elevating systems of governance in the world, reflecting best the power of her mind, the purity of her soul and potency of her new institutions.

## II. Shaping India's New Destiny

This book has nine chapters. Chapter I presents a broad picture of what was thought in August 1947 and what has actually happened.

Chapters II, III and IV trace the deeper roots of the grim challenges that have arisen in Kashmir, Assam and Naxal-affected regions of the country. They reveal how these challenges constitute a grave threat to India's security, integrity and general well-being.

The blood-dimmed tide of contemporary terrorism and its savage impact on India and other parts of the globe is discussed in Chapter V. A strategy to end the turmoil caused by this menace is also unfolded. The folly of ignoring the ideological front in the 'war on terror' is particularly brought out.

In Chapter VI, it is shown how the future of India depends on the manner in which the formidable problems of urban planning, urban poverty, urban pollution and urban productivity are handled.

Chapter VII expounds the true meaning of Governance. It scans the performance of various components of the State's power-structure – its economy, its executive organs, including the civil services and the police, and its parliamentary and judicial institutions.

Chapter VIII is devoted to the nature of the present-day world order and its linkages with the efforts that are needed to reshape India's destiny.

The larger issues have been dealt with in the last chapter which show what great potential India possesses for fashioning out new foundational planks on the shoulders of which a life-nurturing and life-elevating edifice of a reshaped destiny could be built.

## III. My Frozen Turbulence in Kashmir

The eleventh updated edition of this book has 24 chapters. Apart from the historical backdrop and roots embedded in subversion and terrorism, these chapters show how India has imposed upon itself a tyranny of shallowness and prolonged the collective agony of its people. So far, unfortunately, the 'spirit of Munich' has determined the attitude of its decision makers towards Kashmir. A vague hope has been entertained: tomorrow it will be all right. But it will never be all right. The logic of history is against it.